EMPLOYMENT LAW AT INTERNATIONAL ORGANIZATIONS: AN INTRODUCTION TO INTERNATIONAL ADMINISTRATIVE LAW

What is the employment law at international organizations? The answer – international administrative law – implements treaty-based employment at all international organizations, including the United Nations, International Labour Organization and the World Bank. It governs an encounter between the status of the international civil service, administrative authority at international organizations and the jurisprudence of international administrative tribunals. For the first time, the universal legal basis of international administrative law is concisely and clearly introduced, tracking the employee lifecycle, from selection, through remuneration, performance management and integrity to ending service. Drawing on the judgments of multiple administrative tribunals, a clear and useable interpretative framework of interconnected legal principles and legal duties is established. Intended for all staff at international organizations, Member State representatives, legal practitioners and scholars, this book serves as the basis for a shared understanding of international administrative law, equal to the enormity of the endeavours entrusted to the international civil service.

PETER QUAYLE is an international lawyer specializing in the law, governance and effectiveness of international organizations. He advises the United Nations, multilateral development banks and other international organizations worldwide. He also lectures, researches and publishes on international organizations law, including at Harvard Law School, the University of Cambridge and Peking University.

EMPLOYMENT LAW AT INTERNATIONAL ORGANIZATIONS

An Introduction to International Administrative Law

PETER QUAYLE

Shaftesbury Road, Cambridge CB2 8EA, United Kingdom

One Liberty Plaza, 20th Floor, New York, NY 10006, USA

477 Williamstown Road, Port Melbourne, VIC 3207, Australia

314–321, 3rd Floor, Plot 3, Splendor Forum, Jasola District Centre, New Delhi – 110025, India

Cambridge University Press is part of Cambridge University Press & Assessment, a department of the University of Cambridge.

We share the University's mission to contribute to society through the pursuit of education, learning and research at the highest international levels of excellence.

www.cambridge.org
Information on this title: www.cambridge.org/9781108729215
DOI: 10.1017/9781108679428

When citing this work, please include a reference to the DOI 10.1017/9781108679428

First published 2026

A catalogue record for this publication is available from the British Library

Library of Congress Cataloging-in-Publication Data
Names: Quayle, Peter author
Title: Employment law at international organizations : an introduction to international administrative law / Peter Quayle.
Description: Cambridge, United Kingdom ; New York, NY : Cambridge University Press, 2026. | Includes bibliographical references and index.
Identifiers: LCCN 2025053501 | ISBN 9781108492300 hardback | ISBN 9781108679428 ebook
Subjects: LCSH: International administrative courts | International officials and employees | International agencies – Law and legislation | Labor laws and legislation, International
Classification: LCC KZ5274 .Q83 2026
LC record available at https://lccn.loc.gov/2025053501

ISBN 978-1-108-49230-0 Hardback
ISBN 978-1-108-72921-5 Paperback

CONTENTS

PREFACE

The term 'international administrative law' has its detractors, who argue that it compounds misunderstanding and analytical imprecision.[1] Yet the first comprehensive study of international organizations law – Wilfred Jenks' *The Proper Law of International Organisations* (1962) – heads a significant section: 'The International Administrative Law Governing the Internal Legal Relations of International Organisations'. The independent, judicial and binding bodies established by Member State governance organs to resolve employment-related disputes at international organizations are almost all called 'administrative tribunals' and the Statutes of some obligate the application of 'principles of international administrative law'. Discontent with 'international administrative law' mostly seems to stand in for legitimate concern about the law's obscurity – a criticism this book seeks to counter.

The Law Governing Employment in International Organizations (1967) by Michael Akehurst is considered the first in-depth examination of this law. Clearly, the expression 'law governing employment' is as general as 'international administrative law' is specialized. Although readily understandable, 'employment law' is not enough to convey the international status of employees at international organizations – a treaty-based feature this book regards as fundamental. Whereas, *The Law of the International Civil Service: As Applied by International Administrative Tribunals* (1994) by C. F. Amerasinghe prominently features the 'international civil service', it is a two-volume treatise – this book is avowedly an introduction.

This book paradigmatically structures international administrative law as an encounter between treaty-based employees and employers – between the status of international civil servants and the administrative

[1] For example, see Ago 2020, 88: Ago argues, 'that "international administrative law" obscures uncertainty about the sources of law governing the employment relationships' at international organizations.

authority of international organizations – secured by international administrative tribunals. The judgments of administrative tribunals afford an interpretative framework, comprising legal principles – ensuring accountability – and legal duties – governing decision-making. The intention is that a concise and comprehensible introduction to international administrative law emerges, contributing to both shared understanding and endeavour. The inherent generalizations of this book – treading a fine line between forgivable omissions and inexplicable oversights – are in service to this aim.

Each chapter was reviewed by a different jurist – on a personal basis – as follows: Philippa Webb (Chapter 1, 'Introduction'), Kristina Daugirdas (Chapter 2, 'International Organizations'), Santiago Villalpando (Chapter 3, 'International Civil Service'), Olufemi Elias (Chapter 4, 'International Administrative Tribunals'), Kieran Bradley (Chapter 5, 'Employment-Related Dispute Resolution'), Chris de Cooker (Chapter 6, 'Selection'), Mercedes Carrillo (Chapter 7, 'Remuneration'), Dražen Petrović (Chapter 8, 'Performance Management'), Estelle Martin (Chapter 9, 'Standards of Conduct'), Joan Powers (Chapter 10, 'Misconduct'), Rishi Gulati (Chapter 11, 'Administration'), Anne Trebilcock (Chapter 12, 'Ending Service') and Eva Gröniger-Voss (Chapter 13, 'Conclusion').

Their corrections, comments and criticisms improved this published text immeasurably, albeit all errors and idiosyncrasies are my own fault. Laurent Germond commented formatively on an early version of a chapter. Iskender Bakaev both helped with research and discussion of the scope of this book. John Cavanagh prompted me to start out on this project and Gerard Sanders encouraged me to keep going. My students and Yifeng Chen in Beijing sparked my analysis of international administrative law as universally treaty-based, rather than drawing on national traditions restraining governmental authority. Peking University Law School, the Lauterpacht Centre for International Law and Harvard Law School all provided supportive surroundings to my thinking and writing. Lastly, my parents and partner have both sustained and cheered me throughout this undertaking.

NOTES ON STYLE, REFERENCES AND ABBREVIATIONS

General Approach

To achieve the greatest accessibility, this book does not closely follow the traditional stylistic conventions of legal publishing. Each chapter starts with an overview, followed by a conversational and mostly unreferenced discussion responding to a rhetorical question, which introduces – and is substantiated by – the remainder of the chapter.

This book features most case materials in-text and academic writing is cited sparingly. It uses short-form footnotes, together with alphabetically organized References. The approach is designed to be sufficient to guide the reader to the complete entry in the References, to both corroborate the text and suggest further reading. This is complemented by a comprehensive Table of Cases.

Spelling follows UK English. 'Organization' is always spelled with a 'z'. This convention overwrites cited material without using square brackets, but not the titles of books and names of institutions. Otherwise, the spelling of cited material is faithful to the source. All cited text is introduced in the present tense.

Administrative Tribunal Cases

The judgments of international administrative tribunals are almost all first featured in-text, with a full, neutral case citation, for example:

> UNAT Judgment No. 840, *Alcañiz and Others v. Secretary-General of the United Nations* (2018)

This uses the following structure: the abbreviated name of the administrative tribunal; followed by the word Judgment; the serial number adopted by the tribunal; then the italicized claimant surname or initials used by the tribunal, followed by any sequence number and, 'and Others' for more than two claimants; then 'v.' for versus; followed by the full name of the respondent; followed by the year of issuance. Each case citation is usually accompanied by some brief description of the case. If repeated in-text, the case is referenced again in italicized short form: *UNAT No. 840.*

When quoting the text of administrative tribunals judgments, all internal references and related quotation marks are removed.

Footnotes

The use of 'ibid.' is avoided; successive identical citations repeat the short form:

Sands and Klein 2009, 5.
Sands and Klein 2009, 7.

Books and articles take an author–date format. Page numbers are given without prefixes – so no 'p.', 'pp.' or 'page(s)'. As necessary, cases and other references use 'para.' to indicate paragraph numbers. When already introduced in-text, administrative tribunal cases are footnoted as follows: UNAT No. 840, para. 15. If cases appear only in the footnotes, they are presented using the full neutral citation.

Quotations and Overwriting

For consistency and clarity, certain terms are used to overwrite quoted material using square brackets:

- [they] and [their] are used to maintain gender neutrality, replacing 'he', 'she', 'him', 'her', 'his' and 'hers'.
- [claimant] replaces 'applicant' or 'complainant'.
- [challenge] replaces 'claim', 'application', 'grievance' or similar.
- [respondent] refers to the employing international organization or its legal representative.
- [UN], [United Nations] and [international organization] replace 'Organization' or 'Administration', and one-off or inconsistent terms. (Although 'Bank', meaning the World Bank, is usually retained.)
- [principal executive official] replaces 'Secretary-General', 'Director-General', 'President' and so forth.

Treaties

The terms 'treaty-basis' and 'treaty-based' refer to the *constituent instrument* of international organizations. Treaties and constituent instruments are cited both in-text and in footnotes using a short form, for example:

Vienna Convention on the Law of Treaties
UN Charter, or
Charter of the UN

Dates of treaties are omitted in-text and from footnoting (but see References), except where chronology is relevant to discussion. However, the date of UN General Assembly resolutions are included. In footnotes, references follow this format: UN Charter, Article 1.

Abbreviations

Abbreviations for international organizations and treaties are introduced in-text when first used (except for the UN, which is treated as a universal shorthand for the United Nations). For example: International Labour Organization (ILO).

Abbreviations for the following administrative tribunals are introduced in-text where they are part of an institutional narrative; otherwise these abbreviations are used pervasively:

- ILOAT: International Labour Organization Administrative Tribunal
- UNAT: United Nations Appeals Tribunal
- WBAT: World Bank Administrative Tribunal

This is complemented by the list of Abbreviations that follows.

ABBREVIATIONS

ADB	Asian Development Bank
ADBAT	Asian Development Bank Administrative Tribunal
AT	administrative tribunal
ECtHR	European Court of Human Rights
FAO	Food and Agriculture Organization
GAVI	Global Alliance for Vaccines and Immunization
ICJ	International Court of Justice
IFI	international financial institution
ILC	International Law Commission
ILO	International Labour Organization
ILOAT	ILO Administrative Tribunal
IMF	International Monetary Fund
IMFAT	IMF Administrative Tribunal
ITU	International Telegraph Union (historic), International Telecommunication Union (now)
LoNAT	League of Nations Administrative Tribunal
MAS	mutually agreed separation
OECD	Organisation for Economic Co-operation and Development
UN JIU	UN Joint Inspection Unit
UNAdT	UN Administrative Tribunal
UNAT	UN Appeals Tribunal
UNDT	UN Dispute Tribunal
UNDT/AT	UN Dispute Tribunal and UN Appeals Tribunal
UNESCO	UN Educational, Scientific and Cultural Organization
VCLT	Vienna Convention on the Law of Treaties
WBAT	World Bank Administrative Tribunal
WFP	World Food Programme
WHO	World Health Organization

1

Introduction

This chapter begins by asking the question, what is the employment law at international organizations? The answer – international administrative law – implements the treaty-basis of international organizations. Second, the chapter sets out how this book paradigmatically structures international administrative law as the encounter between the status of the international civil service, administrative authority at international organizations and the influence of judgments of international administrative tribunals. Third, this book interprets international administrative law as a framework of interconnected legal principles and legal duties. Fourth, and in conclusion, the chapter identifies ways in which this book may be useful to different types of readers, namely: the employees and managers at international organizations; Member States; lawyers and students of the law; and those wanting to apply the employment law at international organizations to circumstances that seem advanced, rather than introductory.

1.1 What Is the Employment Law at International Organizations?

Established in moments of global rupture and renewal, international organizations – like the United Nations, the World Bank and International Labour Organization (ILO) – occupy a prominent position in international affairs. They represent a consensus to institutionalize common endeavour and confront crisis that transcend both the boundaries and unilateral influence of Member States. Their purposes are comparably ambitious – global peace and security, economic development, social advancement, technical convergence – and once established, even as their fortunes fluctuate, international organizations are irrepressible.

Whilst their mandates are multitudinous, unlike states formed from colloquial combinations of military might and political movements, the basis of all international organizations is uniform: a written instrument, contracted by states, governed by international law: in other words, a 'treaty'.[1] In the same way that corporations are controlled by, but separate from their shareholders, so too are international organizations constituted by Member States, but attributed their own independent legal personalities. International organizations can act – like companies – within national legal orders, but also – like states – on the plane of international law. However, unlike the open-ended and general powers of states, the powers of an international organization are limited, confined to the achievement of its purposes, in accordance with the expressly – and impliedly – stated terms of its treaty-basis; see Chapter 2, 'International Organizations'.

The employees of these international – sometimes termed, 'intergovernmental' – organizations are known as international civil servants. Just as the treaty-basis of an international organization ultimately governs how its Member States meet and make decisions, it also governs the employment of staff. In all but identical terms, these employees have a treaty-based status, possessing three attributes: 'efficiency and competence', 'geographic diversity' and 'integrity and independence'. Likewise, administrative authority at international organizations is treaty-based. Uniformly, staff are subordinated to the principal executive official, subject to regulation by a Member State governance organ; see Annex 1, 'Compendium of Employment-Related Clauses from Constituent Instruments'.

So, fundamentally, the status of the international civil service and the authority to administer an international organization is governed by international law: treaty-based terms, interpreted in accordance with rules of treaty interpretation.[2] The resultant extrapolation, implementation and obligations – international administrative law – is the employment law at international organizations.

1.2 The Basis of International Administrative Law

This book introduces international administrative law as the interaction between the status of the international civil service, the administrative

[1] Whilst a treaty-basis is conventionally regarded as indispensable to classification as an international organization under international law, exceptionally states extend privileges and immunities through their national law to an entity established in other ways, thereby in some respects simulating 'international organization status'. See Chapter 2, 'International Organizations'.

[2] There are four sources of international law: treaties, customary international law, general principles of law and subsidiarily, judicial decisions and teachings; see ICJ Statute, Article 38. However, its treaty-basis is the exclusive source of an international organization's (limited) powers. See Chapter 2, 'International Organizations'.

authority at international organizations and judgments of international administrative tribunals. These bases are now considered in turn.

Basis 1: Status of the International Civil Service

The powers of international organizations – including the power to appoint, manage and dismiss employees – are fundamentally treaty-based, governed by international law. This treaty-basis possesses the employees of international organizations with an official status – comprising three attributes: efficiency and competence; geographic diversity; and integrity and independence. These attributes are obligated by international law and are attained by the application of international administrative law; see Chapter 3, 'International Civil Service'.

Importantly, the resultant paradigm structuring this book is distinguishable from other conceptualizations of employment law. It is not, for example, ordered through a right of access to justice – with some basis in customary international law or a general principle of law, if then transposable to international organizations. Neither is it ordered as a societal compact, balancing fairness with organizational output – a basis for national employment laws. Nor is it ordered as the result of an individualized bargain – a basis for contractual relations between employers and employees. However, this is not to say that justice, fairness and contracts are absent from the treaty-based paradigm of international administrative law, but that these concepts take on unfamiliar guises.

Justice – access to impartial and independent judicial employment-related dispute resolution – is in practice the only recognized method to secure the status of the international civil service, since the establishment of the first international administrative tribunal by the League of Nations. Or, in other words, employment-related disputes at international organizations are in fact status disputes, which are ultimately resolved by the authority of administrative tribunals, established by Member State governance organs. The treaty-based paradigm sees securing the status of the international civil service as legally obligated; see Chapter 4, 'International Administrative Tribunals'.

Whereas, fairness is inherent to the non-arbitrariness that governs administrative authority at international organizations. But this applies since the powers of an international organization are limited to the achievement of its purposes. Arbitrary – including unfair – administration is the misuse of authority. Misuse invalidates this authority and so the related administration is unlawful; see Chapter 5, 'Employment-Related Dispute Resolution'.

Likewise, the legal power at an international organization to appoint staff descends from the treaty-basis, so a contract of employment or letter of appointment held by an international civil servant cannot confound their treaty-based status. Legally, the treaty-basis is paramount. The treaty-based international administrative law paradigm sees appointment terms as – in practice – uncontentious evidence of the assumption of the status of international civil servant, subject to the administrative authority of an international organization.

Basis 2: Administrative Authority at International Organizations

International civil servants are subordinated to the treaty-based administrative authority at international organizations. This authority is manifested in two ways: (1) Internal law; and (2) Discretionary decision-making.

1 Internal Law

The internal law of an international organization is the written expression of administrative authority.[3] It constitutes codified instructions to all the staff.[4] For this reason, internal law is impersonal and legislative not personalized and contractual. In other words, it can be issued and reissued without the mutual consent of employees. But, to obligate staff it must be publicized. For this reason, international organizations produce *Regulations*, *Rules*, *Administrative Orders* and so forth.

The internal law may complement, implement and interpret the treaty-basis of an international organization, but not contradict it. If it was contradictory, then administrative authority is misused, and the internal law negated. Internal law establishes the uniform application of administrative authority in order to achieve the purposes of international organizations. Typically, it occasions employment-related disputes when adherence to the internal law is contested, the internal law is allegedly ambiguous, or when the internal law is contended to be arbitrary, contradicting the treaty-basis of an international organization.

[3] The term 'internal law' features in League of Nations Administrative Tribunal Judgment No. 1, *di Palma Castiglione v. International Labour Office* (1929); the first ever international administrative tribunal judgment.

[4] In formal terms, internal law adopted by governance organs instructs and regulates the principal executive official and their administrative authority. In turn, it is the principal executive official who instructs the staff; see Chapter 3, 'International Civil Service'.

2 Discretionary Decision-Making

Whilst much internal law has an automated application, it also calls for considerable individualized decision-making. Administrative decision-making is a treaty-based authority attributed to – and delegated from – the principal executive official of an international organization, such as the Secretary-General of the UN. The internal law identifies a decision-maker, together with the character – and the consequences – of the decision to be made. It sometimes also describes factors which may – or must – be taken into account when making the decision. But the internal law does not say what the decision-maker decides. The power of the principal executive official – and their delegates, the 'management' of an international organization – to administer the staff, requires them to draw upon their own judgment. This, in other words, is discretionary decision-making.

Whilst many – but not all – national legal orders now restrain governmental authority, the treaty-based paradigm of international administrative law considers deference to discretionary decision-making results from the legal authority of the principal executive official, which may be regulated by a Member State governance organ, but not replaced. In other words, whilst governance organs may establish international administrative tribunals, the treaty-based job of principal executive official – and their discretionary decision-making authority – cannot be handed over to tribunal judges.

Basis 3: Judgments of International Administrative Tribunals

The disputed interaction between the status of the international civil service and the application of administrative authority is ultimately resolved by an international administrative tribunal, established by a Member State governance organ. Many international organizations submit to the jurisdiction of one of several international administrative tribunals which allow for this. Whereas, other international organizations establish a proprietary tribunal. However, proliferation of administrative tribunals is accompanied not by diversity of judgments, but by 'a general convergence of jurisprudence'.[5] The treaty-based paradigm of international administrative law anticipates this, since the status of the international civil service and administrative authority is universal to

[5] De Cooker 2022, 11.

international organizations. So an introduction to international administrative law need not attempt to synthesize an incalculable number of tribunal judgments.

Rather, this book selectively draws upon the judgments of three international administrative tribunals, namely: the ILO Administrative Tribunal, UN Appeals Tribunal and the World Bank Administrative Tribunal (WBAT).[6] This cohort is chosen for both pragmatic and principled reasons. On the one hand, they are indisputably significant to the effectiveness of multilateralism – possessing jurisdiction over the preponderance of the international civil service, totalling at least 150,000 international officials.[7] On the other hand, they adjudicate disputes arising from multiple international organizations, implying systemic rather than institutional precedents.[8]

Sampling judgments from these three administrative tribunals aims to useably account for the doctrine of legal precedent. Legal precedent means 'that decisions of earlier cases sufficiently like new cases should be repeated in a new case'.[9] This doctrine has been said to have strict and relaxed conventions. On the one hand, '[t]he strict doctrine *obliges* judges to follow the earlier decisions of certain other courts ... even if they believe those decisions to have been wrong'.[10] On the other hand, relaxed legal precedent 'demands only that a judge give some weight to past decision on the same issue, that [they] must follow these unless [they think] them sufficiently wrong to outweigh the initial presumption in their favour' and 'may embrace the past decisions not only of courts above [them] or at the same level in [their] jurisdiction but of courts in other states and countries'.[11]

[6] Once, a leading case of the Asian Development Bank Administrative Tribunal figures as the basis of a WBAT judgment (see Chapter 4, 'International Administrative Tribunal') and as in this chapter, the League of Nations Administrative Tribunal illustrates the provenance of the term 'internal law'.

[7] This is a crude tally based upon published employee numbers (in 2025) of the UN and the World Bank online and a figure of 74,000 staff members of international organizations subject to the jurisdiction of the ILO Administrative Tribunal (ILOAT), from Politakis 2021, para. 2.

[8] However, it should be noted that international administrative tribunals established since the International Monetary Fund Administrative Tribunal (IMFAT), in 1992, typically emulate a provision of the Statute of the IMFAT (Article III) and apply 'generally recognised principles of international administrative law'.

[9] Dworkin 1986, 24.

[10] Dworkin 1986, 24, original emphasis.

[11] Dworkin 1986, 25.

In the context of international administrative tribunals, the doctrine of legal precedent follows the relaxed convention. Seldom does a judgment of an administrative tribunal identify a controlling precedent it regards as conclusive. Rather, several past cases are mentioned, as sustaining how the tribunal will rule on the present occasion.[12] Similarly, it has been said that 'the various international administrative tribunals do not consider themselves bound by each other's decisions' but they are 'free to take note of solutions worked out in sufficiently comparable conditions by other administrative tribunals'.[13] To structure its account of legal precedent, this book interprets international administrative law as providing a framework of legal principles and legal duties.

1.3 Legal Framework: Principles and Duties

International administrative law is interpreted by this book as occasioning a framework comprising legal principles and legal duties. Legal principles intend standards for judicial review by international administrative tribunals. They test the legality of contested administrative authority and structure how discretionary decision-making is scrutinized, ascertaining whether it was taken: (1) by a competent authority; (2) in accordance with the applicable procedure established by the respondent international organization; and (3) was not arbitrary or otherwise abusive. Legal duties, by contrast, comprise constraints on the administrative authority of international organizations. They function as binding obligations to be adhered to when administrative decisions are made. These may be thought of as norms of administration, rather than the structure of legal review.

This distinction is also meant as a deliberate aid to introducing international administrative law, concisely and comprehensibly. It also captures the dual potential of the law: governing both the way in which administrative decisions are legally analyzed and adjudicated – through legal principles – and the way in which administrative authority is exercised and discretionary decisions are made – through legal

[12] The relaxed convention of precedent creates methodological uncertainty for international administrative law. Should the earliest case which tried an issue be cited, or the latest case restating the law? Since administrative tribunals do not formally resolve this dilemma, this book adopts a pragmatic approach – presenting cases that state the law most clearly, whilst mentioning if necessary that the case has been repeatedly applied with approval since, or represents a particularly comprehensive discussion of the law.

[13] WBAT Judgment No.1, *de Merode and Others v. The World Bank* (1981), para. 28.

duties. Together, this interpretative framework interrelates the status of the international civil service with administrative authority at international organizations; see Annex 2, 'Summary of International Administrative Law'.

Lastly, throughout this book, an effort is made not to abstract international administrative law, but to anchor it in a recognizable workplace. For this reason, the judgments of international administrative tribunals occasioning this framework are almost always introduced with a brief description of the character of the dispute, before passing onto legal interpretation.

1.4 How to Use This Book

The structure of this book merges both international law – the treaty-basis of international administrative law – with a basic version of the 'employee lifecycle', experienced by employees of international organizations – from their appointment through to the end of their service as international civil servants. The supposition is that many readers of this book first want to understand international administrative law in the context of some specific employment-related circumstance.

Following this Chapter 1, 'Introduction', Part I, 'Legal Basis', of the book moves from the legal foundations of international organizations (Chapter 2, 'International Organizations'), to the status and attributes of the international civil service (Chapter 3, 'International Civil Service'), then the underpinnings of international administrative tribunals (Chapter 4, 'International Administrative Tribunals'), ending with resultant general legal principles of employment-related dispute resolution (Chapter 5, 'Employment-Related Dispute Resolution'). This succession of chapters also constructs international administrative law, as building from broad to specialist international law. The second and third parts of the book are broadly organized around the implementation of the legal attributes of the international civil service. Part II, 'Efficiency, Competence and Geographic Diversity', addresses 'Selection' (Chapter 6), 'Remuneration' (Chapter 7) and 'Performance Management' (Chapter 8). Part III, 'Integrity and Independence' addresses 'Standards of Conduct' (Chapter 9) and the interlocking breach of these standards, namely 'Misconduct' (Chapter 10). Part IV, 'Administrative Authority', focuses on impersonal administration (Chapter 11, 'Administration') and the ending of service in situations outside performance- and integrity-related termination of appointment (Chapter 12, 'Ending Service'). The final chapter – Chapter 13,

'Conclusion' – briefly considers, after a century of international administrative law, what should come next.

The intention throughout this book is to *introduce* international administrative law. Rather than address any one constituency, this book aims to forge, for the first time, a shared basis of understanding of the employment law at international organizations. How different readers could use this book differently is proposed under the following headings: (1) Employees and managers; (2) Member States; (3) Lawyers; and (4) Beyond an introduction.

1 *Employees and Managers*

This is a book written for the international civil service, both as employees and as managers. The style and structure attempts to explain legal concepts clearly and introduce an overarching framework to international administrative law, not readily ascertained from the individual judgments of administrative tribunals. Reading this book cover to cover affords a thorough overview of the law and familiarity with its essential conventions. This may be recommended for a new employee or new manager say, during their first week in the job. A wider understanding of what international administrative law is – and importantly, is not – could result in more cohesive and collegial working cultures. In other circumstances, employees and managers may want to focus on a specific chapter – when, for example, they are an unsuccessful candidate for promotion, or must look into allegations of misconduct. Then turning to the corresponding chapter equips the reader with confidence in the applicable international administrative law. If there is time to spare, reading some of the chapters in Part I, 'Legal Basis' – especially the general legal principles in Chapter 4, 'Employment-Related Dispute Resolution' – adds helpful context.

2 *Member States*

At all international organizations, Member State governance organs regulate the principal executive official, contribute to the internal law, establish international administrative tribunals and stand as the guarantors of multilateral mandates. This book affords Member State representatives and advisors an introduction to the law that they play a significant part in establishing and enforcing. It aids understanding of the status of the international civil service, the way this is inherent to the achievement of the purposes of international organizations and expounds upon both the limits to – but also the potential for – organizational reforms.

3 Lawyers

Lawyers and students of the law may approach this book from a wide range of standpoints. They may be advisors to international organizations, counsel to international civil servants, jurists appointed to international administrative tribunals or academically engaged in the law and accountability of international organizations. For lawyers already conversant with international administrative law, this book proposes a treaty-based paradigm and interpretive framework. It prompts thinking about the employment law at international organizations in a way that prioritizes accessibility. The jurisprudence unexamined by this book could then populate the same structure. The interpretative framework adopted by this book could influence international administrative tribunals. For scholars, international administrative law may also function as a case study of broader dynamics, including the sources and subjects of international law, and the status and effectiveness of international organizations.

4 Beyond an Introduction

This book endeavours to introduce an international administrative law that can be both readily understood and consistently applied. But has it gone too far? Is the resulting version of the law oversimplified or otherwise insufficient? Plenty of administrative controversies would seem to lie outside the pages of this book. For example, not long ago, a hot topic was whether an international organization was empowered to impose a Covid-19 vaccine mandate. In other words, could unvaccinated employees be lawfully excluded from the physical workplace, and their appointment terminated, if after time, they refused to return (vaccinated) to their office?

How then, to approach this controversy? In Chapter 11, 'Administration', a legal principle of administration is stated: 'Administration is unilateral, but may not be arbitrary'. So, whilst a vaccine mandate could be introduced by administrative authority, it must be non-arbitrary: there has to be convincing evidence, related to the effectiveness of an international organization and the achievement of its mandate. This is read alongside a legal duty of administration, 'Administration must ensure safety' and relatedly, 'Foreseeable on-duty risks must be prevented'. During the pandemic, Covid-19 infections in unvaccinated workplaces – assuming the consequences were proven 'unsafe' – would have had to be stopped. Lastly, a component of the employment law of ending service, as shown in Chapter 12, 'Ending Service', is: 'An international organization may unilaterally determine conditions of service – including fitness, format and place – and in accordance with its internal law, terminate the appointment of staff who do not adhere to these conditions'. Or, in other words, successfully working remotely does not negate the administrative authority of an international organization to require you to work from an office.

The premise of this book is that its treaty-based paradigm and interpretative legal framework enables the structured application of international administrative law to any employment-related controversy, including as yet unencountered circumstances.

PART I

Legal Basis

2

International Organizations

This chapter begins by introducing international organizations, historically constituted and governed in accordance with international law. Second, the conventional legal characteristics of international organizations are identified, namely: (1) Treaty-basis; (2) State membership; and (3) Independence. Third, an examination is made of the ways in which the powers of international organizations are sufficient to achieve – but not exceed – their purposes. Fourth, the privileges and immunities that states typically extend to international organizations within their jurisdictions are considered. Fifth, and in conclusion, this legal basis of international organizations is restated.

2.1 What Is an International Organization?

What is an international organization? One way to answer this question, is to start with a short history. This may be divided into three eras. The first era (1815–1914) begins with the end of the Napoleonic Wars and continues until the outbreak of World War I. This period opens with the Congress of Vienna of 1815, in which the states that defeated Napoleon redrew some of the borders in Europe and attempted the containment of France. The Congress inaugurated a series of episodic international summits of the strongest states in Europe – known as the Concert of Europe – which together aimed to maintain stability and ensure that no single state (or alliance) again overwhelmed the continent.[1] Whilst not a formal organization, the Concert of Europe is a deserving antecedent of international organizations for four reasons. First, it represents the emergence of an idea that international affairs cannot be addressed through bilateral relations alone; second, that an entirely ad hoc system is deficient compared to the expectation of regular multilateral conferences;

[1] Sands and Klein 2009, 3.

third, that multilateral cooperation keeps the peace and that, by itself, is a valid aim of the practice of international affairs; and fourth, that the strongest states have responsibilities to protect smaller states, which they should – idealistically speaking – carry out disinterestedly.

Whilst the preoccupation of the Concert of Europe was geopolitical, other developments in this era represent the regulation of cross-border resources. Continent-spanning rivers afforded the rationale for the earliest institutionalized multilateral cooperation. The Congress of Vienna itself established the 'first international organization', the Central Commission for the Navigation of the Rhine, a regime that entered into force in 1831.[2] The Central Commission advised upon and underpinned cooperation between the states sharing the River Rhine. It possessed general administrative powers. Each state had one vote but, in certain matters, voting power was proportionate to river length through or bordering a Member State.[3] It was not long before other river commissions were established: for the Elbe (1821), the Douro (1835), the Po (1849) and the Danube (1856).[4]

This era was rounded out by the establishment of international administrative unions, an early type of international organization that coordinated a globalizing economy and emergent technologies. In 1865, the merger of two regional European telegraphy unions created the International Telegraph Union (ITU), with a permanent bureau in Berne, Switzerland. (Nowadays, ITU stands for International Telecommunication Union and represents a remarkable transition from regulating the defunct telegraph, to a UN agency that allocates geostationary satellite orbits.) The establishment of the Universal Postal Union followed (in 1874), as did the International Bureau of Weights and Measures (1875), International Copyright Union (1886, the forerunner of today's World Intellectual Property Organization), International Union of Railway Freight Transportation (1890), International Sugar Union (1902), International Office of Public Health (1903, from which the World Health Organization (WHO) is descended) and International Institute of Agriculture (1905, now replaced by the Food and Agriculture Organization (FAO)).[5] The promise of this early era was interrupted by the commencement of World War I.

[2] Schermers and Blokker 2018, 24.
[3] Sands and Klein 2009, 6.
[4] Sands and Klein 2009, 6.
[5] Sands and Klein 2009, 6–7.

The second era coincides with the short lifetime of the League of Nations, headquartered in Geneva, constituted by the Versailles Peace Treaty of 1919, after the conclusion of World War I. The League afforded a permanent basis for multilateral cooperation and a formal role for the strongest states, institutionalizing arrangements and ideas familiar from the Concert of Europe.[6] It was intended to reduce armaments, police the peace and regulate colonialism.[7] Whilst the outbreak of World War II (1939–1945) condemned the League to failure, it formed the basis for the third and – for now – enduring era of international organizations, instigated by the foundation of the IMF and the World Bank (officially called the International Bank for Reconstruction and Development) in 1944 and the UN in 1945. The UN was designed to remedy the institutional faults of the League by, generally: (1) incorporating all of the world's then strongest states – as the five permanent members of the Security Council, namely China, France, the United States of America, United Kingdom and USSR (now Russia) – into its establishment; (2) attributing to it the powers to wage war to secure the peace in accordance with Chapter VII of the UN Charter; and (3) ensuring that the body representing all Member States – the UN General Assembly – and the executive body – the UN Security Council – possess distinct, rather than overlapping and competing, responsibilities.[8]

It is apparent, across these three eras, through to the present day – and the continuing proliferation of international organizations – that there is no end to the political, economic and technical domains amenable to institutionalized multilateral cooperation. Yet to understand why institutions with functions as dissimilar as the UN, World Bank and ILO, are

[6] See League of Nations Covenant, Article 4, first sentence: 'The Council shall consist of Representatives of the Principal Allied and Associated Powers, together with Representatives of four other Members of the League'. These permanent members were the US (which did not ratify membership of the League, so the seat remained vacant), UK, France, Italy and Japan – see Tams 2007, para. 16.

[7] See League of Nations Covenant, Articles 8, 11 and 22.

[8] Sands and Klein 2009, 11. Regarding the League's shortcomings, these included:

> Certain matters were within the exclusive jurisdiction of the Council (expulsion of members, for example) others were within the exclusive jurisdiction of the Assembly (admission of new members, revision of treaties); there was, however, concurrent jurisdiction in the most important matter of maintaining the peace and the lack of any clear separation of powers in this matter (or of any priority in the right to deal with them) might give rise to difficulty where the Council and the Assembly differed in their approaches to the solution of a given problem affecting international peace.

nevertheless all comparable *international organizations*, it is necessary to turn to their legal characteristics – which are the same.

2.2 Legal Characteristics of International Organizations

Importantly, it must first be noted that there is not 'some eternally valid blueprint' for international organizations.[9] Rather, international organizations are created with multilateral objectives in mind, and their legal characteristics may be said to follow.[10] However, over time, the legal characterization of international organizations remains stable. For example, in a report to the International Law Commission (ILC) – established by the UN General Assembly to promote the 'progressive development of international law and its codification'[11] – preparatory to the Vienna Convention on the Law of Treaties (VCLT), the rapporteur proposes:

> The term 'international organization' means a collectivity of States established by treaty, with a constitution and common organs, having a personality distinct from that of its member-States, and being a subject of international law with treaty-making capacity.

Whereas, the ILC's Draft Articles on the Responsibility of International Organizations (issued in 2011), states:

> 'international organization' means an organization established by a treaty or other instrument governed by international law and possessing its own international legal personality. International organizations may include as members, in addition to States, other entities.

It may therefore be said that international organizations conventionally possess three characteristics. First, international organizations are based upon a written agreement – a treaty – between states, governed by international law. Second, international organizations are constituted by Member States. Yet, third, international organizations possess an independence, distinguishing them from their Member States. Each of these characteristics are now considered in turn.

9 Klabbers 2022, 7.

10 See Klabbers 2022, 8: '[M]any entities aspire to attain an image of flexibility by styling themselves as something other than an organization … but quite a few of these entities nonetheless display most or all of the characteristics of international organizations'.

11 International Law Commission Statute, Article 1.

Characteristic 1: Treaty-Basis

All international organizations are based upon a governing document. This may be called an 'Agreement', 'Articles', 'Charter', 'Convention', 'Statute' and so forth. Almost always, regardless of the title, this document is a *treaty*. The VCLT states:

> 'treaty' means an international agreement concluded between States in a written form and governed by international law, whether embodied in a single instrument or in two or more related instruments and whatever its particular designation.[12]

The VCLT terms the treaty that forms the basis of an international organization, a 'constituent instrument'.[13] States first negotiate the text of the constituent instrument, then once the text is agreed, it is formally adopted by a treaty conference or signed.[14] Adoption or signature of a constituent instrument is usually the first of two stages, before it enters into force and the resultant international organization commences operations. The second stage – ratification – expresses a state's consent to assume membership of the international organization, 'in accordance with their respective constitutional processes'.[15] Typically, the entry into force of an international organization's treaty-basis is scheduled by the constituent instrument itself. For example, the Charter of the UN states: 'The present Charter shall come into force upon the deposit of ratifications by the [five permanent members of the UN Security Council], and by a majority of the other signatory states.'[16] Thereafter: 'The states signatory to the present Charter which ratify it after it has come into force will become original Members of the United Nations on the date of the deposit of their respective ratifications.'[17] Of course, states that are not original members of an international organization have to apply to join.

However, although a treaty-basis is conventionally regarded as characteristic of an international organization, occasionally entities constituted in other ways are nevertheless regarded as multilateral institutions.

[12] VCLT, Article 2(1)(a).

[13] VCLT, Article 5.

[14] For example, the Bretton Woods Conference in 1944 ended with the adoption by attendees of the Articles of Agreement of the World Bank and IMF; for portrayal of these negotiations, see Conway 2014.

[15] UN Charter, Article 110(1).

[16] UN Charter, Article 110(3).

[17] UN Charter, Article 110(4).

For example, the Global Alliance for Vaccines and Immunization (GAVI Alliance) is an independent non-profit foundation within the meaning of the Swiss Civil Code, as its Statute establishes.[18] The basis of the Green Climate Fund is its Governing Instrument, a text adopted by resolution of the Conference of the Parties of the UN Framework Convention on Climate Change.[19] So, in other words, the basis of these international organizations are national law and the resolution of a treaty organ, respectively. Critically, such entities depend on states extending them privileges and immunities commonly granted to treaty-based international organizations, most importantly at their headquarters. This then simulates some aspects of an international organization, including, as becomes apparent later, application of the attributes of the international civil service.

Importantly, treaties are agreements governed by – which is to say, interpreted in accordance with – international law. The International Court of Justice (ICJ), the 'principal judicial organ of the United Nations',[20] draws upon four sources of international law: treaties, customary international law, general principles of law and subsidiarily, judicial decisions and teachings.[21] Only their parties are obligated by treaties, whereas customary international law governs all subjects of international law. Whilst the VCLT establishes a general rule of interpretation, the ICJ has determined that this also expresses customary international law.[22] The ICJ notes: 'From a formal standpoint, the constituent instruments of international organizations are multilateral treaties, to which the well-established rules of treaty interpretation apply.'[23] Foremost, the VCLT's general rule states: 'a treaty shall be interpreted in good faith in accordance with the ordinary meaning to be given to the terms of the treaty in their context and in the light of its object and purpose'.[24] However, the ICJ also notes, 'the constituent instruments of international organizations are also treaties of a particular type; their object is to create new subjects of law endowed with a certain autonomy, to which the parties entrust the task of realising

[18] GAVI Alliance Statute, Article 1.

[19] The UN Framework Convention contemplates (Article 11) the establishment of a 'mechanism for the provision of financial resources on a grant or concessional basis'; although it also states the mechanism's 'operation shall be entrusted to one or more existing international entities'.

[20] UN Charter, Article 92.

[21] See ICJ Statute, Article 38.

[22] ICJ *Nuclear Weapons*, 13.

[23] ICJ *Nuclear Weapons*, para. 19.

[24] VCLT, Article 31(1).

common goals'.[25] The significance of this re-emerges when considering the resultant powers of international organizations later in this chapter.

Characteristic 2: State Membership

As already noted, whilst international organizations are 'a collectivity of States', they can also 'include as members, in addition to States, other entities'. But most commonly, membership of international organizations is limited to states. For example, only states may be original members of the UN and subsequently membership is 'open to all other peace-loving states which accept the obligations contained in the present Charter and, in the judgment of the [UN], are able and willing to carry out these obligations'.[26] In turn, membership of the UN entitles states to membership of the UN Specialized Agencies. These are autonomous international organizations 'having wide international responsibilities, as defined in their basic instruments, in economic, social, cultural, educational, health, and related fields', which have entered into relationship with the UN,[27] such as the WHO and the UN Educational, Scientific and Cultural Organization (UNESCO).[28] Of course, unlike the UN family, many international organizations do not aspire to universal membership. Although sometimes a functional focus may be deceptive. For example, regional multilateral development banks allow non-regional members, such as the Asian Development Bank (ADB) – the purpose of which is to 'foster economic growth and co-operation in the region of Asia and the Far East' – which not only admits regional members, but also 'non-regional developed countries which are members of the United Nations'.[29]

An important legal consequence of states becoming members of international organizations – either once the constituent instrument enters into force or through subsequent admission – is that they become obligated by the treaty-basis. Whilst it sometimes appears as though states are represented at international organization by diplomatic envoys – in the same way as they exchange ambassadors – and so national self-interests are unchecked, this is misleading. Once states are members, they are

[25] ICJ *Nuclear Weapons*, para. 19.
[26] See UN Charter, Articles 3 and 4(1).
[27] UN Charter, Article 57.
[28] See UNESCO Constitution, Article II(1) and WHO Constitution, Article 3.
[29] ADB Establishing Agreement, Articles 1 and 3(1).

committed to the impartial and multilateral status of an international organization, including the terms of the constituent instrument's preamble and purposes. This extends to the participation of Member States in governance organs, even the UN Security Council or UN General Assembly.[30] The ICJ states: 'The political character of an organ cannot release it from the observance of the treaty provisions established by the [UN] Charter when they constitute limitations on its powers or criteria for its judgment.'

Although states predominate, there are three kinds of 'other entities' that occasionally figure as members of international organizations. First, and most often, other international organizations. For example, the European Investment Bank, itself a multilateral development bank, is a founding member of the European Bank for Reconstruction and Development.[31] Indeed, international organizations, with the authorization of their Member State governance organs, can even band together and create new entities on the international legal plane – for example, the World Food Programme (WFP) is jointly established by the UN and FAO.[32] Second are territorial entities which, although not states, have an economic autonomy, for example Hong Kong, China, is a member of the ADB.[33] Third are philanthropic entities, such as the Gates Foundation, which participates as a member of the Board of the GAVI Alliance.[34] Nevertheless, as already noted, some state involvement is a prerequisite characteristic of an international organization, even if limited to the extension of privileges and immunities; for example, together with the UN and FAO, Italy is necessarily party to the Rome-based WFP's Headquarters Agreement.[35]

Characteristic 3: Independence

There are three ways in which an international organization may typically be said to have a personality distinct from that of its Member States. First is the possession of 'at least one organ which has a will

[30] Indeed, UN Charter, Article 24(2), first sentence, states: 'In discharging [its] duties the Security Council shall act in accordance with the Purposes and Principles of the United Nations'.

[31] Sands and Klein 2009, 190.

[32] See WFP General Regulations and General Rules, Article I.

[33] See www.adb.org/publications/hong-kong-china-fact-sheet, accessed 3 September 2025.

[34] GAVI Alliance Statute, Article 9; the Gates Foundation is a member of the Board, together with the WHO, UNICEF, World Bank, various states and other stakeholders.

[35] Agreement regarding the Headquarters for the WFP.

distinct' from merely expressing the 'aggregate opinion of its members'.[36] Second is the capacity to act within a national legal setting. Third is a capacity on the international legal plane, in some – but not all – ways, equivalent to states.

Of course, all international organizations are a 'tool in the hands' of their membership, in the sense that Member State governance organs are ultimately in control.[37] But, importantly, the decisions of almost all governance organs may be made on the basis of a majority vote – even if there is a non-binding practice of striving for consensus. For example, each Member State of the UN has one vote in the General Assembly; decisions 'shall be made by a majority of the members present and voting' and for decisions on 'important questions', a two-thirds majority is necessary.[38] However, once a decision is made, every Member State of the UN is bound by it. For example, peacekeeping operations authorized by the General Assembly constitute obligations of the UN, to be paid for even by Member States opposed to them.[39]

Usually, the capacity of an international organization in a national legal context – distinguishable from its Member States – is embedded in its constituent instrument. For example, the UN Charter states: 'The [UN] shall enjoy in the territory of each of its Members such legal capacity as may be necessary for the exercise of its functions and the fulfilment of its purpose.'[40] The constituent instrument of the World Bank specifies: 'The Bank shall possess full juridical personality, and, in particular, the capacity: (i) to contract; (ii) to acquire and dispose of immovable and movable property; (iii) to institute legal proceedings.'[41]

Unlike their legal capacity in national legal settings, most constituent instruments do not state that an international organization enjoys its own international legal personality. However, the ICJ regards this capacity to be inseparable from the functioning of international organizations. When considering circumstances involving the assassination of a UN official, can an 'international claim' for reparations against the state allegedly responsible be brought by the UN? The ICJ finds:

[36] Klabbers 2022, 12.
[37] Klabbers 2022, 13.
[38] UN Charter, Articles 18(1) and 18(2).
[39] See generally, ICJ *Certain Expenses*.
[40] UN Charter, Article 104.
[41] World Bank Articles of Agreement, Article VII, Section 2.

> In the opinion of the Court, the [UN] was intended to exercise and enjoy, and is in fact exercising and enjoying functions and rights which can only be explained on the basis of the possession of a large measure of international legal personality and the capacity to operate upon an international plane ... the Court has come to the conclusion that the [UN] is an international person.[42]

However, importantly, although international organizations possess their own international legal personality, their powers are not as expansive as states.

2.3 Powers of International Organizations

What are the powers of international organizations? Or in other words, what is it they are lawfully empowered to do? Whereas states are in principle all equally sovereign, the names alone of international organizations are sufficient to suggest specialist functions.[43] The constituent instruments of international organizations confirm their limited legal purposes, sometimes also called 'objectives' or their 'mandate'. For example, the purposes of the UN are to: 'maintain international peace and security'; 'develop friendly relations among nations'; 'achieve international cooperation in solving international problems'; and 'be a centre for harmonizing the actions of nations in the attainment of these common ends'.[44]

By contrast, the purposes of the World Bank are to: 'assist in ... reconstruction and development'; 'promote private foreign investment'; 'promote the long-range balanced growth of international trade'; arrange loans and guarantees; and bring 'about a smooth transition from a wartime to a peacetime economy'.[45] The purposes of the ILO include the achievement of: 'full employment and the raising of standards of living'; 'the employment of workers in the occupations in which they can have the satisfaction of giving the fullest measure of their skill and attainments and make their greatest contribution to the common well-being'; and 'policies in regard to wages and earnings, hours and other conditions of work'.[46]

Although often ambitiously expressed, the purposes of international organizations are fundamental to both their (1) functional powers and (2) functional limitations.

42 ICJ *Reparation for Injuries*, 9.

43 See UN Charter, Article 2(1).

44 UN Charter, Article 1.

45 World Bank Articles of Agreement, Article 1.

46 ILO Constitution, Annex Section II.

1 *Functional Powers*

All constituent instruments contain a statement of the functions and powers of the international organization as well as those attributed to its organs. For example, the UN Charter sets out the authority of the Security Council, including pivotally: 'The [Member States] of the United Nations agree to accept and carry out the decisions of the Security Council in accordance with the present Charter.'[47] Another article empowers the Security Council to 'determine the existence of any threat to the peace, breach of the peace, or act of aggression and shall make recommendations, or decide what measures shall be taken in accordance with [the UN Charter], to maintain or restore international peace and security'.[48]

Most importantly, constituent instruments establish the function of the international organization as a whole. For example, the functions of the WHO include, 'to act as the directing and co-ordinating authority on international health work' and 'to stimulate and advance work to eradicate epidemic, endemic and other disease'.[49] Albeit these expressly stated functional powers of an international organization are already extensive, further powers may be implied by the constituent instrument. What enables this is the legal assumption that the expressly stated purposes of an international organization are intended by Member States to be achieved, even if it becomes necessary to call upon unstated powers. The ICJ finds:

> The powers conferred on international organizations are normally the subject of an express statement in their constituent instruments. Nevertheless, the necessities of international life may point to the need for organizations, in order to achieve their objectives, to possess subsidiary powers which are not expressly provided for in the basic instruments which govern their activities. It is generally accepted that international organizations can exercise such powers, known as 'implied' powers.[50]

However, the boundaries of these implied powers are that they are 'conferred upon [an international organization] by necessary implication as being essential to the performance of its duties'.[51] In other words, if not essential to the achievement of an international organization's

47 UN Charter, Article 25.

48 UN Charter, Article 39.

49 WHO Constitution, Articles 2(a) and 2(g).

50 ICJ *Nuclear Weapons*, para. 25.

51 ICJ *Reparations for Injuries*, 12.

treaty-based functioning, then the possession of a power unexpressed by the constituent instrument cannot be implied.

2 *Functional Limitations*

The limitations on the powers of international organizations are also related to their functions. Albeit that an international organization possesses international legal personality, this 'is not the same thing as saying that it is a State, which it certainly is not, or that its legal personality and rights and duties are the same as those of a State'.[52] Unlike a state, the functional powers of a multilateral institution are limited. In determining the limits of the powers of the WHO not to extend to the health risks of nuclear fallout, despite its otherwise expansive purposes,[53] the ICJ states:

> The Court need hardly point out that international organizations are subjects of international law which do not, unlike States, possess a general competence. International organizations are governed by the 'principle of speciality', that is to say, they are invested by the States which create them with powers, the limits of which are a function of the common interests whose promotion those States entrust to them.[54]

Are international organizations otherwise constrained? The ICJ states: 'International organizations are subjects of international law and, as such, are bound by any obligations incumbent upon them under general rules of international law, under their constitutions or under international agreements to which they are parties.'[55] So, importantly, customary international law and general principles of law that may obligate states do not necessarily encumber international organizations.[56] Whilst the general rules of treaty interpretation incontrovertibly govern constituent instruments, international organizations are not prominently constrained under other international law.[57] Or, in other words, it

[52] ICJ *Reparations for Injuries*, 9.

[53] The ICJ considers the question, 'In view of the health and environmental effects, would the use of nuclear weapons by a State in war or other armed conflict be a breach of its obligations under international law including the WHO Constitution?' (ICJ *Nuclear Weapons*, para. 1).

[54] ICJ *Nuclear Weapons*, para. 25.

[55] ICJ *Agreement between WHO and Egypt*, 21.

[56] For example, throughout Klabbers 2022, customary international law is mentioned twice; neither reference is in the context of restraining the powers of international organizations.

[57] However, for a rival view, see generally, Daugardis and Schuricht 2020.

is the constituent instruments of international organizations that both fundamentally enable – and limit – their powers. The paramountcy of the treaty-basis of international organizations is further secured by their possession of privileges and immunities.

2.4 Privileges and Immunities

Besides their multilateral functions, perhaps the most noticed – and often controversial – feature of international organizations is their possession of privileges and immunities. Typically, privileges and immunities exempt international organizations – and their officials – from most forms of state authority, including the jurisdiction of national courts.[58] But these are not inherent to international organizations; instead, they are granted by states. Why do states follow this practice? The European Court of Human Rights (ECtHR) answers this question in a judgment considering an employment-related challenge to the privileges and immunities of the European Space Agency:

> [T]he attribution of privileges and immunities to international organizations is an essential means of ensuring the proper functioning of such organizations free from unilateral interference by individual governments. The immunity from jurisdiction commonly accorded by States to international organizations under the organizations' constituent instruments or supplementary agreements is a long-standing practice established in the interest of the good working of these organizations. The importance of this practice is enhanced by a trend towards extending and strengthening international cooperation in all domains of modern society.[59]

An example of a constituent instrument affording privileges and immunities is the UN Charter, which states:

> (1) The [UN] shall enjoy in the territory of each of its [Member States] such privileges and immunities as are necessary for the fulfilment of its purposes.
>
> (2) Representatives of the [Member States] of the UN and officials of the [UN] shall similarly enjoy such privileges and immunities as are necessary for the independent exercise of their functions in connection with the [UN].[60]

[58] See Amerasinghe 2005, 320–328.
[59] ECtHR *Waite and Kennedy*, para. 63.
[60] UN Charter, Article 105.

The UN is also afforded privileges and immunities by the Convention on the Privileges and Immunities of the UN (the 'General Convention') – an example of a 'supplementary agreement'. Notably, the UN Charter affords the UN so-called *functional* immunity – in terms similar to the powers possessed by an international organization – whereas the General Convention recasts this as *absolute* immunity:

> The United Nations, its property and assets wherever located and by whomsoever held, shall enjoy immunity from every form of legal process except insofar as in any particular case it has expressly waived its immunity. It is, however, understood that no waiver of immunity shall extend to any measure of execution.[61]

Privileges and immunities are also always the focus of additional agreements between an international organization and states where it is headquartered and operates. For example, the UN's seat in New York is the subject of a bilateral agreement, governed by international law, between the UN and the United States of America.[62] However, even when an international organization is otherwise not afforded immunity: 'The history of judicial precedent in many national legal systems is … weighted heavily in favour of recognising the immunity of organizations in employment-related matters, even where, as in the case of [the World Bank], immunity is not explicitly granted by the conventional law except in special cases.'[63] The consequence of such privileges and immunities is that neither the international organization as an employer nor their employees, may be subject to national employment law or access the employment tribunals of states. Hence, the employment law of international organizations resulting from their treaty-basis necessarily exists on the international – not national – legal plane.

When states extend privileges and immunities to non-treaty-based entities, they afford the 'simulated' international organization the opportunity to attribute international civil service status to its employees, secured by an international administrative tribunal. For example, the Global Fund to Fight AIDS, Tuberculosis and Malaria (Global Fund) is a Geneva-based 'multi-stakeholder international financing institution duly formed as a non-profit foundation under the laws of Switzerland',[64] with

61 General Convention, Article II, section 2.
62 Agreement between the United Nations and the United States of America regarding the Headquarters of the United Nations.
63 Amerasinghe 2005, 323.
64 By-Laws of the Global Fund, Article 1.

a 'Headquarters Agreement which recognizes the international juridical personality and legal capacity of the Global Fund in Switzerland and provides to the Global Fund a similar set of privileges and immunities as those enjoyed by other international organizations in Switzerland.'[65] Consequently, the Global Fund is enabled to submit its employment-related disputes to the jurisdiction of the ILOAT – and the employment law at international organizations.[66]

2.5 The Legal Basis of International Organizations

Although their multitudinous purposes extend to every domain of human endeavour, conventionally all international organizations share three legal characteristics, namely: a treaty-basis, state membership and independence. Their constituent instruments afford the basis of – and limits to – all their powers, so that in every dimension of their governance, operations and administration, they are ultimately subject to international law. The privileges and immunities typically extended to multinational institutions necessarily result in a treaty-based – not nationally regulated – employment law at international organizations.

The legal basis of international organizations may be restated as:

Legal Characteristics of International Organizations

- Conventionally, international organizations are based upon treaties, governed by international law.
- International organizations are constituted by states and may include as members, in addition to states, other entities.
- International organizations possess independence from Member States, in terms of their governance, legal capacity under national laws and status as an international legal person.

[65] Zeidan and Abboud 2020, 164.

[66] ILOAT Statute, Annex 1(1), states:

> To be entitled to recognize the jurisdiction of the [ILOAT], an international organization must either be intergovernmental in character, or fulfil the following conditions: (a) it shall be clearly international in character, having regard to its membership, structure and scope of activity; (b) it shall not be required to apply any national law in its relations with its officials, and shall enjoy immunity from legal process as evidenced by a headquarters agreement concluded with the host country; and (c) it shall be endowed with functions of a permanent nature at the international level and offer, in the opinion of the [ILO], sufficient guarantees as to its institutional capacity to carry out such functions as well as guarantees of compliance with the Tribunal's judgments.

Powers of International Organizations

- International organizations possess the functional powers both expressly stated and necessarily implied by their treaty-basis.
- The powers of international organizations are limited to the achievement of their treaty-based purposes.

Privileges and Immunities

- States extend privileges and immunities to international organizations – and officials – freeing them from unilateral state authority, to secure the multilateral status and paramountcy of the constituent instrument of an international organization.

3

International Civil Service

This chapter begins by introducing the international civil service – the employees of international organizations, possessing a treaty-based status, inherent to instrumentalizing the mandates of multilateral institutions. Second, the legal attributes of the international civil service are identified, namely: (1) Efficiency and competence; (2) Geographic diversity; and (3) Integrity and independence. Third, the authority to administer the international civil service – possessed by the principal executive official, appointed and regulated by the governance organs of international organizations – is considered. Fourth, and in conclusion, this legal basis of the international civil service is restated.

3.1 What Is the International Civil Service?

The mandates of all international organizations are instrumentalized by their employees: administrators, doctors, economists, financiers, lawyers, logisticians, scientists and security experts – the variety of occupations is matched only by the multiplicity of multilateral institutions. However, collectively, all employees of all international organizations are termed the *international civil service*. It is necessary to turn first to the ideals of national civil service, then to the approach taken to staffing the Secretariat of the League of Nations (established in 1920), to understand why.

Dag Hammarskjöld was the storied, second Secretary-General of the UN – 'the epitome of the impartial, non-partisan international civil servant'.[1] When called upon to defend their officials, the starting point was the traditions of national civil servants: 'In the United Kingdom, as

[1] Sinclair 2015, 755: 'For many in the UN and outside it, Hammarskjöld was the epitome of the impartial, non-partisan international civil servant.' Importantly, Sinclair essays a critique of this reputation.

in certain other European countries, a system of patronage, political or personal, had been gradually replaced in the course of the nineteenth century by the principle of a permanent civil service based on efficiency and competence and owing allegiance only to the State which it served.'[2] In other words, a modern national civil service is permanent, professionally qualified and politically impartial – a civil servant is a 'non-partisan administrator'.[3] At first it seemed as though the Secretariat of the League of Nations would bypass this heritage. The Covenant of the League Nations headquarters the Secretariat in Geneva, Switzerland, and simply states: 'The Secretariat shall comprise a Secretary-General and such secretaries and staff as may be required.'[4]

Hence, '[i]n the earliest proposals for the Secretariat of the League, it was apparently taken for granted that there not be a truly international secretariat but that there would have to be nine national [secretariats]' – since there were to be nine Member States on the League's Council – each reporting to the Secretary-General.[5] This scheme enlarged upon 'precedents set by the various international bureau established' before World War I – see Chapter 2, 'International Organizations' – 'which were staffed by officials seconded by [Member States] on a temporary basis'.[6]

Yet, the first Secretary-General of the League of Nations, Sir Eric Drummond, envisaged not these fragmentary national staffs, but instead, one consolidated multinational secretariat. To Drummond, it was imperative that the League was not simply the site for conferences between states, but was rather, an impartial and international entity. This necessitated the 'constitution of a truly international civil service – officials who would be solely the servants of the League and in no way representative or responsible to the Governments of the countries of which they were nationals'.[7] Or, in other words, a secretariat whose 'duties are not national but international'.[8] Drummond's approach

[2] Hammarskjöld [1961] 2021, 331.
[3] Hammarskjöld [1961] 2021, 331.
[4] League Covenant, Article 6, second sentence.
[5] Hammarskjöld [1961] 2021, 330.
[6] Hammarskjöld [1961] 2021, 330; Hammarskjöld is quoting from a report to the Council of the League of Nations, delivered by Arthur Balfour, the representative on the Council for the UK.
[7] Drummond 1931, 229.
[8] Hammarskjöld [1961] 2021, 330; quoting Balfour.

prevailed and the Council established Staff Regulations to secure the international status of the League's officials.[9]

Subsequently, this status was reproduced in the constituent instrument of the UN – the UN Charter features Chapter 15, titled 'The Secretariat', comprising five Articles, 97–101. Such treaty terms constitute legally obligated attributes – governed by international law – of international officials. The legal significance of all of the articles of the UN Charter is consistent and mandatory. In other words, the staff of the UN possess attributes with a status under international law no different from how – for example – each Member State of the UN General Assembly has one vote (Article 18(1)) or France is a permanent member of the UN Security Council (Article 23(1)) or the principal judicial organ of the UN is the International Court of Justice (Article 92).

In terms all but identical to the UN Charter's Chapter 15, these attributes – this international status – are established by the constituent instrument of almost all other international organizations, instrumentalizing every multilateral mandate, with identical legal significance; see Annex 1, 'Compendium of Employment-Related Clauses from Constituent Instruments'. It is this uniform treaty-basis of the employees of multilateral institutions that establishes the international civil service, as universal to international organizations.

3.2 Legal Attributes of the International Civil Service

What are the attributes of the international civil service – obligated by international law – integral to the success of institutionalized multilateralism? First, as with modern national civil servants, international officials are meritocratically appointed on the basis of efficiency and preeminent competence. Second, since multilateralism without multinationalism would be unobtainable, international civil servants must be geographically diverse. Third, to ensure that international civil servants are impartial – and independent – administrators, they must be both uncorrupted and uninfluenced by outside instructions, especially from states. In other words, international officials must possess integrity and independence. These attributes are now considered in turn.

[9] See Tams 2007, para. 19, citing Article 1(1) of the League of Nations Staff Regulations, 'The officials of the Secretariat of the League of Nations are exclusively international officials and their duties are not national but international'.

Attribute 1: Efficiency and Competence

Rather than obtain employment with international organizations on the basis of personal ties, or political affiliations or nationality preferences, international officials are appointed – and retained – on the basis of efficiency and competence.[10] The UN Charter states: 'The paramount consideration in the employment of the staff and in the determination of the conditions of service shall be the necessity of securing the highest standards of efficiency, competence, and integrity'.[11] (Integrity – together with independence – is considered separately.)

The constituent instrument of the World Bank (its Articles of Agreement), likewise states, 'In appointing the officers and staff the President shall, subject to the paramount importance of securing the highest standards of efficiency and of technical competence ...'.[12] Whereas the Constitution of the International Labour Organization (ILO) – originally contemporaneous with the Covenant of the League of Nations – refers to, 'due regard to the efficiency of the work of the Office'.[13] Yet, as with the League, competence is codified by the ILO's Staff Regulations: 'The paramount consideration in the filling of any vacancy shall be the necessity to obtain a staff of the highest standards of competence, efficiency and integrity.'[14]

It is consequential that these standards are to be 'secured' or 'obtained'. In other words, they are not preferences, ranges or intentions, but obligated by international law. But secured, how? What are the moments in the careers of international officials that need to be governed in order to obtain such standards? Perhaps, most obviously, first at the time of recruitment: procedures must be established to ensure transparent and merit-based appointment to the staff of international organizations. Then, compensation must be sufficient to both attract and incentivise the most competent international officials. Lastly, rigorous processes must ensure the effective management of performance, obtain the advancement of competent officials and address substandard performance,

10 In the constituent instrument of international organizations, 'efficiency' and 'competence' typically double up, similar to 'privileges and immunities', which are always paired together. However, assuming that privileges are distinguishable from immunities, it seems that efficiency is an organizational trait – attributed to the international civil service as a whole – whereas competence is an attribute an individual international civil servant may possess. Nevertheless, no related distinction emerges in international administrative law.

11 UN Charter, Article 101(3), first sentence.

12 World Bank Articles of Agreement, Article 5(5)(D).

13 ILO Constitution, Article 9(2).

14 ILO Staff Regulations, Article 4.2.

potentially – in irretrievable situations – by termination of employment. Necessarily, this treaty-based attribute of efficiency and competence is implemented in the employment law at international organizations – see Chapter 6, 'Selection', Chapter 7, 'Remuneration' and Chapter 8, 'Performance Management'.

Attribute 2: Geographic Diversity

The constituent instruments of multilateral institutions also obligate the recruitment of a multinational staff. As was noted during debate about the staffing of the League of Nations: 'Evidently, no one nation or group of nations ought to have a monopoly in providing the material for this international institution.'[15] The UN Charter states: 'Due regard shall be paid to the importance of recruiting the staff on as wide a geographical basis as possible.'[16] Whilst the World Bank's Articles of Agreement establish that the 'highest standards of efficiency and of technical competence' are of paramount importance, they also require 'due regard to the importance of recruiting personnel on as wide a geographical basis as possible'.[17] Likewise, the ILO Constitution reads in full, 'So far as is possible with due regard to the efficiency of the work of the Office, the Director-General shall select persons of different nationalities.'[18]

Notably, the highest standards of efficiency and competence – these are 'paramount' – always take precedence over geographic representation – this possesses 'importance'. But functionally, the latter may be considered to complement the former, since a multinational staff is inherent to the achievement of multilateral purposes. With competence secured, geographic diversity may be weighed.[19] So, for example, between two equally competent candidates for appointment – or promotion say – the person of an underrepresented nationality is preferable.[20] But rather than obtaining

15 Hammarskjöld [1961] 2021, 330, quoting Balfour.

16 UN Charter, Article 101(3), second sentence.

17 World Bank Articles of Agreement, Article 5(5)(D).

18 ILO Constitution, Article 9(2).

19 Nowadays, the achievement of a diverse international civil service is considered inherent to the highest overall standards of competence, but as with geographic representation, the balance of other characteristics – such as gender equity – cannot be prioritized over competence. See Chapter 6, 'Selection'.

20 However, ascertaining under- and over-representation is a minefield. Does it mean equal numbers of nationals, with, for example, Chinese officials numbering the same as Chilean staff? Or is it based on population size or is it regional? Asia balancing Europe? Or is it tied

this attribute on a case-by-case basis, the achievement of geographic diversity is chiefly served by seeking to attract and retain a multinational staff. Or, in other words, the UN Office at Geneva, must be as attractive a workplace to Cameroonian, Canadian, Chinese, Chilean and other employees, as it is to Swiss nationals. So, benefits at international organizations must contribute to achieving geographic diversity.[21] This legitimates a degree of differentiation consistent with this due regard. The impediments to geographic diversity to be mitigated, may include: relocation costs, local language training, the greater expense and lower return of renting, not owning property, the education of children in their own language in pursuit of national examinations, and an accompanying, unemployed or underemployed spouse or partner. Necessarily, this treaty-based attribute of geographic diversity is implemented in the employment law at international organizations – see Chapter 7, 'Remuneration'.

Attribute 3: Integrity and Independence

Once appointed to the multinational staff – exemplify the highest standards of efficiency and technical competence – of a multilateral institution, the conduct of international officials is regulated by a demanding ethical framework, implementing the treaty-based attribute of integrity and independence. As with efficiency and competence, the highest standards of integrity must be 'secured'.[22] Necessarily, international officials must be uncorrupted and irreproachable. So, the Standards of Conduct for the International Civil Service state, 'The concept of integrity enshrined in the Charter of the UN embraces all aspects of an international civil servant's behaviour, including such qualities as honesty, truthfulness, impartiality and incorruptibility.'[23]

Yet, in addition to this requirement, to obtain the impartiality of international officials, constituent instruments establish further obligations upon both international civil servants on the one hand, and Member States of an international organization on the other hand. Article 100 of the UN Charter states:

to financial contribution or shareholding (for international financial institutions), which is connected to the economic magnitude of Member States? So implementing 'due regard' on an individualized basis is fraught.

21 Appropriate benefits are also consistent with attaining a highly competent staff with integrity, since self-subsidy both dissuades employment and could cause a vulnerability to corruption.

22 See UN Charter, Article 101(3) and World Bank Articles of Agreement, Article 5(5)(D). This is also the basis for background-checking candidates before appointment to the staff of international organizations.

23 Standards of Conduct for the International Civil Service, para. 5, first sentence.

> (1) In the performance of their duties the Secretary-General and the staff shall not seek or receive instructions from any government or from any other authority external to the [UN]. They shall refrain from any action which might reflect on their position as international officials responsible only to the [UN].
>
> (2) Each [Member State] of the United Nations undertakes to respect the exclusively international character of the responsibilities of the Secretary-General and the staff and not to seek to influence them in the discharge of their responsibilities.

This interlocking dual prohibition is fundamental to the independent, international status of the employees of international organizations. On the one hand, it prohibits international officials from seeking or receiving illegitimate instructions, and on the other hand, it enjoins Member States to refrain from exerting such unallowed influence. In other words, the lawful influence of states upon international organization is exclusively channelled through the governance arrangements of international organizations.[24] As the Standards of Conduct for the International Civil Service state, 'It cannot be too strongly stressed that international civil servants are not, in any sense, representatives of Governments or other entities, nor are they proponents of their policies.'[25]

Similar to the UN Charter, the constituent instrument of the World Bank states:

> The President, officers and staff of the Bank, in the discharge of their offices, owe their duty entirely to the Bank and to no other authority. Each member of the Bank shall respect the international character of this duty and shall refrain from all attempts to influence any of them in the discharge of their duties.[26]

Likewise, the ILO Constitution:

> The responsibilities of the Director-General and the staff shall be exclusively international in character. In the performance of their duties, the Director-General and the staff shall not seek or receive instructions from any government or from any other authority external to the [ILO]. They shall refrain from any action which might reflect on their position as international officials responsible only to the [ILO].

24 Of course, this treaty law is overlaid by practicalities. Notwithstanding the one Member State one vote basis of most governance organs of UN-style international organizations, the sway of states contributing the most financially to the organization is inevitably enhanced.

25 Standards of Conduct for the International Civil Service, para. 5, third sentence.

26 World Bank Articles of Agreement, Article 5(5)(C).

> Each [Member State] of the [ILO] undertakes to respect the exclusively international character of the responsibilities of the Director-General and the staff and not to seek to influence them in the discharge of their responsibilities.[27]

Furthermore, the constituent instruments of some international organizations also complement this with an express prohibition on the staff of international organizations weighing the 'political character' of Member States in their decision-making.[28]

The integrity and independent international character of the international civil service – although developed further by treaty terms than efficiency, competence and geographic diversity – must also be implemented in practice. In this way, international organizations adopt standards of conduct within their internal law intended to prevent the integrity and independence of international civil servants being compromised. They also establish procedures for notifying and reliably investigating employees suspected of breaching standards of conduct – featuring an opportunity for international officials accused of misconduct to respond. Lastly, they adopt internal laws intended to proportionately sanction international officials found culpable of misconduct. In the most serious circumstances, such sanction could be disciplinary termination of employment and the referral of the matter to local law enforcement authorities. Necessarily, this treaty-based attribute of integrity and independence is implemented in the employment law at international organizations – see Chapter 9, 'Standards of Conduct' and Chapter 10, 'Misconduct'.

3.3 Principal Executive Official

Since the limited powers possessed by international organizations arise from the terms of their constituent instruments, the authority to instruct and regulate international civil servants is likewise, treaty-based and ultimately governed by international law. All constituent instruments establish a paramount official, although their titles vary. For example, the Secretariat of the UN is prominently led by the Secretary-General;

[27] ILO Constitution, Article 9(4)–(5).

[28] See, for example, World Bank Articles of Agreement, Article 4(10): 'The Bank and its officers shall not interfere in the political affairs of any member; nor shall they be influenced in their decisions by the political character of the member or members concerned. Only economic considerations shall be relevant to their decisions, and these considerations shall be weighed impartially in order to achieve the purposes [of the Bank]'.

the World Bank – and all other multilateral development banks – has a President; whereas the ILO has a Director-General. For the purposes of this, and subsequent, chapters, the term *principal executive official* is adopted, drawing upon a clause in the Convention on the Privileges and Immunities of the Specialized Agencies which uses the term 'executive head', defined as the 'principal executive official' of an international organization, regardless of the formal treaty-based title used. The reason to prefer principal executive official is that it importantly conveys – in a stronger way than executive head – that this paramount officer is themselves, an international civil servant.

In other words, the principal executive official shares the legal attributes of the international civil service.[29] In ILOAT Judgment No. 2232, *JMB v. Organisation for the Prohibition of Chemical Weapons* (2003) – in which the former principal executive official successfully contests their premature and politicized removal from office – the Tribunal determines its jurisdiction over officials of international organizations extends to the principal executive official, since they are in fact the 'foremost official' of an international organization.[30] This, because as already noted, constituent instruments attribute to principal executive officials – as with say, the Secretary-General of the UN – responsibilities of an 'exclusively international character'.[31]

All principal executive officials are appointed through treaty-based governance processes, and possess an autonomous authority to instruct the staff, subject to regulation by Member State governance organs. These characteristics are considered under the following headings: (1) Appointment; and (2) Administrative authority.

1 *Appointment*

The power to appoint the principal executive official of any international organization is attributed by its constituent instrument to a governance organ. There are two types of governance organ, ubiquitous to international organizations.[32] First, a 'plenary body' representing all Member

[29] However, since the principal executive official could not be subordinated to their own authority, this is not identical to the status of a 'staff member' – although much about this status may be replicated in the terms and conditions of an appointment concluded with a principal executive official.

[30] ILOAT No. 2232, para. 7.

[31] UN Charter, Article 100(2).

[32] See Klabbers 2022, 211–212.

States of the multilateral institution. This resonates with one of the foundational principles of international law, namely the sovereign equality of states.[33] Second, an 'executive body' – a limited membership body – composed of a subset of all Member States of the organization. With some exceptions, the plenary body must meet at least biennially. Whereas, the executive body meets more frequently and in most cases repeatedly throughout the year.[34] Typically, membership of the executive body is chosen by the plenary body – for example, the UN General Assembly elects the non-permanent members of the UN Security Council.[35] The treaty-basis of all international organizations possess executive bodies with their own powers separate from – not only delegated by – the plenary body.[36]

The treaty-basis of international organizations attributes the authority to appoint the principal executive official to a governance organ. When this is by decision of the plenary body, the executive body typically has a nominating function. The UN Charter states: 'The Secretary-General shall be appointed by the General Assembly upon the recommendation of the Security Council.'[37] Hence, whilst the General Assembly – the plenary body – possesses the formal power to appoint the Secretary-General, candidacy is controlled by the Security Council. In accordance with the constituent instrument of the World Bank, its President is appointed by its executive body, the Executive Directors.[38] Whereas, the Board of Governors is the plenary body – the Articles of Agreement state: 'All the powers of the Bank shall be vested in the Board of Governors consisting of one governor and one alternate appointed by each [Member State] in such manner as it may determine.'[39] The Director-General of the ILO is appointed by the Governing Body,[40] an executive body composed not only of Member States, but also equal numbers of 'employer' and 'worker' representatives.[41]

33 UN Charter, Article 2(1), states: 'The [UN] is based on the principle of the sovereign equality of all its Members'.

34 Whereas the Board of Executive Directors of the World Bank usually meets at least biweekly and the UN Security Council is effectively in constant session.

35 See UN Charter, Article 23(3).

36 For example, UN Charter, Article 24, possesses the Security Council with 'primary responsibility for the maintenance of international peace and security'.

37 UN Charter, Article 97, second sentence.

38 See World Bank Articles of Agreement, Article (5)(5)(a).

39 World Bank Articles of Agreement, Article 5(2)(a), first sentence.

40 ILO Constitution, Article 8(1).

41 ILO Constitution, Article 3(1).

In all circumstances, appointment of the principal executive official is by resolution of the governance organ, achieved if not through consensus, then by voting. (Terms of appointment are then concluded between the appointee and the organization.) Notably, this power of appointment is limited – the only international civil servant almost all governance organs are empowered by the constituent instrument to appoint is the principal executive official.[42] As emerges later in this chapter, it is the principal executive official who is competent to appoint the other staff of the international organization, not a governance organ.

The power to appoint the principal executive official is accompanied both by the authority to limit their term upon appointment and justifiably remove them from office, before their term of appointment expires. So, whilst the UN Charter does not fix a duration for the appointment of the Secretary-General, in practice the General Assembly resolution appointing them expresses their term of office to last for five years.[43] Now, influenced by trends in corporate governance, there is an expectation that candidates will be selected through a transparent and merit-based procedure.[44] Typically, incumbent (and reasonably competent) principal executive officials may expect to be reappointed only once.[45]

The power to remove an incumbent principal executive official is unexpressed by constituent instruments, but is necessarily implied.[46] However, it would be incompatible with the integrity of a principal executive official – complemented by security of tenure during the term of

[42] Regional multilateral development banks – such as the Asian Development Bank – also allow, 'One or more Vice-Presidents shall be appointed by the Board of Directors on the recommendation of the President.' (See ADB Articles of Agreement, Article 35(1), first sentence.) Whereas UN office-holders, such as judges of the ICJ and members of the ILC – in other words, falling outside the UN Secretariat – are 'elected' by the UN General Assembly and UN Security Council (see Statute of the ICJ, Article 4(1)) and by the General Assembly (see Statute of the ILC, Article 3), respectively.

[43] UN General Assembly Res. 75/286 (2021).

[44] See, for example, UN General Assembly Res. 69/321 (2015), requesting Member States 'present candidates with proven leadership and managerial abilities, extensive experience in international relations and strong diplomatic, communication and multilingual skills' for the role of UN Secretary-General.

[45] This is achieved either by a non-binding practice – which could of course be set aside – or by treaty-based term limits; for example, the Director-General or the UN Educational, Scientific and Cultural Organization (UNESCO) may serve a maximum of two four-year terms (see UNESCO Constitution, Article VI(2)).

[46] The UN Joint Inspection Unit (JIU) recommends, 'The legislative bodies of United Nations system organizations that have not yet done so should develop and adopt appropriate formal procedures for the investigation of complaints of misconduct by executive heads and adopt appropriate policies' (UN JIU Report 2020, vi, Recommendation 7).

their appointment – for a governance organ to discontinue their appointment arbitrarily. In other words, this implied treaty-based power is also limited by international law. Hence, in *ILOAT No. 2232*, the Tribunal contemplates removal by governance resolution 'may, exceptionally, be justified in cases of grave misconduct'.[47] However, 'such a measure, being punitive in nature, could only be taken in full compliance with the principle of due process, following a procedure enabling the individual concerned to defend [their] case effectively before an independent and impartial body'.[48]

2 *Administrative Authority*

The constituent instruments of all international organizations attribute administrative authority to the principal executive official. The UN Secretary-General is the 'chief administrative officer' of the UN; the World Bank's President is 'chief of the operating staff of the Bank'; and the ILO's Director-General is 'responsible for the efficient conduct of the International Labour Office'.[49] However, albeit that the principal executive official is the 'chief administrative officer', this authority is not absolute. In the case of all international organizations, this power to appoint, direct and dismiss the staff is subject to regulation by the governance organ possessing the power to appoint the principal executive official.

The UN Charter states: 'The staff shall be appointed by the Secretary-General under regulations established by the General Assembly.'[50] The Articles of the Agreement of the World Bank state: 'Subject to the general control of the Executive Directors, [the President] shall be responsible for the organization, appointment and dismissal of the officers and staff.'[51] Under the ILO Constitution, the Director-General, 'subject to the instructions of the Governing Body, shall be responsible for the efficient conduct of the International Labour Office and for such other duties as may be assigned' to them.[52] Hence, the administrative authority of the principal executive official is subordinated to 'regulations', 'general control' and 'instructions' of the governance organ that appoints them.

[47] ILOAT No. 2232, para. 16.
[48] ILOAT No. 2232, para. 16.
[49] UN Charter, Article 97; Articles of Agreement of the World Bank, Article 5(5)(b); and ILO Constitution, Article 8(1).
[50] UN Charter, Article 101(1).
[51] World Bank Articles of Agreement, Article 5(5)(B), second sentence.
[52] ILO Constitution, Article 8(1).

In practice, this competence to regulate the staffing of an international organization, possessed by the governance organ that is empowered to appoint the principal executive official, is discharged by the issuance of *Staff Regulations* or such-like. Whereas, the principal executive official issues complementary instructions, such as *Staff Rules*. For example, the preamble of the Staff Regulations and Staff Rules of the UN states:

> Under Article 101 of the Charter of the United Nations, the General Assembly establishes staff regulations which set out the broad principles of human resources policy for the staffing and administration of the Secretariat ... The Secretary-General is required by the staff regulations to provide and enforce such staff rules, consistent with these principles, as the Secretary-General considers necessary.

Together, these and any other written instruments expressing the administrative authority of an international organization are termed – since the first ever international administrative tribunal judgment – the *internal law* of an international organization. League of Nations Administrative Tribunal Judgment No. 1, *di Palma Castiglione v. International Labour Office* (1929) – in which the claimant unsuccessfully seeks retroactive inclusion in the Staff Provident Fund – states, 'The Tribunal must apply the internal law of the League of Nations, as set out either in general regulations or in decisions and texts governing specific cases'[53] (See also Chapter 1, 'Introduction'.)

These treaty-based arrangements, uniform to international organizations, are the basis for three significant dimensions to the employment law at international organizations. First, the principal executive official of a multilateral institution is possessed of an administrative authority in their own right. In other words, although this authority is subject to regulation, it is possessed through attribution by the constituent instrument, not because it is delegated from a governance organ. Consequently, since the treaty-basis can never be nullified, nor can the administrative authority of the principal executive official.[54] However, the degree to which regulatory authority is imposed upon the principal executive official is ultimately determined by the governance organ.

Second, this arrangement constitutes a governance hierarchy whereby the principal executive official is empowered to implement, clarify and supplement regulation by the governance organ, but not to override it.

[53] League of Nations Administrative Tribunal (LoNAT) No. 1, para. II(A).

[54] See Quayle 2016, 858: '[T]he ICJ sets forth its own proposition governing contextualization so as to prohibit interpretation that nullifies the examined text'.

In other words, the regulatory authority of the UN General Assembly, the Executive Directors of the World Bank, and the Governing Body of the ILO, take precedence – in accordance with their constituent instrument – over the authority of the Secretary-General, President and Director-General, of these respective multilateral institutions.

However, third, the competence to instruct international civil servants is exclusively attributed to the principal executive official, not shared with the regulatory governance organ. Or in other words, international organizations possess only one chief administrative officer – the principal executive official. Whilst the governance organ may regulate principal executive officials' authority over employees of an international organization, they are not competent to instruct the staff. The only international civil servant that the governance organ is competent to instruct is the principal executive official. The principal executive official delegates their chief administrative officer authority, internally to subordinate officers of the multilateral institution – 'management' – consistent with an organizational and functional hierarchy. Necessarily, this treaty-based administrative authority of the principal executive official, regulated by the governance organ, is implemented in the employment law at international organizations – see especially, Chapter 11, 'Administration' and Chapter 12, 'Ending Service'.

3.4 The Legal Basis of the International Civil Service

The status of the international civil service is integral to the treaty-basis of international organizations. In order to instrumentalize the purposes of all international organizations, employees possess three irreducible attributes. First, international officials are selected and managed on the paramount basis of efficiency and competence. Second, there is due regard to obtaining geographic diversity of the staff of international organizations. Third, the international civil service must possess integrity and independence. This not only means an absence of corruption in the conventional sense. It necessitates that international officials must be impervious to instructions from all exterior authorities, most notably from states. Member States of international organizations are forbidden from instructing international civil servants – only a principal executive official is competent to do so. The sway of Member States over multilateral institutions is lawfully limited to activity within the organization's governance organs. All international organizations possess a principal executive official, appointed by a governance organ, with administrative authority over the international civil service, subject to regulation by a governance organ. Necessarily, these attributes and authority to instruct and regulate the international civil service are to be transposed from clear yet concise treaty terms, into the employment law at international organizations.

The legal basis of the international civil service may be restated as:

Legal Attributes of the International Civil Service

- International law obligates the selection and management of international officials on the paramount basis of efficiency and competence.
- International law obligates due regard is paid to achieving a geographically diverse staff of an international organization.
- International law obligates the integrity of international officials and their independence from states and other external authorities, and prohibits states from such interference.

Principal Executive Official

- The principal executive official is an international civil servant, possessed of a treaty-based office, through appointment by the governance organ of an international organization.
- The administrative authority of the principal executive official, as chief administrative officer, is autonomous but subordinated to regulation by their appointing governance organ.

4

International Administrative Tribunals

This chapter begins by introducing international administrative tribunals – independent, judicial, subsidiary organs of international organizations, competent to compulsorily adjudicate employment-related disputes involving international officials – that whilst ubiquitous, are implied, but not expressly stated, by the treaty-basis of all multilateral institutions. Second, the legal characteristics of international administrative tribunals are identified, namely: (1) Capacity to establish administrative tribunals is treaty-based; (2) Administrative tribunals possess an independent and judicial status; and (3) The jurisdiction of administrative tribunals is determined by their Statute. Third, the chapter considers the ability – and related approach – of administrative tribunals to impose administrative relief upon, and financial awards against, the employing international organization. Fourth, and in conclusion, this legal basis of international administrative tribunals is restated.

4.1 What Is an International Administrative Tribunal?

An *international administrative tribunal* – or administrative tribunal (AT) – is nowhere mentioned in the treaty-basis of any international organization. Yet they are an ubiquitous feature of the governance of multilateral institutions: independent, judicial, subsidiary organs of international organizations, empowered to compulsorily adjudicate employment-related disputes involving international officials. This coexistence of international administrative tribunals and international organizations began with the constitution of the international civil service itself to staff the League of Nations. Following the ad hoc resolution of the first documented employment-related dispute between an international official employee and employing international organization (see Chapter 5, 'Employment Related Dispute Resolution'), the League of Nations Administrative Tribunal was established in 1927.[1]

[1] See Petrović 2017, 21.

In addition to jurisdiction over members of the League's Secretariat, the Tribunal was also accessible by the officials of the International Labour Organization (ILO).[2] Like the League, the ILO was established in the aftermath of World War I and headquartered in Geneva.

When the League was disbanded to make way for the UN at the end of World War II, its Tribunal was adopted by the ILO, becoming the International Labour Organization Administrative Tribunal (ILOAT) in 1946.[3] Like the League before it, the UN, newly formed in 1945, soon established an administrative tribunal. The UN Administrative Tribunal (UNAdT) was founded in 1949, and superseded in 2009 by a two-tier internal justice system: the first-instance UN Dispute Tribunal and appellate UN Appeals Tribunal (UNDT, UNAT and together, the UNDT/AT).[4]

Like their predecessor, LoNAT, both the ILOAT and UNDT/AT adjudge challenges brought by the employees of multiple international organizations. The Statutes of the ILOAT and UNDT/AT allow other multilateral institutions to recognize – to utilize and enforce – their jurisdictions. In this way, about sixty international organizations around the world engage the jurisdiction of the ILOAT for a last resort hearing and judgment of employment-related disputes.[5] Whereas, about a dozen UN Specialized Agencies use the UNDT/AT in the same way.[6] International organizations that decide not to utilize the jurisdiction of the ILOAT or UNDT/AT establish their own, proprietary international administrative tribunals.[7]

This brief chronology would seem to suggest that international organizations automatically establish administrative tribunals. However, the elapse of over three decades, between the founding of the World Bank in 1944 and its creation of the World Bank Administrative Tribunal in 1980, demonstrates otherwise.[8] Yet, if international administrative tribunals are unmentioned by the treaty-basis of international organization, why are they inevitable?

Necessarily, international administrative tribunals are derived from the – limited – legal powers of international organizations (see Chapter 2, 'International Organizations'). So, the capacity to establish an international

[2] Schermers and Blokker 2018, 405.
[3] Petrović 2017, 23–24.
[4] UN General Assembly Res. 351 (1949) and UN General Assembly Res. 63/253 (2008).
[5] De Cooker 2022, 3.
[6] De Cooker 2022, 4.
[7] De Cooker 2022, 4–6.
[8] See WBAT Statute.

administrative tribunal must exercise a competence necessarily intended but not expressly stated by the treaty-basis of multilateral institutions. In doing so, this orchestrates several treaty-based stated legal powers possessed by international organizations. These include the authority to create subsidiary organs, enter into budgetary obligations, regulate the employment framework, secure the attributes of the international civil service – efficiency and competence, geographic diversity, integrity and independence – together with responding to the jurisdictional immunities typically possessed by multilateral institutions (see Chapter 2, 'International Organizations'). Governance organs converge this authority in a *Statute* of the AT – equipping the tribunal with an independent and judicial status, of limited jurisdiction. Or, in other words, whilst international administrative tribunals are not expressly constituted, they are necessarily intended, by the treaty-basis of international organizations.

4.2 Legal Characteristics of International Administrative Tribunals

As noted in Chapter 3, 'International Civil Service', the treaty-basis of all international organizations legislates for a plenary body – a governance organ intended to represent the authority and interests of all Member States. Most constituent instruments also enact an executive body – a subset of Member States, selected from amongst the totality of the membership (whether elected or in accordance with some functional criteria) to meet more frequently and carry out specialist functions. The principal executive official can be said to lead a third institutional organ, namely the *Secretariat* – or in other words, an administrative organ.

Taking the UN as an example, the General Assembly is the plenary body, the Security Council is an executive body, and the administrative organ is the Secretariat, led by the Secretary-General. Whereas, at an international financial institution (IFI), such as the World Bank or IMF, the all-membership governance organ is the Board of Governors – which meets once or twice a year. The more frequently convened, compact executive body is the Board of Executive Directors – meeting as often as weekly or even daily. Under an IFI's President is the administrative organ, which tends to be thought of simply as 'the Bank' or 'the Fund' rather than a 'secretariat' as it would be at an UN-style multilateral institution. However, despite this variety of terms, these are all principal organs of an international organization. In other words, there are expressly constituted by the constituent instrument of an international organization.

Yet, the UN Charter states that the organs of the UN are not limited to the expressly mentioned principal organs: 'Such subsidiary organs as may be found necessary may be established in accordance with the present Charter.'[9] When not expressly stated, this authority to establish subsidiary organs is necessarily intended by the treaty-basis of other international organizations.[10] And this, together with the competence to regulate the employment framework of international organizations – as with the UN General Assembly, for example – or the paramount competency of an IFI's Board of Governors, enables the establishment of administrative tribunals. Tribunals align with the treaty-based powers possessed by international organizations.[11]

Accordingly, the first legal characteristic that international administrative tribunals may be said to possess is a treaty-basis. Consequently, administrative tribunals are to be ultimately understood as deriving from and regulated by the international law that enables the constitution and governance of international organizations themselves. Second, the Statute adopted by a principal organ that establishes an administrative tribunal, possesses this subsidiary organ with an independent and judicial status. It may do so, even though necessarily, this is not the status of the principal organ itself. Third, this Statute delimits the jurisdiction of international administrative tribunals, largely confining the exercise of their authority to international officials appointed to the staff of international organizations, who have brought an in-time challenge against an adverse administrative decision, following the exhaustion of any recourse that is preconditional to accessing the tribunal. These legal characteristics are now considered in turn.

Characteristic 1: Capacity to Establish Administrative Tribunals Is Treaty-Based

Notwithstanding the uncontested establishment of LoNAT in the 1920s, express provision for an international administrative tribunal was not incorporated into the UN Charter in the 1940s. In the 1950s,

9 UN Charter, Article 7(2).

10 Klabbers 2022, 217–218.

11 UN Charter, Article 101(1): 'The staff shall be appointed by the Secretary-General under regulations established by the General Assembly.' See Chapter 2, 'International Civil Service'.

the UN General Assembly was sufficiently disconcerted by the administrative tribunal it had created to request from the International Court of Justice (ICJ) an Advisory Opinion, *Effect of Awards of Compensation Made by the United Nations Administrative Tribunal* (1954).[12] The question the Court is asked to answer is whether the General Assembly has legal grounds to renege on the financial awards made by judgments of the UNAdT going against the UN Secretary-General – the respondent – in cases concerning the unilateral termination of staff appointments. (However, the resulting Advisory Opinion is broader, settling all of the legal characteristics of international administrative tribunals.) Fundamentally, the ICJ considers whether the UN has exceeded its powers in establishing the UNAdT. Of the UN Charter, the ICJ notes, '[t]here is no express provision for the establishment of judicial bodies or organs and no indication to the contrary', yet:

> Under international law, the [UN] must be deemed to have those powers which, though not expressly provided in the Charter, are conferred upon it by necessary implication as being essential to the performance of its duties. The Court must therefore begin by enquiring whether the provisions of the Charter concerning the relations between the staff members and the [UN] imply for the [UN] the power to establish a judicial tribunal to adjudicate upon disputes arising out of the contracts of service.[13]

The Court next investigates the arrangement of employment relations at the UN – which resemble those at all international organizations. Namely, that staff members are subordinated to the administrative authority of the principal executive official – the UN Secretary-General – themselves regulated by a Member State governance organ – the General Assembly. The internal law of the UN is comprised of Staff Regulations issued by the General Assembly and implemented by Staff Rules, issued by the Secretary-General – securing the legal attributes of the international civil service: efficiency and competence, geographic diversity, integrity and independence together with subordination to administrative authority. (See Chapter 3, 'International Civil Service'.) Drawing upon this arrangement, in conjunction with the Statute of the UNAdT, the ICJ finds:

[12] In requesting an Advisory Opinion, the UN General Assembly was preoccupied by the fact that the Secretary-General had been forced to seek 'a supplementary [financial] appropriation ... for the purpose of covering the awards made by the United Nations Administrative Tribunal in eleven cases'; see ICJ *Effects of Awards*, 5.

[13] ICJ *Effects of Awards*, 13.

> [T]hat the power to establish a tribunal, to do justice as between the [UN] and the staff members, was essential to ensure the efficient working of the Secretariat, and to give effect to the paramount consideration of securing the highest standards of efficiency, competence and integrity. Capacity to do this arises by necessary intendment out of the Charter.[14]

Although the Court prefaces this with a pointed observation about the inconsistency of an international organization such as the UN – existing to 'promote freedom and justice for individuals' – not affording a 'judicial or arbitral remedy to its own staff for the settlement of any disputes which may arise between it and them',[15] the overall scheme of the Advisory Opinion rests upon the intention of the General Assembly – expressed through adoption of the UNAdT Statute – to establish an independent, judicial, subsidiary organ, competent to compulsorily adjudicate employment-related disputes, to secure the status of the international civil service. In this regard, the Statute of the ILOAT – adopted by the International Labour Conference – and the Statute of the WBAT – adopted by the Board of Governors of the World Bank – are similar to the Statute of the UNDT/AT – adopted by the UN General Assembly.[16]

Characteristic 2: Administrative Tribunals Possess an Independent and Judicial Status

Essential to the International Court of Justice's consideration of the legal status of international administrative tribunals is, 'whether the [UNAdT] is established either as a judicial body, or as an advisory organ or a mere subordinate committee of the General Assembly'.[17] To determine the status of the UNAdT, the ICJ examines the Tribunal's Statute. It finds: 'This examination of the relevant provisions of the Statute shows that the Tribunal is established, not as an advisory organ or a mere subordinate

[14] ICJ *Effects of Awards*, 14.

[15] ICJ *Effects of Awards*, 14.

[16] Notably, the authority to regulate the principal executive official of the World Bank and ILO is attributed to the executive body – the Executive Directors and Governing Body, respectively – not the plenary body. (See Chapter 3, 'International Civil Service'.) Whereas, the Statutes of the WBAT and ILOAT are adopted by the plenary body, the Board of Governors and International Labour Conference, respectively. This has fundamental governance consequences, since the UNAT cannot overrule decisions and internal law adopted by the General Assembly, as incompatible with international administrative law, whereas the WBAT and ILOAT are competent to set aside unlawful administration, even when attributable to the executive body that instructs and regulates the principal executive official.

[17] ICJ *Effects of Awards*, 8.

committee of the General Assembly, but as an independent and truly judicial body pronouncing final judgments without appeal within the limited field of its functions.'[18] The basis for this is the way in which the provisions of the Statute, 'and the terminology used are evidence of the judicial nature of the Tribunal. Such terms as "tribunal", "judgment", competence to "pass judgment upon applications", are generally used with respect to judicial bodies'.[19] The UN General Assembly itself confers upon the UNAdT the power to pronounce 'final judgments without appeal within the limited field of its functions'.[20] Comparable provisions are found in the Statutes of all international administrative tribunals – for example, the Statute of the present-day UNAT states:

> A tribunal is established by the present statute as the second instance of the two-tier formal system of administration of justice, to be known as the United Nations Appeals Tribunal. The Appeals Tribunal shall be competent to hear and pass judgement on an appeal filed against a judgement rendered by the United Nations Dispute Tribunal.[21]

The Statute of the ILOAT states:

> There is established by the present Statute a Tribunal to be known as the International Labour Organization Administrative Tribunal. The Tribunal shall be competent to hear complaints alleging non-observance, in substance or in form, of the terms of appointment of officials of the International Labour Office, and of such provisions of the Staff Regulations as are applicable to the case.[22]

The Statute of the WBAT states:

> There is hereby established a Tribunal of the International Bank for Reconstruction and Development ... the International Development Association and the International Finance Corporation ... to be known as the World Bank Administrative Tribunal. The Tribunal is a judicial body that functions independently of the management of the Bank Group. The independence of the Tribunal shall be guaranteed and respected by the Bank Group at all times. The Tribunal shall hear and pass judgment upon any application by which a member of the staff of the Bank Group alleges non-observance of the contract of employment or terms of appointment of such staff member.

[18] ICJ *Effects of Awards*, 10.
[19] ICJ *Effects of Awards*, 9.
[20] ICJ *Effects of Awards*, 10.
[21] UNAT Statute, Articles 1–2.
[22] ILOAT Statute, Articles 1–2.

But are non-judicial principal organs – such as the UN General Assembly, ILO's International Labour Conference and the World Bank's Board of Governors – empowered to establish judicial subsidiary organs? The ICJ is untroubled by this controversy. It finds: 'By establishing the Administrative Tribunal, the General Assembly was not delegating the performance of its own [non-judicial] functions: it was exercising a power which it had under the Charter to regulate staff relations.'[23] In other words, it was not delegating a judicial competence it did not possess. It was selecting a suitable modality to resolve employment-related disputes – a competence derived from its authority to regulate employment relations at the UN's Secretariat. Likewise, the budgetary authority of the General Assembly[24] is not usurped by the establishment of an international administrative tribunal with binding judicial competence:

> [T]he function of approving the budget does not mean that the General Assembly has an absolute power to approve or disapprove the expenditure proposed to it; for some part of that expenditure arises out of obligations already incurred by the [UN], and to this extent the General Assembly has no alternative but to honour these engagements. The question, therefore, to be decided by the Court is whether these obligations comprise the awards of compensation made by the Administrative Tribunal in favour of staff members. The reply to this question must be in the affirmative.[25]

The ICJ finds analysis of the Tribunal's Statute establishes that the UN is obligated by judgments and consequent financial awards by its administrative tribunal. The related analysis in *Effect of Awards* also underlines the finality of the judgments of international administrative tribunals.

Administrative tribunals are terminal judicial venues.[26] For example, the Statute of the ILOAT states that judgments are 'final and without appeal'; the Statute of the WBAT is expressed identically.[27] As the ICJ notes, a governance organ could create an administrative tribunal

[23] ICJ *Effects of Awards*, 18.
[24] See UN Charter, Article 17.
[25] ICJ *Effects of Awards*, 16.
[26] Both the UNAdT and ILOAT once had arrangements whereby their judgments could be appealed to the ICJ, through the Advisory Opinion mechanism. However, this was ultimately discontinued. The UN General Assembly resolution ending the mechanism for the UNAdT notes that after forty years, it 'has not proved to be a constructive or useful element in the adjudication of staff disputes' at the UN. (See UN General Assembly Res. 50/54 (1996).)
[27] See ILOAT Statute, Article VI and WBAT Statute, Article XI.

with different features, but the General Assembly did not – or in other words, whilst a tribunal's Statute may be repealed it cannot be disregarded.[28]

Likewise, the judgments of international administrative tribunals – inherent to their independent and judicial status – must be (promptly) enforced. In ILOAT Judgment No. 4324, *S (No. 3) v. European Patent Office* (2020) – in which the claimant unsuccessfully contends that the employing international organization has failed to execute an earlier judgment – the Tribunal recalls that its judgments are 'immediately operative' and 'international organizations that have recognised the Tribunal's jurisdiction are bound to take whatever action the decision in a judgment may require, which must be executed by the parties as ruled'; and the Tribunal adds: 'Judgments must be executed within a reasonable period of time.'[29] Similarly, in WBAT Judgment No. 673, *EO (No. 3) v. International Finance Corporation* (2022), the claimant contends that an adjustment to their benefits – previously awarded by the Tribunal – was incorrectly calculated and payment was delayed. The Tribunal relates the enforceability of judgments to its judicial status:

> The Bank Group's obligation to comply with judgments delivered by the Tribunal is foundational to the legitimacy of the Tribunal's establishment as a judicial body charged with responsibility for determining issues of conflict between the Bank Group and its staff in a manner that is wholly independent and impartial.[30]

The Tribunal finds that its judgments must be implemented 'in a reasonable manner and within a reasonable time'.[31] This is unsurprising since, within the internal governance of an international organization, administrative tribunals are the deployment of authority of their parent governance organ, taking precedence over the principal executive official.

Characteristic 3: The Jurisdiction of Administrative Tribunals Is Determined by Their Statute

As subsidiary organs, the jurisdiction of an international administrative tribunal is necessarily determined by its Statute. As with any judicial organ, the jurisdiction of an administrative tribunal is limited by: the nature of the events which are legally challengeable before it; the

[28] ICJ *Effects of Awards*, 18.
[29] ILOAT No. 4324, para. 3.
[30] WBAT No. 673, para. 32.
[31] WBAT No. 673, para. 34.

nature of the person capable of bringing such legal challenge; and the deadline following the challengeable event within which time any related legal challenge must be brought. Although the Statutes of international administrative tribunals address all three of these dimensions of jurisdiction, the legal basis for challengeable events requires the most exposition by ATs and is expressed as a general legal principle – see Chapter 5, 'Employment-Related Dispute Resolution'. Whereas, it may be said that administrative tribunals are statutorily limited, so that conventionally: (1) only international civil servants may access administrative tribunals, and (2) administrative tribunals may only admit in-time challenges. These limitations are now considered in turn.

1 Only International Civil Servants May Access Administrative Tribunals

Since international administrative tribunals exercise the authority of governance organs to regulate international organizations, then limiting access to administrative tribunals may be understood as functionally justified. Or, in other words, international administrative tribunals secure the legal attributes of the international civil service, subject to administrative authority at international organizations. However, not without controversy, this deliberately excludes jurisdiction over the many non-staff 'consultants' and 'contractors' retained by international organizations. But it is possible, as becomes apparent later in this chapter, for international administrative tribunals to recategorize non-staff as international civil servants, thus attributing to them the status and all of the legal consequences of employment at the international organization.

The Statute of the ILOAT states that the following categories of person have access to the Tribunal: 'the official, even if [their] employment has ceased, and to any person on whom the official's rights have devolved on [their] death' and also 'any other person who can show that [they're] entitled to some right under the terms of appointment of a deceased official or under provisions of the Staff Regulations on which the official could rely'.[32]

[32] ILOAT Statute, Article II(6). Notably, however, the ILO itself may utilize the ILOAT to adjudicate disputes involving non-staff contractors, further to ILOAT Statute, Article II(4): 'The Tribunal shall be competent to hear disputes arising out of contracts to which the International Labour Organization is a party and which provide for the competence of the Tribunal in any case of dispute with regard to their execution.' In this scenario, one expects the contract terms to govern the dispute, not international administrative law. Rarely, some Statutes also allow disappointed (external) applicants for vacancies at an international organization to bring a claim before an administrative tribunal; see Chapter 6, 'Selection'.

The WBAT is accessible to 'members of staff':

> For the purposes of [the WBAT] Statute: the expression 'member of the staff' means any current or former member of the staff of the Bank Group, any person who is entitled to claim upon a right of a member of the staff as a personal representative or by reason of the staff member's death, and any person designated or otherwise entitled to receive a payment under any provision of the Staff Retirement Plan.[33]

Likewise, the Statute of the UNDT (from which judgments are appealed to the UNAT) permits access by:

> (a) Any staff member of the United Nations, including the United Nations Secretariat or separately administered United Nations funds and programmes;
> (b) Any former staff member of the United Nations, including the United Nations Secretariat or separately administered United Nations funds and programmes;
> (c) Any person making claims in the name of an incapacitated or deceased staff member of the United Nations, including the United Nations Secretariat or separately administered United Nations funds and program.[34]

Consequently, any other contractual relationship with an international organization is insufficient to access international administrative tribunals. The tribunal-user must hold an appointment to the staff of the multilateral institution, issued by or on behalf of its principal executive official. For this reason, long-term non-staff contractors and consultants – although embedded amongst the staff of almost all international organizations – attempting to resort to an administrative tribunal have first sought to establish that they should be reclassified by the administrative tribunal as employees.

The most influential case of contractual miscategorization before an international administrative tribunal is Asian Development Bank Administrative Tribunal [ADBAT] Judgment No. 24, *Amora v. Asian Development Bank* (ADB) (1997). The claimant worked at the ADB for fourteen years as a 'consultant', before being converted to a staff member and retiring less than two years' later. Throughout this whole period the claimant worked as a copy machine operator. They contended that they were entitled to retirement benefits reflecting the entire time of their engagement at the ADB, alleging that they were contractually misclassified as a consultant and were instead throughout, de facto staff. Having not

[33] WBAT Statute, Article II(1) and Article II(3).
[34] UNDT Statute, Article 3.

addressed the issue before, the ADBAT surveys the existing jurisprudence on contractual miscategorization before the ILOAT and the (now discontinued) UNAdT. The Tribunal rules:

> The Tribunal holds that recourse to successive short-term or temporary contractual appointments to jobs which are essentially of a permanent nature is not a fair employment practice, particularly if such appointments can be shown to have been made only to deny employees security of tenure or other conditions and benefits of service. Such appointments are permissible only if they have a clear functional justification and rationale in the exigencies of management and the nature of the job in question, and are subject to limitations based on norms of good administration.[35]

The ADBAT finds the ADB abused its power, and the claimant was a de facto employee when designated a 'consultant', awarding the claimant retirement benefits (and other payments) commensurate with this period of service.

In WBAT Judgment No. 214, *Caryk v. IBRD* (1991),[36] in which the claimant unsuccessfully seeks to rely on *ADBAT Amora* to obtain retirement benefits, the Tribunal finds:

> In the *Amora* case, two features appear salient. First, the [claimant] was an essentially unskilled office labourer whose tasks could readily have been performed by practically anyone. To consider someone in that position to be an 'independent contractor' seems an abuse of language. [Their] work was routine and fungible, not a specific task in the framework of a mission limited in time or expected to be terminated with the achievement of particular goals, or in the context of a program … which was explicitly designed as potentially transitional. The ADBAT properly refused to accept a characterisation which did not reflect the true relationship between the parties. Second, [the claimant] was never offered a regular position until a time when it was almost too late to be a practical benefit to [them], given the decision to retire [them] within less than two years.
>
> In the *Amora* case, there appeared to be no valid reason for having treated the [claimant] as an 'independent contractor' and denying [them] the benefits of a regular staff member. Indeed, the [respondent international organization] practically admitted as much in portions of its pleadings quoted in the judgment, when it spoke of 'expediency' and 'efficient functioning.' An authority which seeks to justify its miscategorisation of persons subject to its power on such grounds is likely to be found guilty of abuse.[37]

35 ADBAT No. 24, para. 27.

36 WBAT Judgment No. 215, *Madhusudan v. International Bank for Reconstruction and Development* (1991) was decided at the same time and in identical terms.

37 WBAT No. 214, paras. 22–23.

However, this judgment does not turn on contested access to the WBAT, since the claimant was not seeking reclassification from non-staff to staff status to first utilize the Tribunal's jurisdiction, but rather reclassification between different types of staff. Such differentiation between different types of international official, entitled to different appointment terms and conditions, if not arbitrary, is permissible. For example, the World Bank utilizes 'Short-Term Temporary', 'Short-Term Consultant', 'Extended Term Temporary' and 'Extended Term Consultant' appointment types, together with 'Term' appointments. Albeit some of this terminology is confusing, all these types of appointees are employees, but the international organization seeks to benefit from 'added flexibility for rapid scalability (expansion and contraction) and quick adaptation to business needs and requisite skill changes'.[38] (However, see Chapter 12, 'Ending Service'.)

2 Administrative Tribunals May Only Admit In-Time Challenges

As with many forms of justice – and especially administrative jurisdictions – challenges must be submitted to international administrative tribunals within a statutory deadline, to be admissible. For example, the ILOAT's Statute states, 'To be receivable, a complaint [by a claimant] must also have been filed within ninety days after the [claimant] was notified of the decision impugned.'[39] Before the UNDT/AT, claimants have ninety days to file a challenge to the UNDT, and then sixty days following judgment to file an appeal with the UNAT.[40] (Decisions of the UN Joint Staff Pension Fund must be appealed to the UNAT within ninety days.)[41]

The deadline to file a challenge with the WBAT is longest – 120 days – and the Tribunal also has the competence to extend even this time limit, 'under exceptional circumstances'.[42] The WBAT summarizes its approach to applying this exception in WBAT Judgment No. 675, *GU v. International Bank for Reconstruction and Development* (2022) – in which the claimant unsuccessfully seeks to overturn a 'mutually agreed separation' agreement, concluded seven years earlier – and states:

[38] World Bank Guidance (2024), para. 1.01.
[39] ILOAT Statute, Article VII(2).
[40] UNAT Statute Article 7(1)(c).
[41] UNAT Statute Article 7(2).
[42] WBAT Statute, Article II(2).

> The Tribunal [has] held that the statutory requirement of timely action may be relaxed in exceptional circumstances. Such circumstances, it added, are determined by the Tribunal from case to case on the basis of the particular facts of each case. … [T]he Tribunal clarified that exceptional circumstances are real and serious impediments to exhausting internal remedies, and that mere inconvenience is not sufficient. The Tribunal follows a strict approach in determining what constitutes exceptional circumstances in the context of [statutory time limits]. Under this strict approach, exceptional circumstances cannot be based on allegations of a general kind but require reliable and pertinent contemporaneous proof.[43]

4.3 Remedies

The remedies that international administrative tribunals may impose are delimited by their Statute, but have also been iterated through their judgments. There are two types of remedy: (1) administrative relief; and (2) financial awards.

1 *Administrative Relief*

All international administrative tribunals are possessed of the competence to order administrative relief – in other words, to order actions that place successful claimants into the administrative circumstances that they would be experiencing, had the employing international organization not acted unlawfully. The multilateral institution must take action, either to reverse the unlawful administrative act or to perform an act that has been unlawfully withheld. This is respectively referred to as *rescission* on the one hand, and *specific performance* on the other hand. The Statute of the ILOAT states, 'if satisfied that the complaint was well founded, [the Tribunal] shall order the rescinding of the decision impugned or the performance of the obligation relied upon'.[44] The Statute of the WBAT states: 'If the Tribunal finds that the application is well-founded, it shall order the rescission of the decision contested or the specific performance of the obligation invoked.'[45] Likewise, the Statute of the UNAT empowers the Tribunal to order, 'Rescission of the contested administrative decision or specific performance.'[46] However, these powers to order administrative relief are constrained in two important respects.

[43] WBAT No. 675, paras. 24–26.

[44] ILOAT Statute, Article VIII, first sentence.

[45] ILOAT, Article XII(1), first sentence.

[46] UNAT Statute, Article 9(1)(a).

First, the Statutes of international administrative tribunals obligate consideration of the efficiency of the international civil service in the imposition of administrative relief. The ILOAT must consider if administrative relief is 'not possible or advisable'.[47] The WBAT, whether it 'would not be practicable or in the institution's interests'.[48] If so, the Tribunals are obligated to commute such administrative relief to a financial award. Whereas, the UNAT, if 'the contested administrative decision concerns appointment, promotion or termination, the Appeals Tribunal shall also set an amount of compensation that the respondent may elect to pay as an alternative to the rescission of the contested administrative decision or specific performance ordered'.[49] In other words, in such circumstances it falls to the employing international organization to determine whether to undertake the administrative relief or pay the alternative financial award.[50] However, on this basis, if the unlawful administrative action is unrelated to appointment, promotion or termination, then the UNAT should not itself commute administrative relief to a financial award.

Second is the circumspection demonstrated by the jurisprudence of international administrative tribunals as to what administrative relief may precisely be ordered. In ILOAT Judgment No. 1213, *El Mahjoub v. International Labour Organization* (1993), wherein the claimant unsuccessfully seeks as administrative relief, essentially appointment to the post they want, and on the terms they set,[51] the Tribunal circumscribes its powers of specific performance, to include disencumbering a position but exclude encumbering one:

> What [ILOAT Statute, Article VIII] means, as the case law has construed it, is that the Tribunal may not order an organization to put a staff member on any particular post. All it may do is set aside an unlawful decision putting someone on a post or refusing to do so or order specific performance where the [international organization] has failed to discharge an obligation.[52]

[47] ILOAT Statute, Article VIII.
[48] WBAT Statute, Article XII(1).
[49] UNAT Statute, Article 9(1)(a).
[50] The UNAT has clarified that this choice must be offered; see UNAT Judgment No. 587, *Faraj v. Commissioner-General of the United Nations Relief and Works Agency for Palestine Refugees in the Near East* (2015), para. 48, 'It follows that, in principle, in cases concerning appointment, promotion or termination, the Tribunal should not limit itself to only granting compensation. It has to provide the [respondent] with a choice between on the one hand, rescinding the decision or performing an obligation and, on the other hand, paying compensation.'
[51] See ILOAT No. 1213, para. 1.
[52] ILOAT No. 1213, para. 3.

2 *Financial Awards*

The authority to make a financial award to a successful claimant is possessed by most international administrative tribunals in the alternative – not concurrently – to ordering administrative relief. The Statute of the ILOAT, makes clear this contingency: 'If such rescinding of a decision or execution of an obligation is not possible or advisable, the Tribunal shall award the complainant compensation for the injury caused to [them].'[53] The WBAT Statute is the basis for the Tribunal ordering the respondent to 'pay restitution in the amount that is reasonably necessary to compensate the applicant for the actual damages suffered', instead of administrative relief.[54] However, the UNAT may order financial awards in addition to administrative relief, in the following terms:

> Compensation for harm, supported by evidence, which shall normally not exceed the equivalent of two years' net base salary of the applicant. The Appeals Tribunal may, however, in exceptional cases order the payment of a higher compensation for harm, supported by evidence, and shall provide the reasons for that decision.[55]

The financial quantification by international administrative tribunals of harm done by maladministration by international organizations is an inexact science. Occasionally, the loss to the staff member can be rendered with some arithmetical precision. More often, the administrative tribunal awards an amount indicative of the severity of its disapproval, benchmarked to other financial awards ordered in comparable cases. Although unmentioned in the Statutes of international administrative tribunals, this is achieved by awarding so-called *moral damages*, for which tribunals afford some guidance.

In UNAT Judgment No. 309, *Asariotis v. Secretary-General of the United Nations* (2013) – in which the claimant contests the belated cancellation of a vacancy for which they considered themselves the most likely successful candidate – the Tribunal sets out its approach to moral damages in the first-instance tribunal, and finds that: '[t]o invoke its jurisdiction to award moral damages, the UNDT must in the first instance identify the moral injury sustained by the employee. This identification can never be an exact science and such identification will

[53] ILOAT Statute, Article VIII, second sentence.
[54] WBAT Statute, Article XII(1).
[55] UNAT Statute, Article 9(1)(b).

necessarily depend on the facts of each case.'[56] It goes on, stating that, unlawful administration, breaching a staff members 'substantive entitlements' or a breach of a 'fundamental nature' may occasion moral damages, 'by virtue of the harm to the employee'.[57] Any 'medical, psychological report or otherwise of harm, stress or anxiety caused to the employee' attributable to such substantive or fundamental breaches may also result in moral damages.[58]

In ILOAT Judgment No. 4644, *S (No. 3) v. European Patent Office* (2023) the Tribunal summarizes its approach to moral damages – unsuccessfully sought by the claimant in recompense for a series of prolonged internal appeals broadly related to contested allowance payments – and states:

> Moral damages are awarded for moral injury and the complainant bears the burden of proving that injury and the causal link with the unlawful conduct of the defendant organization. Delay, of itself, does not entitle a [claimant] to moral damages. Without attempting to describe, exhaustively, what might constitute a moral injury, it includes emotional distress, anxiety, stress, anguish and hardship.[59]

4.4 The Legal Basis of International Administrative Tribunals

The first judgment of the World Bank Administrative Tribunal – WBAT Judgment No. 1, *de Merode and Others v. The World Bank* (1981) – contemplates the significance of the Tribunal's establishment and declares:

> [T]he decision of the Board of Governors to establish this Tribunal introduced into the conditions of employment of Bank staff the right of recourse to this Tribunal, in accordance with the conditions laid down in the Statute. This right forms an integral part of the legal relationship between the Bank and its staff members.[60]

Moreover, international administrative tribunals are necessarily intended by the treaty basis of all international organizations. Absent such tribunals – possessed of an independent and judicial status, together with a jurisdiction determined by their Statute, securing the legal attributes of the international civil service and application of administrative

[56] UNAT No. 309, para. 36.
[57] UNAT No. 309, para. 36(i).
[58] UNAT No. 309, para, 36(ii).
[59] ILOAT No. 4644, para. 7.
[60] WBAT No. 1, para. 21.

authority – international organizations would be irredeemably exposed to maladministration on the one hand, and deficient international officials on the other hand. This, in turn, would be injurious to their operational efficiency, effectiveness and legitimacy.

The legal basis of international administrative tribunals may be restated as:

Legal Attributes of International Administrative Tribunals

- Capacity to establish administrative tribunals is treaty-based.
- Administrative tribunals possess an independent and judicial status.
- The jurisdiction of administrative tribunals is determined by their Statute, thereby: (1) only international officials may access administrative tribunals, and (2) administrative tribunals may only admit in-time challenges.

Remedies

- Administrative tribunals may order remedies for the benefit of successful claimants, namely (1) administrative relief and (2) financial awards, including so-called moral damages.

5

Employment-Related Dispute Resolution

This chapter begins by introducing the resolution of employment-related disputes at international organizations – by examining the first ever formal example of this, involving an international civil servant employed by the League of Nations. Second, the general legal principles of reviewing employment-related disputes at international organizations are identified, namely: (1) Only adverse administrative decisions may be contested; (2) Deference is owed discretionary authority; and (3) Arbitrariness invalidates authority. Third, three general legal principles of evidence utilized by international administrative tribunals are considered, namely: (1) Claimants must establish arbitrariness; (2) Unreasoned administrative decisions are evidently arbitrary; and (3) Administrative decisions cannot be based upon withheld evidence. Fourth, and in conclusion, this legal basis of employment-related dispute resolution at international organizations is restated.

5.1 What Is Employment-Related Dispute Resolution?

The League of Nations was the first international organization to be staffed – not by secondees or envoys from states, but – by an independent and international civil service. In other words, staff members were loyal only to the League and subject neither to the civil service regulations nor employment law of their same-nationality states. Or indeed, the labour laws of their headquarters location: Geneva. (See Chapter 3, 'International Civil Service'.) Necessarily, the first employment-related dispute resolved at the League asked and answered the foundational question, what is the legal basis of employment-related disputes at international organizations?[1] The claimant was François

[1] See League of Nations, Committee Conclusions (1925); all quotations in this Section 5.1 draw on the report of the judicial committee appointed by the Council of the League to determine Monod's employment-related dispute.

Monod, appointed to the League's Secretariat on a five-year contract as Director of the Precis-Writing Section. But in February 1921, it was mutually agreed between Monod and Sir Eric Drummond, the League's Secretary-General, that upon the 'reorganisation' of this section, Monod would cease to act as its director and go on a leave of absence. Then, he 'would be reabsorbed as soon as a permanent post occurred with the Secretariat'; but it never did.

The ensuing dispute was referred to the executive body, the Council of the League of Nations – since it predated the establishment of the League of Nations Administrative Tribunal – which formed a commission, comprised of three international jurists: Italian, Dutch and Swedish. The commission reported in 1925. It finds that Monod's employment was not 'contractual' – or, in other words simply a private and negotiated bargain between employer and employee, but instead:

> [P]ublic administration [by the League of Nations] accomplishes an act of authority for an object of public utility and by such act it confers on private persons public duties thus endowing them with the status of officials, inasmuch as it is this delegation of public duties that characterises appointment to public offices.

The commission regards this transformation from private person to public office-holder as inherent to the international civil service, since the League was an intergovernmental entity acting in the public interest. The commission then asserts, '[r]elations connected with public employment are always governed by the exigencies of the public interest, to which the private and personal interests of the officials must necessarily give way'. However, the commission cautions that the demands of the public interest are not unregulated:

> This does not mean that a public administration can exercise its powers in an arbitrary manner. The public administration must always, in all its acts, have regard to the public interest and respect the principles of justice. If it exceeds its powers for private ends or ends not authorized by law or if it commits an injustice, it is guilty of unlawful acts.

Consequently, the commission finds that the only legal question at issue is whether the claimant had been relieved of their duties 'dictated solely by a regard for the interests' of the League of Nations. If there is no reason to think otherwise, then the discretion of the Secretary-General is unquestionable. The commission upholds the termination of Monod's appointment; but finds that they were owed sums unpaid before the end of their appointment plus an amount – what may today be termed, moral damages (see Chapter 4, 'International Administrative Tribunals') – because they were induced to step down, by an empty promise of future responsibilities.

Whilst the committee's decision is 100 years old, its identification of the legal basis of employment-related disputes at international organizations remains consequential. First, the claimant contests an administrative act – usually termed by administrative tribunals, an *administrative decision* – that is allegedly adverse to their interests and compromises their employment at an international organization. Second, deference is owed the judgment underlying the exercise of administrative authority to achieve the purposes of international organizations – in other words, *discretionary authority*. Third, the administrative authority exercised at international organizations cannot be utilized arbitrarily – if it is, this abuse illegitimates the authority, so nullifying the legal effect of the administrative decision. Similarly integral to the resolution of any employment-related dispute are principles concerning proof – the commission in *Monod* were persuaded by the evidence, mostly produced by the party seeking to rely upon it.

5.2 General Legal Principles of Review

The review of challenged administrative decisions at international organizations is structured in accordance with three general legal principles, overarchingly applicable to any contested subject matter. Essentially, these arise from the fundamental character of the treaty-based employment relationship between international officials and international organizations. First, to dispute the exercise of administrative authority of an international organization, there must be an adverse and final administrative decision. This principle expounds upon the bare terms – 'decision', 'administrative decision' and 'non-observance' – found in some Statutes of international administrative tribunals.[2] In doing so, administrative tribunals ascertain both whether administrative authority has been exercised with finality, and if this administration damages the official interests of an international civil servant. Second, the competence of administering international

[2] ILOAT Statute, Article VII(1), 'A complaint shall not be receivable unless the decision impugned is a final decision and the person concerned has exhausted such other means of redress as are open to her or him under the applicable Staff Regulations'; UNDT Article 2(1), references 'administrative decision'; whereas WBAT Statute, Article II(1) states: 'The Tribunal shall hear and pass judgment upon any application by which a member of the staff of the Bank Group alleges non-observance of the contract of employment or terms of appointment of such staff member.'

officials is attributed by the treaty basis of an international organization to its principal executive official – and officials to whom this authority is delegated – regulated by a governance organ. (See Chapter 3, 'International Civil Service'.) This competence engages the exercise of personal judgment that cannot be separated from the principal executive official or overridden by the governance organ that establishes an international administrative tribunal. Consequently, this discretionary authority is owed deference. Third, authority used in ways inconsistent with the purposes for which the authority is possessed, illegitimates administration. So, whilst discretion is presumed to be lawfully exercised, arbitrary administration is always abusive. These general principles are now considered in turn.

General Principle 1: Only Adverse Administrative Decisions May Be Contested

Routinely, international officials challenge actions by international organizations which are indisputably administrative decisions adverse to their interests: performance-related termination of employment, for example. (See Chapter 8, 'Performance Management'.) The administrative authority of the international organization has been conclusively addressed to the international official and consequently, their interests are disadvantaged – the dispute turns on the lawfulness of this administration. Hence, in practice, international organizations endeavour to render administrative decisions contemporaneously in writing. Ideally, this is accompanied by a statement that 'this is an administrative decision', and so clearly amenable to legal challenge – and transparently starting the clock ticking on a filing deadline. (See Chapter 4, 'International Administrative Tribunals'.) However, since an adverse administrative decision is the substance of what may be legally challenged, what constitutes an adverse administrative decision may be disputed before – and is clarified by – international administrative tribunals.

In UNAT Judgment No. 840, *Alcañiz and Others v. Secretary-General of the United Nations* (2018), the Secretary-General successfully contends that a downwardly revised Unified Salary Scale cannot be challenged – since it reflects the exercise of authority by the UN General Assembly, to which the Secretary-General is subordinate – and is not a contestable administrative decision. The Tribunal finds:

> An administrative decision is a unilateral decision of an administrative nature taken by the administration involving the exercise of a power or the performance of a function in terms of a statutory instrument, which

> adversely affects the rights of another and produces direct legal consequences. A decision of an administrative nature is distinguished from other governmental action of a regulatory, legislative or executive nature.
>
> Deciding what is and what is not a decision of an administrative nature may be difficult and must be done on a case-by-case basis and will depend on the circumstances, taking into account the variety and different contexts of decision-making in the [international organization]. The nature of the decision, the legal framework under which the decision was made, and the consequences of the decision are key determinants of whether the decision in question is an administrative decision. What matters is not so much the functionary who takes the decision as the nature of the function performed or the power exercised. The question is whether the task itself is administrative or not.[3]

In ILOAT Judgment No. 1674, *Gosselin v. European Patent Organisation* (1998) – in which the claimant with a medical complaint challenges the decision to convene an Invalidity Committee they had acquiesced to – the Tribunal relies upon a two sentence-formulation, to similar effect: 'The case law says that a complaint is irreceivable when the decision at issue is not one that adversely affects the complainant. A decision is an act by an officer of an organization which has a legal effect on the staff member's status.'[4] Or, in other words, as the Tribunal decides, 'the instigation of proceedings' is no such decision.[5] Indeed, stages of any procedure are not to be regarded as an administrative decision. In ILOAT Judgment No. 3697, *MJ v. European Patent Organisation* (2016) – in which the claimant challenges the receipt of written notification of their unsatisfactory performance – the Tribunal finds that such notification is not an administrative decision occasioning a legal claim:

> Consistent case law holds that a written notification issued within the context of a performance evaluation is not a final measure adversely affecting an employee … As the written notification itself had no adverse effect on the complainant, the complaint in relation to that notification is irreceivable and will be dismissed.[6]

In WBAT Judgment No. 188, *Briscoe v. International Bank for Reconstruction and Development* (1992) – in which the claimant challenges a general rule that is not applied to them but they consider unfair – the Tribunal finds:

[3] UNAT No. 840, paras. 61–62.
[4] ILOAT No. 1674, para. 6(a).
[5] ILOAT No. 1674, Decision, para. 1.
[6] ILOAT No. 3697, para. 5.

> The Tribunal, along with other international administrative tribunals, has consistently held that a claim of non-observance of a staff member's contract or terms of appointment must be directed not against the organization's promulgation of some general rule or policy but rather against an application of that rule or policy – be it reflected in an action or an omission – that directly affects the employment rights of a staff member in an adverse manner.[7]

However, once an administrative decision applies the internal law directly to an employee, an indirect challenge to this internal lawmaking may be constructed. It has been observed, 'tribunals do pronounce on the validity of legislative acts more or less directly'.[8] Some administrative tribunals are competent to review these 'regulatory decisions' – the issuance of internal law, rather than its application – challenged by a staff member, not directly adversely affected. The Statute of the International Monetary Fund Administrative Tribunal (IMFAT) allows for this.[9] Although, notably the IMFAT's statutory jurisdiction excludes any resolutions adopted – which is to say any internal lawmaking – by the Board of Governors of the Fund, the paramount governance organ of which the Tribunal is a subsidiary organ. (See Chapter 4, 'International Administrative Tribunals'.)

The approach to staff representatives before most international administrative tribunals is comparable. A staff representative has standing to challenge an administrative decision that is adverse to their status as a staff representative, but not otherwise. In ILOAT Judgment No. 3644, *A (No. 10) and Others v. World Intellectual Property Organization* (2016) – settling the Tribunal's approach – elected members of the Staff Council challenge an appointment to the staff of the respondent as procedurally flawed.[10] The Tribunal affirms that the statutory basis of its jurisdiction 'is directed to the vindication or enforcement of the rights of an individual officer'.[11] It finds:

> It might be thought all officials have a 'right' to have the organization which employs them comply with and observe the organization's [internal law] irrespective of whether any failure to comply or non-observance had any bearing on their own situation as an official of the organization. If this was so, all officials would have standing to commence proceedings in the Tribunal in relation to any non-observance of the [internal law]. It is highly improbable that the Statute intended this result.[12]

7 WBAT No. 188, para. 30.
8 Thomas and Elias 2012, 409.
9 See IMFAT Statute, Article II(2)(b).
10 See ILOAT No. 3644, paras. 1–6.
11 ILOAT No. 3644, para. 11.
12 ILOAT No. 3644, para. 14.

This is so, even for staff representatives:

> Consistent with the entire focus of the [ILOAT] Statute, the right of an elected representative to enforce the [internal law] for the benefit of all staff is limited to circumstances where the provision (which has allegedly not been observed) confers a right on the elected representative as a member of staff. It might be a right limited to the staff representative (such as the right to be consulted) or it might be a right enjoyed by all staff (such as the right to freedom of association).[13]

General Principle 2: Deference Is Owed Discretionary Authority

Since *Monod* was decided a century ago, employment-related dispute resolution at international organizations has been pervaded by the general principle of deference to the discretionary authority of the employing international organization. In other words, when appointed to the international civil service, an individual becomes an official – and has not entered into some private contractual bargain – and servant of the international organization and its mandate. (See Chapter 2, 'International Organizations'.) The treaty-basis of international organizations attribute administrative authority to the principal executive official – regulated by a governance organ – to obtain such purposes. The authority of the principal executive official over the staff prevails and is accompanied by a rebuttable presumption of legality. Hence, international administrative tribunals – established by governance organs – may review the lawfulness of an administrative decision, but not usurp the principal executive official's administrative authority, by imposing their own preferences. Almost every judgment by an international administrative tribunal invokes this general legal principle.

For example, in ILOAT Judgment No. 4881, *K v. United Nations Educational, Scientific and Cultural Organization (UNESCO)* (2024) – in which the claimant challenges their reporting line – the Tribunal emphasizes that the preferences of an international organization, such as how staff are organized, are unreviewable:

> It is well established in the case law that an international organization has broad discretion over the organization of its services and the Tribunal cannot judge the wisdom of measures that it deems necessary to adopt in this regard ... It is also a general rule that an [international] organization's staff members are, in the performance of their duties, placed in a position of hierarchical subordination to its executive head and the various supervisors to whom they report ... The Tribunal considers that it follows from these considerations that staff members cannot ordinarily be allowed the opportunity

[13] ILOAT No. 3644, para. 14.

> to challenge measures determining their reporting lines or the choice of persons designated to exercise supervisory functions in their respect. It is the [international] organization's prerogative to take such decisions and they cannot therefore be considered to adversely affect those staff members.[14]

This deference is shared by the UNAT, as exemplified by a comparable approach to organizational structuring. In UNAT Judgment No. 1135, *Timoth v. Secretary-General of the United Nations* (2017), the Tribunal states:

> The [international organization] has broad discretion to reorganize its operations and departments to meet changing needs and economic realities. According to the [UN] Appeals Tribunal's well-settled jurisprudence, an international organization necessarily has power to restructure some or all of its departments or units, including the abolition of posts, the creation of new posts and the redeployment of staff. This Tribunal will not interfere with a genuine organizational restructuring even though it may have resulted in the loss of employment of staff.[15]

Likewise, in WBAT Judgment No. 147, *Lopez v. International Bank for Reconstruction and Development* (1996) – continually cited with approval since – the Tribunal reiterates, 'The Tribunal has repeatedly stated that it will not substitute its judgment for the discretionary decisions of the Bank's management', such as the unsuccessfully challenged administrative decision to terminate the claimant's probationary appointment.[16]

General Principle 3: Arbitrariness Invalidates Authority

In the first judgment of the World Bank Administrative Tribunal – WBAT Judgment No. 1, *de Merode and Others v. The World Bank* (1981) – the Tribunal pronounces: 'Discretionary power is not absolute power.'[17] But why is this? The answer: since administrative power is possessed for a purpose – ultimately derived from the treaty-basis of an international organization – and if such power is exercised in a way inconsistent with this purpose, then this delegitimizes the power. This general principle – arbitrariness invalidates authority – governs employment-related dispute resolution at international organizations. Whereas, international administrative tribunals tend to use a series of near-synonyms, 'arbitrary' itself may be said to encompass 'capricious',

[14] ILOAT No. 4881, para. 4.
[15] UNAT No. 1135, para. 25.
[16] WBAT No. 147, para. 36.
[17] WBAT No. 1, para. 44.

'uncertain', 'varying', 'not based on the nature of things' and 'uncontrolled power or authority'.[18]

For example, taking (almost) at random, ILOAT Judgment No. 3652, *P (Nos. 1 and 2) v. Food and Agriculture Organization* (2016) – the Tribunal defers to the administrative determination not to select the claimant for an internal vacancy: 'The Tribunal's case law has it that a staff appointment by an international organization is a decision that lies within the discretion of its' principal executive official.[19] Nevertheless, the Tribunal states that such discretionary decision is subject to so-called limited review and finds for the claimant.[20] What this means is that an administrative decision is upheld by the Tribunal, unless it is invalidated by arbitrariness. The ILOAT expounds upon this – setting aside a challenged administrative decision if it possesses any one of the following seven defects:

(1) taken without authority, or
(2) in breach of a rule of form or of procedure, or
(3) if it was based on a mistake of fact, or
(4) [mistake] of law, or
(5) if some material fact was overlooked, or
(6) if there was abuse of authority, or
(7) if a clearly wrong conclusion was drawn from the evidence.[21]

Likewise, in WBAT Judgment No. 100, *Jassal v. International Bank for Reconstruction and Development* (1991) – in which the claimant successfully challenges their non-selection for an internal vacancy – the Tribunal states that this administrative decision is subject to review by the Tribunal, 'only for abuse of discretion'.[22] Again, arbitrariness is expounded upon: '[T]he Tribunal is charged with determining whether the Bank's decision was the product of bias, prejudice, arbitrariness, manifest unreasonableness, or unfair or improper procedure'.[23] The Tribunal observes, if an administrative decision 'altogether lacks support in factual evidence or reasonable inference', then the 'conclusion must be found to be an abuse of discretion'.[24] Like the WBAT, this book interchanges 'abuse of discretion' and 'arbitrariness'.

[18] See *Shorter Oxford English Dictionary.*
[19] ILOAT No. 3652, para. 7.
[20] ILOAT No. 3652, para. 7.
[21] ILOAT No. 3652, para. 7, numbering added.
[22] WBAT No. 100, para. 37.
[23] WBAT No. 100, para. 37.
[24] WBAT No. 100, para. 37.

In a foundational judgment – UNAT Judgment No. 82, *Sanwidi v. Secretary-General of the United Nations* (2010), in which the claimant's misconduct-related termination is upheld – the Tribunal remarks:

> Administrative tribunals worldwide keep evolving legal principles to help them control abuse of discretionary powers. There can be no exhaustive list of the applicable legal principles in administrative law, but unfairness, unreasonableness, illegality, irrationality, procedural irregularity, bias, capriciousness, arbitrariness and lack of proportionality are some of the grounds on which tribunals may for good reason interfere with the exercise of administrative discretion.[25]

However, since 'capriciousness' and 'irrationality' say, have much the same flavour, it seems that this – as with an itemized basis for 'limited review', or interchanging 'abuse of discretion' with 'arbitrariness' – iterates administrative defects which are all abusive and arbitrary. Indeed, the UNAT addresses the limited review of discretionary administrative authority in conventional terms:

> When judging the validity of the [principal executive official's] exercise of discretion in administrative matters, the [administrative tribunal] determines if the decision is legal, rational, procedurally correct, and proportionate. The Tribunal can consider whether relevant matters have been ignored and irrelevant matters considered, and also examine whether the decision is absurd or perverse. But it is not the role of the [administrative tribunal] to consider the correctness of the choice made by the [principal executive official] amongst the various courses of action open to [them]. Nor is it the role of the Tribunal to substitute its own decision for that of the [principal executive official].[26]

In other words, to survive legal challenge before an administrative tribunal, any administrative decision must be taken: (1) by a competent authority; (2) in accordance with the applicable procedure established by the respondent international organization; and (3) not be arbitrary or otherwise abusive.

5.3 General Legal Principles of Evidence

As with any other judicial process, an international administrative tribunal applies the law to the facts in arriving at its judgment. So, to begin, how to find out these facts? Three general legal principles apply

25 UNAT No. 82, para. 38.
26 UNAT No. 82, para. 40.

to evidence in order to resolve employment-related disputes at international organizations. These general principles may be expressed as: (1) Claimants must establish arbitrariness; (2) Unreasoned administrative decisions are evidently arbitrary; and (3) Administrative decisions cannot be based upon withheld evidence. These are now considered each in turn.

General Principle 1: Claimants Must Establish Arbitrariness

It is seldom that an employment-related dispute before an international administrative tribunal turns upon an authentic factual controversy. In other words, a disagreement over whether or not an event in fact occurred – rather than divergent interpretations to be applied to the same event, or whether an event should be construed as substantiating (or compromises) a lawful administrative decision. The presumption then, is that administrative decisions are not arbitrary – indeed, it would be both incompatible with its treaty-basis to deem international organizations as arbitrary by default and conflict with the reasoned basis of lawful administrative decisions. Hence, claimants must convince an administrative tribunal that a challenged administrative decision is abusive – that it is arbitrary. This is the so-called, burden of proof. It is not for an employing international organization to demonstrate that an administrative decision was not arbitrary – except in circumstances limited to misconduct, when the international organization becomes burdened with demonstrating lawfulness, to a standard either articulated by an administrative tribunal or by the internal law of an international organization. (See Chapter 10, 'Misconduct'.)

The degree to which the claimant must convince – the so-called, standard of proof – an international administrative tribunal is not fixed by most Statutes (see Chapter 4, 'International Administrative Tribunals'), but is instead alluded to by tribunals in their judgments, when finding or not finding facts. Hence, the claimant should – to draw upon terms used across judgments cited in this chapter – set out to 'prove', 'persuade', 'establish', 'substantiate' and 'reasonably infer' allegations of arbitrariness; whereas 'mere suspicion' and 'unsupported allegations' are unconvincing.

In ILOAT Judgment No. 4382, *B v. International Federation of Red Cross and Red Crescent Societies* (2021) – in which the claimant unsuccessfully contends that their performance appraisal is procedurally and substantively unlawful – the Tribunal recalls:

> It is well settled that the [claimant] bears the burden of proving allegations of bias and that, moreover, the evidence adduced to prove the allegations must be of sufficient quality and weight to persuade the Tribunal. It is also recognized that bias is often concealed and that direct evidence to support the allegation may not be available. In these cases, proof may rest on inferences drawn from the circumstances. However, reasonable inferences can only be drawn from known facts and cannot be based on suspicion or unsupported allegations. With regard to prejudice, the Tribunal has stated that although evidence of personal prejudice is often concealed and such prejudice must be inferred from surrounding circumstances, that does not relieve the [claimant], who has the burden of proving [their] allegations, from introducing evidence of sufficient quality and weight to persuade the Tribunal. Mere suspicion and unsupported allegations are clearly not enough, the less so where the actions of the organization which are alleged to have been tainted by personal prejudice are shown to have a verifiable objective justification.[27]

The UNAT casts this obligation that claimants must establish arbitrariness as an expectation that an administrative decision is by default, not arbitrary – a so-called 'presumption of regularity'. In UNAT Judgment No. 122, *Rolland v. Secretary-General of the United Nations* (2011) – in which the claimant unsuccessfully challenges their non-selection for several vacancies – the Tribunal holds:

> [T]here is always a presumption that official acts have been regularly performed. This is called the presumption of regularity, but it is a rebuttable presumption. If the management is able to even minimally show that the [claimant's] candidature was given a full and fair consideration, then the presumption of law is satisfied. Thereafter the burden of proof shifts to the [claimant] who must be able to show through clear and convincing evidence that [they were] denied a fair chance of promotion.[28]

In other words, reasonableness in international administrative law is like the glue sticking together lawfulness with an administrative decision. Dissolving this bond is no easy task for the claimant – but establishing arbitrariness always means the administrative decision comes unstuck.

General Principle 2: Unreasoned Administrative Decisions Are Evidently Arbitrary

Interconnecting with the general principle that claimants must establish arbitrariness – or, in other words, the administration of international

[27] ILOAT No. 4382, para. 11.
[28] UNAT No. 122, para. 5

organizations is assumed to be rules-based and reasonable – is the principle that administrative decisions must be reasoned. This is to say, that to be relied upon by an international organization, adverse administrative decisions must be accompanied by an explanation. Since, without such reasoning, the affected staff member is unable to assess whether they have a plausible legal challenge. In turn, an international administrative tribunal is frustrated in determining whether such administration is lawfully exercised, unless the international organization explains itself at the time.

In ILOAT Judgment No. 4937, *L v. International Organization for Migration* (2025) – in which the claimant unsuccessfully challenges the abolition of their post and resulting termination of their appointment – the Tribunal states, 'the need to give reasons in support of adverse administrative decisions arises precisely because the affected staff member must be given an opportunity of knowing and evaluating whether or not the decision should be timely contested'.[29]

In UNAT Judgment No. 1042, *Nuugroho v. Secretary-General of the United Nations* (2020) – in which the claimant successfully contests the termination of their appointment – the Tribunal establishes its approach as: 'The duty to give reasons for a decision, as this Tribunal has long held, is essential for the Tribunal to exercise their judicial review of administrative decisions, assessing whether they were arbitrary, capricious, or unlawful'.[30] The UNAT sees 'a threefold purpose for providing reasons for decisions, which is intelligibility (enabling both implementation and acceptance), accountability and reviewability',[31] and suggests:

> It is therefore good practice for the [international organization] to provide a general guidance for its managers that a well written statement of reasons, albeit sometimes succinct depending on the circumstance, is fundamental for the correct identification of the matters, concerns and reasoning process of the decision-maker, as well as for the accurate implementation, which will more likely reflect the decision maker's intent. At the same time, this practice provides better grounds of adequate explanation for those adversely affected by these decisions, perhaps even facilitating their acceptance and hence diminishing instances of disputes. What is more, when a justification is given by the [international organization] for the exercise of its discretion, it must be supported by the facts.[32]

[29] ILOAT No. 4937, para. 2.
[30] UNAT No. 1042, para. 39.
[31] UNAT No. 1042, para. 4.
[32] UNAT No. 1042, para. 4.

As the Tribunal conveys, adverse administrative decisions should be accompanied by unambiguous written reasons. However, whilst these reasons must be sufficient, then need not exhaustive. In other words, the reasons must establish the fact-based motivation of the international organization, but these facts may be stated concisely and go narrowly to the administrative decision at hand. Impliedly, an international organization should show extenuating circumstances if this 'good practice' is set aside.

General Principle 3: Administrative Decisions Cannot Be Based on Withheld Evidence

In the same way that the reasons for an administrative decision must be imparted – almost always contemporaneously in writing – to employees of international organizations, so too must the evidence upon which the decision depends. If this evidence does not accompany an administrative decision, it is 'disclosable' by an international organization responding to a challenge before an international administrative tribunal. Or, in other words, administrative decisions cannot be based upon withheld evidence.

In ILOAT Judgment No. 4023, *A-M v. International Atomic Energy Authority* (2018) – in which the claimant was an unsuccessful internal applicant for a vacancy – the Tribunal finds:

> [A] staff member must, as a general rule, have access to all evidence on which the authority bases or intends to base its decision against [them], and, under normal circumstances, such evidence cannot be withheld on grounds of confidentiality. It follows that a decision cannot be based on a material document that has been withheld from the concerned staff member.[33]

However, this principle is not unqualified. It may be balanced against maintaining the integrity of discretionary authority. In this way, 'records of the discussions regarding the merits of the applicants for a post', for example, may be withheld.[34] The ILOAT (and the UNAT) discuss this concept in terms of 'confidentiality', but this approach could be more clearly explained: judgments state that 'confidentiality' cannot be a blanket reason to withhold evidence, but sometimes withholding 'confidential' evidence is justified.

Where evidence deemed relevant by an international administrative tribunal is withheld by an international organization, the tribunal may

[33] ILOAT No. 4023, para. 5.
[34] ILOAT No. 4023, para. 5.

draw so-called adverse inference. This means that the allegation the undisclosed evidence goes to resolving is assumed to have been proven. In UNAT Judgment No. 121, *Bertucci v. Secretary-General of the United Nations* (2011) – in which the claimant contests their non-selection for an internal vacancy – the Tribunal finds:

> The Tribunal is ... entitled to draw appropriate conclusions from the refusal [to produce evidence]. Based on these conclusions, it could, depending on the circumstances, go so far as to find that, by virtue of its refusal, the [international organization], whatever the scope of its discretionary power, must be regarded as having accepted the allegations made by the other party regarding the facts.[35]

Although instructive for claimants and respondents, this also demonstrates the way in which international administrative tribunals are essentially competent to evaluate the evidence in proceedings, as they deem appropriate in all the circumstances.

5.4 Legal Basis of Employment-Related Dispute Resolution

Distinct from the substantive law applied by international administrative tribunals – see Part II, 'Competence and Geographic Diversity', Part III, 'Integrity and Independence' and Part IV, 'Administrative Authority' – is the legal basis for the resolution of such employment-related disputes before international administrative tribunals.

The legal basis of employment-related dispute resolution may be restated as:

General Legal Principles of Review

- Only adverse administrative decisions may be contested.
- Deference is owed discretionary authority.
- Arbitrariness invalidates authority.

General Legal Principles of Evidence

- Claimants must establish arbitrariness.
- Unreasoned administrative decisions are evidently arbitrary.
- Administrative decisions cannot be based upon withheld evidence.

[35] UNAT No. 121, para. 51.

PART II

Efficiency, Competence and Geographic Diversity

6

Selection

This chapter begins by introducing selection – the appointment, promotion and reassignment of international officials – as an administrative decision exercising discretionary authority, that is inherent to securing the highest standards of efficiency and competence necessitated by the treaty basis of international organizations. Second, the legal principles of selection are identified, namely: (1) Absent abuse of discretion, deference is due selecting managers; (2) Vacancy announcements must be adhered to, but may be revoked; and (3) Selection defects must be manifest, to be contestable. Third, two attendant legal duties of selection are considered, as follows: (1) Selection must be competency-based; and (2) All candidates are entitled to consideration, but not selection. Fourth, non-competitive selection – through direct selection and reassignment – is examined. Fifth, the classification of positions that underpins the objectivity of selection is considered. Sixth, and in conclusion, this employment law of selection at international organizations is restated.

6.1 What Is Selection?

As in most human endeavours, the achievements of international organizations begin with selecting people suited to fulfilling these purposes. Once suitable international officials are appointed to the international civil service, successful multilateral institutions tend to promote their best staff to positions of greater responsibility and more onerous duties. At the same time, suitably skilled international officials are redeployed to different duties and duty stations, as the continuing effectiveness of an evolving international organization determines. These ends are not only operationally desirable, they are also legally obligated. As the UN Charter states: 'The paramount consideration in the employment of the staff and in the determination of the conditions of service shall be the necessity of securing the highest standards of efficiency, competence, and integrity.'[1] The administrative action of selection – in other words, deciding which person encumbers what post – must adhere to this paramount consideration and secure such highest standards.

Selection reoccurs throughout the career of an international official. First, *appointment* is experienced by everyone joining the staff of an international organization, as it transforms a private person into an international civil servant. Second, *promotion* occurs when an international official is the successful candidate for a vacant post, hierarchically superior to the position they presently hold. (Whereas, if an external candidate is successful, then they are newly appointed.) Third, *reassignment* takes place when an international official is transferred to a different post or different duty station, but this is not accompanied by promotion – in other words, it is hierarchically lateral. Of course, if an administrative action results in an international official taking on a hierarchically inferior post to the position they presently hold, this is *demotion* – but this is limited to use as a sanction for misconduct. (See Chapter 10, 'Misconduct'.) Or as an alternative to redundancy, as a consequence of organizational restructuring. (See Chapter 12, 'Ending Service'.)

Throughout all acts of selection, the presumption is that competitive selection best secures the highest standards at – and competency-basis of – international organizations. In order to maintain the integrity of these competitions, the vacancy announcement – informing potential candidates about the role, including the mandatory selection criteria and application deadline – must be adhered to. Typically, these characteristics of fairness and transparency are closely regulated by the internal law of international organizations. The utilization of non-competitive selection to either promote staff members on the one hand, or reassign – or *transfer* – staff members to another hierarchically lateral post on the other hand, must be used openly and accompanied by an organizational justification.

Inherent to the ability to select is the capability to match people to positions. This necessitates an organizational grading structure at multilateral institutions. An objective methodology must be used to hierarchically classify all positions – rather than the staff members who hold

[1] This is the first sentence of UN Charter, Article 101; the second reads, 'Due regard shall be paid to the importance of recruiting the staff on as wide a geographical basis as possible.' This is 'important' but not 'paramount' and is particularly reflected in the benefits extended to employees by international organizations – see Chapter 7, 'Remuneration'.

such positions – according to its duties and responsibilities. Much is then tied to this *classification*, most prominently, pay. (See Chapter 7, 'Remuneration'.)

Although great efforts go into ensuring that selection is an impartial process, resulting in reasoned and facts-based decisions, the extent to which the combining together of many complex factors that comprise a successful candidacy, requires considerable judgment. Consequently, selection is an administrative decision that exercises the discretionary authority of an international organization – against which unsuccessful external candidates typically have no redress, because of the privileges and immunities of multilateral institutions.[2] (See Chapter 2, 'International Organizations'.) Internally, absent abuse, deference is owed decisions taken by selecting managers. Taken together, this is the legal basis of the employment law of selection at international organizations.

6.2 Legal Principles of Selection

Since selection exercises discretionary authority, the first legal principle of selection is that, absent an abuse of their discretion, deference is owed selecting managers. Fundamental to the effectiveness of selection is a second legal principle, obligating adherence to the terms of the vacancy announcement, unless it is revoked. Interlocking with both these principles however is a third – namely, errors in selection must be manifest in order to be contestable. These principles are now considered in turn.

Principle 1: Absent Abuse of Discretion, Deference Is Owed Selecting Managers

The act of selection – for appointment, promotion and reassignment – is an exercise of the discretionary authority of an international organization. In other words, this administrative decision reflects a choice from a range of legitimate options. Conceptually, between the

[2] However, some international organizations do allow disappointed external applicants to challenge the selection decision; for example, the Statute of the Organisation for Economic Co-operation and Development (OECD) Administrative Tribunal, Article 1(c) states:

> The Tribunal shall have jurisdiction over applications filed by persons who are not members of staff of the [OECD], challenging the refusal of their application for appointment to functions governed by the [Staff] Regulations, where it is alleged that such refusal was the result of discrimination based on the grounds of racial or ethnic origin, nationality, opinions or beliefs, gender, sexual orientation, health or disabilities.

same two (evenly matched) candidates, two different managers may select one or other candidate – the managers are entitled to their professional views and judgment. The law is not capable of examining the *merits* of the decision. Determining whether the so-called 'right' or 'best' candidate was chosen would impermissibly replace the treaty-based competence of the principal executive official, with that of the governance organ that established an administrative tribunal. Rather, the law asks whether the successful candidate was chosen lawfully. For this reason, an international administrative tribunal refrains from substituting its views and judgment for those of the multilateral institution's managers. Instead, the preoccupation is whether the selection decision exhibits abuses.

In ILOAT Judgment No. 4467, *R (No. 8) v. International Atomic Energy Agency* (2022) the claimant unsuccessfully challenges the lawfulness of the selection of a rival candidate to a position to which they had also applied. The Tribunal states its established approach:

> The Tribunal's case law has it that a staff appointment by an international organization is a decision that lies within the discretion of its [principal executive official] and is subject to only limited review. Such a decision may be set aside only if it was taken without authority or in breach of a rule of form or of procedure, or if it was based on a mistake of fact or of law, or if some material fact was overlooked, or if there was abuse of authority, or if a clearly wrong conclusion was drawn from the evidence.[3]

Likewise, in WBAT Judgment No. 100, *Jassal v. International Bank for Reconstruction and Development* (1991) – repeatedly cited by the Tribunal with approval since – the claimant was not chosen for several vacancies, in light of their own position being abolished through reorganization. The Tribunal states, 'a decision by the Bank to select a staff member for a particular position rests within the Bank's discretion, and may be overturned by the Tribunal only when it concludes that this discretion has been abused'.[4] It finds:

> [T]he Tribunal is charged with determining whether the Bank's decision was the product of bias, prejudice, arbitrariness, manifest unreasonableness, or unfair or improper procedure. Thus, if the Bank's conclusion regarding the [claimant's] qualifications for selection ... altogether lacks support in factual evidence or reasonable inference, that conclusion must be found to be an abuse of discretion.[5]

3 ILOAT No. 4467, para. 2.
4 WBAT No. 100, para. 30.
5 WBAT No. 100, para. 37.

In UNAT Judgment No. 122, *Rolland v. United Nations Secretary-General* (2011) – featuring a formative examination of selection – the claimant unsuccessfully challenges their non-selection for a role in a newly created department. The Tribunal states the limits to its review: 'Generally speaking, when candidates have received fair consideration, discrimination and bias are absent, proper procedures have been followed, and all relevant material has been taken into consideration, the selection shall be upheld.'[6] It emphasizes that a selection decision in accordance with this scope of review will be 'rescinded under rare circumstances'.[7]

Therefore, the scope of review in challenges to selection is limited to examining the legal authority to take this decision, the procedure that accompanies this use of authority and ensuring that authority is not abused. In other words, to withstand legal challenge before an administrative tribunal, any administrative decision on selection must be taken: (1) by a competent authority; (2) in accordance with the applicable procedure established by the respondent international organization; and (3) not be arbitrary or otherwise abusive.

Principle 2: Vacancy Announcements Must Be Adhered to, but May Be Revoked

Selection competitions are triggered by an announcement describing the duties and responsibilities attached to the vacant post, the mandatory and desirable selection criteria, duty station, job title and the deadline for applications. It is this announcement which enables prospective candidates to decide whether or not the opportunity interests them, to gauge the extent to which they are professionally suited to the position and by when they must express their candidacy. To ensure the integrity of selection, the statements made in the vacancy announcement obligate an international organization. In other words, the application deadline must be adhered to and the successful candidate must satisfy the mandatory selection criteria.

In ILOAT Judgment No. 1549, *Lopez-Cotarelo v. International Atomic Energy Agency* (1996) – in which the Tribunal establishes its approach to application deadlines – the claimant succeeds in challenging the selection of a candidate who had applied after the application deadline had

[6] UNAT No. 122, para. 4.
[7] UNAT No. 122, para. 4.

passed. The Tribunal holds, 'an official of an international organization who applies for a vacancy is entitled to have [their] application considered and assessed according to the set procedure once the organization admits it under the terms of the vacancy notice'.[8] The competitive basis of selection is compromised when late applications are accepted: 'If the organization considers a late application it gives the impression of preferential treatment.'[9]

In ILOAT Judgment No. 2712, *K v. World Intellectual Property Organization* (2008) – in which the ILOAT establishes its approach to mandatory selection criteria – the Tribunal finds 'that an international organization which decides to hold a competition in order to fill a post cannot select a candidate who does not satisfy one of the required qualifications stipulated in the vacancy announcement'.[10] On this basis, the Tribunal's judgment favours the claimant, whose application for a position of director was rejected, whereas the successful candidate does not meet one of the requirements – at least fifteen years of relevant experience – stated in the vacancy announcement.[11] The Tribunal explains why this is a legal obligation:

> Such conduct, which is tantamount to modifying the criteria for appointment to the post during the selection process, incurs the Tribunal's censure on two counts. Firstly, it violates the principle of *tu patere legem quam ipse fecisti*,[12] which forbids the [international organization] to ignore the rules it has itself defined. In this respect, a modification of the applicable criteria during the selection procedure more generally undermines the requirements of mutual trust and fairness which international organizations have a duty to observe in their relations with their staff. Second, the appointment body's alteration, after the procedure had begun, of the qualifications which were initially required in order to obtain the post, introduces a serious flaw into the selection process with respect to the principle of equal opportunity among candidates. Irrespective of the reasons for such action, it inevitably erodes the safeguards of objectivity and transparency which must be provided in order to comply with this essential principle, breach of which vitiates any appointment based on a competition.[13]

[8] ILOAT No. 1549, para. 6.
[9] ILOAT No. 1549, para. 13.
[10] ILOAT No. 2712, para. 5.
[11] ILOAT No. 2712, see para. 4.
[12] The Tribunal uses a legal Latin phrase, but cross-refers to its own English translation in ILOAT Judgment No. 51, *D'Andecy v. Food and Agriculture Organization* (1960), para. 3: 'Any authority is bound by its own rules for so long as such rules have not been amended or abrogated.'
[13] ILOAT No. 2712, para. 5.

Likewise, selection is flawed if the selection criteria – either mandatory or preferential – is supplemented by any criterion unspecified by the vacancy announcement. In ILOAT Judgment No. 4208, *Z v. International Atomic Energy Agency* (2020), the claimant successfully contests a selection decision for 'Senior Safeguards Evaluator' – in which their candidacy was not preferred – influenced by a criterion (namely, 'inspector experience')[14] unmentioned by the vacancy announcement. The Tribunal finds:

> [T]he interview panel's report shows that inspector experience was indeed taken into the panel's consideration as an asset in its evaluation of candidates. It was an irrelevant consideration. The vacancy notice had itself expressly set out the factors which were to be taken into account as assets or advantage and inspector experience was not one of them.[15]

However, the legal obligation to adhere to the vacancy announcement in this way does not impede revoking the announcement. Consequently, the vacancy announcement may then either be reissued with amendment or the vacancy – and selection procedure – cancelled altogether.

In *ILOAT No. 1549*, the Tribunal finds that if an extended application deadline is considered desirable, the international organization must 'announce a new deadline in the same way as it did the vacancy'.[16] In other words, this action effectively revokes and reissues the original vacancy announcement with the amended application deadline. In this way, the Tribunal holds, the organization 'will then commit no breach of equality and the competition will be seen as fair'.[17]

Likewise, if an amended mandatory selection criteria is found to be desirable during the currency of a selection procedure, in *ILOAT No. 2712* the Tribunal finds:

> So long as the notice remained valid the [international] organization was bound by the wording of it and was not free to amend it secretly. The only proper way of doing so would have been to withdraw the notice altogether and open a new competition on terms that better matched actual requirements. The procedure followed must have left the [claimant] with the unfortunate impression that [they] had not been given a fair chance to compete.[18]

[14] ILOAT No. 4208, para. 6.
[15] ILOAT No. 4208, para. 7.
[16] ILOAT No. 1549, para. 13.
[17] ILOAT No. 1549, para. 13.
[18] ILOAT No. 2712, para. 13.

In other words, since fairness is inherent to an effective competitive selection procedure and transparency is inherent to fairness, the vacancy announcement cannot be disregarded, although it may be revoked and reissued.

Principle 3: Selection Defects Must Be Manifest, to Be Contestable

Staff members discontented by selection outcomes must do more than simply assert that they are the superior candidate, disparage their rival or allege that their lack of success is sufficient to show a flawed process. In other words, any defect must be manifest.

For example, in ILOAT Judgment No. 1827, *Ochani v. World Health Organization* (1999) – cited repeatedly by the Tribunal with approval since – the claimant contests their non-selection for a post, based upon their unfaulted past performance. The Tribunal makes clear that this is insufficient to manifest a selection error:

> The selection of candidates for promotion is necessarily based on merit and requires a high degree of judgment on the part of those involved in the selection process. Those who would have the Tribunal interfere must demonstrate a serious defect in it; it is not enough simply to assert that one is better qualified than the selected candidate.[19]

In *WBAT No. 100* the Tribunal states that to be contestable, defective selection must be sufficiently serious that it is ascertainable without an examination of minutiae:

> It is not for the Tribunal, in assessing the validity of the selection or non-selection of a staff member, to undertake its own examination of that staff member's record, or a criterion-by-criterion assessment of [their] qualifications. That is for the [international organization] to do in the first instance, subject to review by the Tribunal only for abuse of discretion.[20]

The UNAT terms this the 'presumption of regularity' (see Chapter 5, 'Employment-Related Dispute Resolution'). In *UNAT No. 122* it holds:

> [T]hat there is always a presumption that official acts have been regularly performed. This is called the presumption of regularity, but it is a rebuttable presumption. If the [international organization] is able to even minimally show that the [claimant's] candidature was given a full and fair consideration, then the presumption of law is satisfied.[21]

[19] ILOAT No. 1827, para. 6.
[20] WBAT No. 100, para. 37.
[21] UNAT No. 122, para. 5.

To set this presumption aside, the claimant must 'show through clear and convincing evidence' that the selection decision was manifestly abusive.[22]

6.3 Legal Duties of Selection

Legal duties of selection govern the administrative authority of an international organization. These duties may be expressed as: (1) Selection must be competency-based; and (2) All candidates are entitled to consideration, but not selection.

Duty 1: Selection Must Be Competency-Based

The treaty-based obligation to obtain the highest standards of international officials means that competency overrides all other candidate attributes, subject of course to integrity. In other words, whilst diversity is a desirable – indeed, an indispensable – organizational trait, gender equity and a wide and diverse geographic basis to the selection of staff are subordinated to securing international officials exhibiting the highest standard of competency. (See Chapter 3, 'International Civil Service'.)

In ILOAT Judgment No. 2004, *Matthews v. World Health Organization* (2001) – notable for its successful assertion of gender-biased selection – the internal (male) claimant alleges that 'reverse' gender discrimination resulted in the preferment of a rival external (female) candidate.[23] The Tribunal underscores its support for a *policy* of gender equity, but not the overriding of competency-based selection:

> The Tribunal wishes to emphasise that there is nothing wrong in having a policy aimed at gender parity. For too long women have been subjected to discrimination in appointments to senior posts which can be proved by statistics. But this policy cannot be achieved by setting quotas and by reverse discrimination, in other words, by the appointment – for particular posts – of women who are less qualified than men.[24]

[22] UNAT No. 122, para. 5.

[23] Of course, discrimination *against* women employees at international organizations has a provenance that can be dated back to the League of Nations; see Macfadyen and Others 2019, 93:

> Women from the Great Powers found that national quotas were filled by male compatriots, who unlike them, had essential experience in international politics ... Those who were selected did not enjoy equal standing with men. [The most senior woman official, Rachel] Crowdy while doing the same job as those heading a Section, was never given the rank of 'Director', but rather that of 'Head of Section' which was remunerated about 25% lower.

[24] ILOAT No. 2004, para. 20.

The Tribunal suggest how such a policy could otherwise – lawfully – be implemented by international organizations: 'The policy can be achieved by different means such as actively encouraging qualified women to apply for senior posts, and by ensuring that work practices do not discourage women from applying.'[25] Nevertheless, 'the bottom line must always be that the person best qualified should be appointed'.[26]

In WBAT Judgment No. 592, *ET v. International Bank for Reconstruction and Development* (2018), the (male) claimant successfully contends that their non-selection for a vacancy was gender-biased since (female) candidates were preferred, after being added to the candidate shortlist after the deadline for applications had passed. The Tribunal finds that between 'evenly matched' male and female candidates,[27] the latter could be preferred, 'given the Bank's focus on achieving gender parity in managerial positions'.[28] However, the Tribunal also finds that this was only the case between the claimant and a rival woman candidate, following (surreptitious) modification of the mandatory selection criteria, to balance-out the candidates' credentials,[29] and states:

> The Tribunal finds that, when the Bank took the decision to look only for female candidates and changed the selection criteria, it denied the [claimant] a fair opportunity to compete for the [advertised] position. The Tribunal holds that the Bank can legitimately pursue gender parity, particularly in managerial positions, as provided for in the Bank's regulatory framework. However, it not only should observe the bottom line of making a choice between candidates who are evenly matched in qualifications but also must be transparent in the selection process such that all candidates are evaluated against the same criteria.[30]

Likewise, whilst at all international organizations, like the UN, 'Due regard shall be paid to the importance of recruiting the staff on as wide a geographical basis as possible', nevertheless, the paramount selection consideration is competency.[31] Albeit this conceivably permits – between equally competent candidates – the lawful selection of the candidate from the Member State underrepresented amongst the staff of an international organization, truly equivalent competence is uncommon. (Instead, the

[25] ILOAT No. 2004, para. 20.
[26] ILOAT No. 2004, para. 20.
[27] WBAT No. 592, para. 116.
[28] WBAT No. 592, para. 119.
[29] WBAT No. 592, see para. 127.
[30] WBAT No. 592, para. 131.
[31] UN Charter, Article 101(3); and see Chapter 3, 'International Civil Service'.

compensation afforded by international organizations contemplates the achievement of geographic diversity – see Chapter 7, 'Remuneration'.)

In ILOAT Judgment No. 1871, *Coates v. Food and Agriculture Organization* (1999) – notable for its successful assertion of geographically biased selection – the claimant succeeds because the Tribunal finds:

> [The international organization] gave paramount importance to the principle of geographic distribution, which resulted in … selecting the applicant who was second in the list recommended by the Selection Committee because that applicant was a national of an 'under-represented' country, while the [claimant], who was in first place, was a national of an 'equitably represented' country … The [treaty basis] of the [international organization] clearly states that 'the highest standards of efficiency and of technical competence' are of paramount importance in appointing staff. The Selection Committee is under the obligation to recommend for selection the candidate whose qualifications most closely meet the requirements of the post. Therefore the essential qualifications required are the priority criterion.[32]

The Tribunal is clear that obtaining wide geographic representation through selection, 'is only envisaged where several candidates are equally well qualified'.[33]

Duty 2: All Candidates Are Entitled to Consideration, but Not Selection

All eligible candidates have a right to be considered for a vacancy, irrespective of the apparent strengths or weaknesses of their candidacy. In *ILOAT No. 4467*, the Tribunal states:

> [A]nyone who applies for a post to be filled by some process of selection is entitled to have [their] application considered in good faith and in keeping with the basic rules of fair and open competition. That is a right which every applicant must enjoy, whatever [their] hope of success may be.[34]

Whilst every staff member has this right to consideration of their candidacy in good faith, in adherence to the vacancy announcement, there is no entitlement to selection – no matter the strengths of a staff member's resumé or their successful track record.

In WBAT Judgment No. 255, *Riddell v. International Bank for Reconstruction and Development* (2001) – repeatedly cited by the

32 ILOAT No. 1871, paras. 9–10.
33 ILOAT No. 1871, para. 10.
34 ILOAT No. 4467, para. 2.

Tribunal with approval since – the claimant challenges the decision not to shortlist them for a vacancy for which they applied. The Tribunal finds that, 'no staff member has a right to be selected to a particular position or to be included in a list of candidates for a position'.[35] As with the selection decision itself, the administrative decision to shortlist a candidate for a vacancy, 'is discretionary and the Tribunal will not overturn such a decision unless it finds that it is tainted by bias or abuse of discretion'.[36] In other words, absent abuse of discretion, deference is owed shortlisting.

Likewise, affording (internal) candidates 'priority consideration' – a widespread feature of the internal law of international organizations – does not entitle selection.[37] In UNAT Judgment No. 88, *Megerditchian v. Secretary-General of the United Nations* (2010) – in which the UNAT forms its approach to 'priority consideration' – the Tribunal finds:

> It should be emphasised that 'priority consideration' cannot be interpreted as a promise or guarantee to be appointed or receive what one is considered in priority for. To hold otherwise would compromise the highest standards of efficiency, competency, and integrity required in selecting the best candidate for staff positions under Article 101 of the [UN] Charter.[38]

The claimant's challenge to their non-selection on the basis that their selection – as an internal candidate – should have been preferred, is unsuccessful.

6.4 Non-competitive Selection

The premise of competitive selection is that it obtains the highest standards, since it allows 'everyone who wants a post to compete for it equally'.[39] Consequently, the utilization of non-competitive selection by international organizations is limited to circumstances in which either non-competitive selection is justified by an exception, or staff are reassigned between different – but hierarchically lateral – posts, to achieve the purposes of the multilateral institution. This is considered under the following headings: (1) Direct selection; and (2) Reassignment.

[35] WBAT No. 255, para. 23.
[36] WBAT No. 255, para. 23.
[37] For example, UN Staff Regulation 4.4 states, 'The Secretary-General may limit eligibility to apply for vacant posts to internal candidates, as defined by the Secretary-General.'
[38] UNAT No. 88, para. 28.
[39] ILOAT No. 1549, para. 13.

1 *Direct Selection*

Direct selection means a chosen international official encumbers a vacant post, without being the successful candidate through an open competition used to evaluate rival applicants. The internal law of international organizations regulates direct selection, as an exception from competitive selection. The example of UN Staff Regulations is widespread: 'So far as practicable, selection shall be made on a competitive basis.'[40] The use of this discretion – to utilize non-competitive selection, in place of competitive selection – must be justified.

In ILOAT Judgment No. 4069, *M (No. 3) v. Organisation for the Prohibition of Chemical Weapons* (2019) the claimant successfully challenges two direct selections to vacancies for which they consider themselves qualified, but are not allowed to compete. The relevant internal law mirrors the UN Staff Regulations and establishes competition as the default mode of selection, with an exception allowing direct selection on the basis of 'practicability'.[41] The Tribunal restates its approach:

> [T]he expression 'so far as practicable' cannot be interpreted to mean that for certain specific posts a competitive selection process can automatically be considered as not practicable … those words confer power on the [principal executive official] to determine whether or not a competition is practicable. However, that is not a general or unfettered discretion. There must be something in the circumstances of the vacancy upon the basis of which the [principal executive official] might reasonably conclude that a competition is not practicable.[42]

Importantly, the Tribunal also underscores that 'the "impracticability" of the competitive selection process cannot be based on the post itself'.[43] Direct selection is also achieved when staff members are selected to posts on a temporary (or so-called, ad interim) basis. In ILOAT Judgment No. 1982, *Barrett v. European Organisation for the Safety of Air Navigation* (2000) – in which the Tribunal examines the alleged misuse of temporary appointment – the claimant is a rejected candidate in competition for a vacant post, but the competition was cancelled and a colleague was temporarily appointed to the vacancy.[44]

40 UN Staff Regulation 4.3, second sentence.
41 ILOAT No. 4069, para. 3.
42 ILOAT No. 4069, para. 4.
43 ILOAT No. 4069, para. 4.
44 ILOAT No. 1982, see para. 1.

Subsequently, the post was readvertised and the colleague who had held it temporarily was competitively selected.[45] The Tribunal finds:

> The temporary appointment of an employee to a vacant post may correspond to the interests of the [international] organization. As such, it cannot be criticised … If the person appointed ad interim is or could also be a candidate for the post open to competition, the temporary appointment may enable the candidate to acquire more easily than [their] rivals the experience or seniority required for definitive appointment to the post. Such an appointment may thereby give the impression that the [international] organization wishes to favour that candidate … [The international organization] therefore has to take the necessary measures in so far as possible to minimise any such disadvantages in cases where it decides that a temporary appointment is justified, when it determines the conditions for it and when it takes steps to fill the post.[46]

The claimant's contention that this was a pretextual arrangement – delaying the competition until the rival colleague (but not the claimant) acquired a requisite two-year period in the preceding grade – is dismissed by the Tribunal trusting, 'The delay in opening the competition perhaps allowed employees to complete the necessary period of seniority, but this was a normal consequence of the measure, not its purpose.'[47]

2 *Reassignment*

The internal law of international organizations features a ubiquitous power of non-competitive selection, namely reassignment. For example, the UN Staff Regulations state: 'Staff members are subject to the authority of the Secretary-General and to assignment by [them] to any of the activities or offices of the United Nations.'[48] This then possesses international organizations with the discretionary authority to reassign staff members between hierarchically lateral posts – and absent abuse of this discretion, deference is owed such reassignment.

In UNAT Judgment No. 1223, *Silva v. Secretary-General of the United Nations* (2022), the claimant challenges their reassignment

[45] ILOAT No. 1982, see para. 1.

[46] ILOAT No. 1982, para. 5(b).

[47] ILOAT No. 1982, para. 6.

[48] UN Staff Regulation 1.2(c), first sentence; similarly, World Bank Staff Rule 5.01 'Reassignment', para. 3.01 states, 'A Staff Member may be reassigned at any time at the initiative of the Bank Group as provided [by this Staff Rule].'

from a legal to a policy function, intended to prevent a conflict of interest arising. The Tribunal finds:

> The crucial issue is whether the reassignment decision was lawful or not. Under our constant jurisprudence, a reassignment decision must be properly motivated, and not tainted by improper motive, or taken in violation of mandatory procedures. It can be impugned if it is found to be arbitrary or capricious, motivated by prejudice or extraneous factors, or was flawed by procedural irregularity or error of law. The accepted method for determining whether the reassignment of a staff member to another position was proper is to assess whether the new post was at the staff member's grade; whether the responsibilities involved corresponded to [their] level; whether the functions to be performed were commensurate with the staff member's competence and skills; and, whether [they] had substantial experience in the field.[49]

Importantly, the Tribunal underscores that whilst staff members are routinely consulted upon contemplated reassignment, there is not 'a need for prior consultation as a procedural prerequisite in every reassignment case'.[50]

Likewise, in WBAT Judgment No. 524, *DB v. International Finance Corporation* (2015) – in which the claimant successfully challenges their reassignment to non-managerial duties – the Tribunal establishes:

> A reassignment decision is a management decision subject to limited review by the Tribunal. When Bank interests dictate reassignment elsewhere, those interests will prevail. Staff members may occasionally be required to accept reassignments which they do not find congenial. However, reassignment decisions must be set aside if they constitute an abuse of discretion, were arbitrary, capricious, and discriminatory or were influenced by a lack of due process. The power to reassign must be exercised through appropriate procedures and with proper motive.[51]

However, the claimant challenges the reassignment on the basis that it was not justified, largely undocumented and that – though they maintained their grade and salary – they were effectively demoted.[52] The Tribunal identifies two elements fundamental to lawful reassignment: first, that there is a demonstrable and substantive basis for reassignment;[53]

[49] UNAT No. 1223, para. 70.
[50] UNAT No. 1223, para. 74.
[51] WBAT No. 524, para. 65.
[52] WBAT No. 524, see paras. 45–48.
[53] WBAT No. 524, see paras. 66–85.

and second, that the reassignment procedure must be adhered to.[54] The Tribunal notes:

> A written record of the decision-making process, the underlying rationale and the consultation which has taken place (be it written exchanges or notes of oral exchanges) will not only assist any subsequent review, but also facilitates transparency and assists all parties in ensuring that no abuse of discretion arises in the first place.[55]

This aligns with the general legal principle, 'Unreasoned administrative decisions are evidently arbitrary' – see Chapter 5, 'Employment-Related Dispute Resolution'.

6.5 Classification

The classification of positions is essential to the integrity of all selection decisions, whether competitive, non-competitive, promotion or reassignment. If classification is faulty, potential candidates may be dissuaded or misled, and the effectiveness and efficiency of international organizations impaired be mismatches between staff and their duties. International administrative tribunals may therefore review, and if necessary rectify, the classification of a position as they may do with any other legal defect of administration. But, this is done sparingly – classification exercises the discretionary authority of an international organization. Absent abuse of discretion, deference is owed classification.

In ILOAT Judgment No. 3589, *V v. Pan American Health Organization* (2016), the claimant alleges that their position should be reclassified. The Tribunal finds:

> It is well established that the grounds for reviewing the classification of a post are limited and ordinarily a classification decision would only be set aside if it was taken without authority, had been made in breach of the rules of form or procedure, was based on an error of fact or law, was made having overlooked an essential fact, was tainted with abuse of authority or if a truly mistaken conclusion had been drawn from the facts. This is because the classification of posts involves the exercise of value judgements as to the nature and extent of the duties and responsibilities of the posts and it is not the Tribunal's role to undertake this process of evaluation.[56]

[54] WBAT No. 524, see para. 103.
[55] WBAT No. 524, see para. 103.
[56] ILOAT No. 3589, para. 4.

The ILOAT finds that the claimant 'does not identify any failure of the classification process or the subsequent review and internal appeal that demonstrates a flaw in the process which would justify the Tribunal quashing the impugned decision'.[57]

The UNAT expressly adopts this same basis of review from the ILOAT. In UNAT Judgment No. 105, *Fuentes v. Secretary-General of the United Nations* (2011) – in which the claimant successfully contends that the correct reclassification procedure was not followed – the Tribunal takes the opportunity to 'note and endorse, in principle' the ILOAT's 'standard of judicial review of classification decisions'.[58]

6.6 The Employment Law of Selection

Selection – the discretionary action of matching people to vacant positions – is integral to perpetuating the international civil service, through its recruitment, deployment and advancement. In doing so, treaty-obligated highest standards of international officials at multilateral institutions must be obtained. Selection – albeit a closely regulated and carefully structured procedure in pursuit of objectivity – necessarily exercises sophisticated judgment by international officials. Necessarily, absent an abuse of direction, deference is owed to decisions to shortlist and select candidates for appointment and promotion, to determine the exercise of direct selection, to reassign staff members (to hierarchically lateral posts) in furtherance of the aims of the international organization and to classify positions. The applicable law may be restated as:

Legal Principles of Selection

- Absent abuse of discretion, deference is owed selecting managers.
- Vacancy announcements must be adhered to, but may be revoked.
- Selection defects must be manifest, to be contestable.

Legal Duties of Selection

- Selection must be competency-based.
- All candidates are entitled to consideration, but not selection.

Non-competitive Selection

- The utilization of non-competitive selection is limited to circumstances in which either, non-competitive selection is justified by an

[57] ILOAT No. 3589, para. 5.
[58] UNAT No. 105, para. 26.

exception – direct selection – or staff are reassigned between different – but hierarchically lateral – posts, to achieve the purposes of the international organization.

Classification

- Classification of the duties and responsibilities of posts must be: (1) by a competent authority; (2) in accordance with the applicable procedure established by the respondent international organization; and (3) not be arbitrary or otherwise abusive.

7

Remuneration

This chapter begins by introducing 'remuneration' – a term encompassing both compensation corresponding to the work an international official performs and benefits addressing their personal circumstances – as integral to the treaty-based obligation upon international organizations to secure staff possessing the highest standards of efficiency and technical competence, with due regard to recruitment on as wide a geographical basis as possible. Second, the legal principles of remuneration are identified, namely: (1) Compensation must secure staff of the highest standard; and (2) Pay must be equal for equivalent work. Third, two attendant legal duties of remuneration are considered, namely: (1) Benefits must ensure geographic diversity; and (2) Remuneration revision methodology must be objective. Fourth, the practice of tax reimbursement is examined. Fifth, and in conclusion, this employment law of remuneration at international organizations is restated.

7.1 What Is Remuneration?

The remuneration – comprising compensation and benefits – offered by any employer is integral to efforts to recruit, motivate and retain their employees.[1] Obviously, this is not to say that other factors – shared values, job satisfaction and career fulfilment, for example – are unimportant. But, even when personally committed and servant to a noble purpose, few people are prepared – or can afford – to work for nothing. So, whilst the culture and context of the workplace are important to recruitment

[1] Broadly, the UN and UN Specialized Agencies refer to 'salary', 'allowances' (UN Staff Regulations, Chapter III) and 'social security', incorporating the UN Joint Staff Pension Fund (UN Staff Regulations, Chapter IV); whereas international financial institutions use 'compensation' (World Bank Staff Rule 6.01), 'benefits' (World Bank Staff Rule 6.14) and the Staff Retirement Plan (World Bank Staff Directive 6.20). However, this book uses the term *remuneration* in the same all-inclusive sense of the ILO Equal Remuneration Convention (No. 100), *compensation* for working in the position encumbered by employees and *benefits* corresponding to their personal circumstances.

and retention, employers must remunerate their employees to work. However, whereas employers generally attempt to attract employees with competitive salaries and appealing benefits, remuneration at international organizations is inherent to achieving the treaty-based attribute of highly efficient and competent staff, with due regard to recruitment on as wide a geographical basis as possible – indeed, all elements of remuneration at multilateral institutions must be connected to this purpose. (See Chapter 3, 'International Civil Service'.)

The compensation of international civil servants is conventionally comprised of three components: (1) pay; (2) post adjustment; and (3) retirement payments.[2] First, pay – regular salary payments – are made for the work an international official performs. Most likely, the greater the decision-making responsibilities, technical expertise or leadership required, the higher the pay. So, pay should correspond to the duties and responsibilities assigned to international officials – not say, their individual capabilities or circumstances. Typically, pay ranges across salary bands related to the hierarchical grade used to classify positions, fixed by the internal law of an international organization.[3] Employees may advance through steps within salary bands over time, even if their grade is unchanged. This increase may be explained as incentivizing sustained satisfactory performance and the potential for greater achievement, the more accustomed the incumbent is to their duties.

Second, since money does not have an absolute value and the workforce of an international organization is invariably global, something must be done to ensure that salary has a uniform effect across the world – in other words, by achieving purchasing parity. This is accomplished by adding to pay a post adjustment – also termed a *cost of living allowance* or *location premium* and so forth – expressed as a percentage or multiplier of the staff member's pay. In other words, international officials of the same grade, but working at different duty stations, would receive identical pay, but differing post adjustments. A duty station where the cost of living is lower

[2] The expression 'post' has two well-established, but entirely different meanings, within international administrative law. On the one hand, it refers to the physical location, the duty station or 'posting' in other words to which an international official is assigned. On the other hand, it refers to the position that the international official encumbers. So, as an example, someone's post in the first sense could be Geneva and in the second sense, Senior Legal Officer. Usually the context makes the distinction tolerably clear.

[3] See, for example, UN Staff Regulation 2.1, 'In conformity with principles laid down by the General Assembly, the Secretary-General shall make appropriate provision for the classification of posts and staff according to the nature of the duties and responsibilities required'.

would attract a lower post adjustment than a duty station where the cost of living was higher. Although complex and fluctuating, all such post adjustment computations must be methodologically objective.

Third, whilst both pay and post adjustments are paid during service, the remaining element of compensation is retirement payments – in a sense, an element of pay deferred – and (mostly) unavailable until service ends. The intended purpose of these retirement payments is to provide financial security to international civil servants after the end of their careers – either through a *pension* or *retirement plan*. Whilst the way these amounts are determined varies, retirement payments are either represented as a known amount paid out to an international official, or a known amount invested for them into the financial markets, then after time the accrued sum is paid out.

Compensation – pay, post adjustments and retirement payments – is related to the position encumbered by an international civil servant. But whilst benefits too, have a cash value, they relate to the personal circumstances of international officials – irrespective of seniority. Chiefly, these are financial inducements intended to make a duty station equally attractive to all international officials, regardless of their nationality – and in this way, enable the wide geographic basis of the international civil service. For example, even a motivated Japanese national official, recruited from Tokyo to work in Paris, may be disadvantaged and so dissuaded, by the costs of resettling, educating their children in Japanese or for Japan's national examinations, the dislocated second income of a partner, and traveling home to Japan periodically to maintain family and cultural ties – contrasted to a French national employed by the same institution faced with none of these impediments. Benefits – relocation, education, spousal and home leave benefits, for example – are intended to counteract this. However, not all the employees of international organizations are recruited on this basis and a distinction is drawn between a post open to international recruitment or to local recruitment. Typically, the latter category are support functions and the roles do not attract the benefits conventionally offered international civil servants.

There is also the question of taxation. Ordinarily, taxes on income are one of life's inevitabilities, but the privileges and immunities of international organizations typically exempt the remuneration of international officials from national taxation – thus both husbanding the resources of multilateral institutions and maintaining equality of treatment amongst their staff. However, since some Member States reserve the right to tax same-nationality international officials, many international organizations reimburse such taxes paid by staff members, thereby equalizing pay after taxation.

So, rather than tempting international officials with an enviable lifestyle, the remuneration offered by international organizations responds to their treaty-based legal obligations to secure staff of the highest standards of efficiency and competence – through compensation – with due regard to recruitment on as wide a geographical basis as possible – through benefits. In other words, this is the legal basis of the employment law of remuneration at international organizations.

7.2 Legal Principles of Remuneration

The administrative action of remunerating international officials exercises the discretionary authority of an international organization, attributed to the principal executive official. Since the financial resources of a multilateral institutions are involved, this is usually closely regulated by the governance organ with control of the budget.[4] It also draws upon considerable technical expertise, prominently provided – for the UN and UN Specialized Agencies – by the International Civil Service Commission.[5] Yet obviously, since not all international civil servants are all paid the same salary is to ask the question, what legal basis enables a distinction to be drawn between lawful and unlawful compensation? First, compensation must secure staff of the highest standard since the treaty-basis of international organizations obligates this outcome. Second, since pay could not be arbitrary – see Chapter 11, 'Administration' – it must be equal for equivalent work.[6] These principles are now considered in turn.

Principle 1: Compensation Must Secure Staff of the Highest Standard

Inevitably, to staff an international organization, international civil servants must be financially incentivized to forego employment elsewhere. Thus, pay is necessarily comparative and should be calibrated to an applicable employment marketplace. But what is the employment marketplace applicable to the international civil service? In 1920, the League of Nations formed an expert committee – 'to examine the organization, method of work, efficiency, number, salaries and allowances of the [s]taff,

4 For example, UN Charter, Article 17(1), 'The General Assembly shall consider and approve the budget of the [UN]'.

5 Established by UN General Assembly Res. 3357/XXIX (1974).

6 This book prefers the term 'equivalent work' over 'equal work', since it makes clearer the crucial discretionary authority to classify functionally comparable positions.

general expenditure of the whole organization, and any other factors' – in order to answer this question.[7] The resulting principle – that the pay of international civil servants should not differ based upon their nationality and should, at the same time, be attractive to individuals otherwise eligible for the world's best paid national civil service – was named after the chair of the committee, a French diplomat called George Noblemaire.

In ILOAT Judgment No. 825, *Beattie and Sheeran v. International Labour Organization* (1987) – repeatedly cited with approval by the Tribunal since – the claimants contend that their pay has been unfairly reduced. The Tribunal states:

> The Noblemaire principle, which dates back to the days of the League of Nations and which the United Nations took over, embodies two rules. One is that, to keep the international civil service as one, its employees shall get equal pay for work of equal value, whatever their nationality or the salaries earned in their own country. The other rule is that in recruiting staff from their full membership, international organizations shall offer pay that will draw and keep citizens of countries where salaries are highest.[8]

Further, the Tribunal notes:

> Ever since the United Nations was founded the United States has been the country deemed to have the highest salaries. Thus the pay of international civil servants is set against the pay of United States federal civil servants stationed in Washington DC, or rather the comparison is between international civil servants in New York, the base city, and national civil servants in Washington, one factor of disparity being the cost of living.[9]

However, international organizations that discharge functions dissimilar to those performed by national civil servants, in practice apply some other employment marketplace. The World Bank, for example, with a focus on international finance expertise competes on pay with 'comparator organizations in the local labour market composed of public and private sector organizations [selected for] the quality and soundness of their compensation programs, their relevance, size and stability'.[10]

When applicable at an international organization, the Noblemaire principle governs all types of compensation, including pension payments. In UNAT Judgment No. 34, *Muthuswami and Others v. United Nations Joint*

[7] 'Report of the Committee of Enquiry adopted by the League of Nations Council, 17 June 1921', (1921) 2 *League of Nations Official Journal*, 651.
[8] ILOAT No. 825, para. 1.
[9] ILOAT No. 825, para. 2.
[10] World Bank Staff Rule 6.01 'Compensation', para. 3.02.

Staff Pension Board (2010) – in which the Tribunal applies the Noblemaire principle for the first time – the claimants, having agreed to the partial commutation of their pensions into lump sums, seek to substitute this with the more advantageous approach of the national civil service pension scheme of India. The Tribunal observes that it is bound by the UN General Assembly's application of the Noblemaire principle: 'Until the application of the Noblemaire principle is changed, the United States federal civil service is the basis of comparison' for all compensation:[11]

> Noblemaire covers both pay and pension. The relations of staff with an international organization do not end when they leave its employ. The pension scheme forms part of the administrative arrangements they may look forward to and, like pay, pensions are governed by basic rules that are binding on the [international] organization.[12]

Since not all positions require internationally recruited staff – for example, the 'General Service' of the UN – locally recruited positions should be attractive to individuals otherwise eligible for the best paid equivalent work opportunities at the duty station – this is known as the Flemming principle.[13] In ILOAT Judgment No. 1000, *Clements and Others v. International Atomic Energy Agency* (1990) – featuring a full examination of the Flemming principle by the Tribunal – the claimants successfully contend that the principle has been misapplied (and an extraneous factor introduced) in setting salaries for locally recruited staff in Vienna. The Tribunal quotes with approval the formulation of the International Civil Service Commission:

> To comply with the standards [of competency and efficiency] established by [Article 101 of] the [UN] Charter as regards the employment of locally recruited staff, the organizations of the United Nations [common system] must be competitive with those employers in the same labour market who recruit staff of equally high calibre and qualifications for work which is similar in nature and equal in value to that of the organizations. Remaining competitive in order to both attract and retain staff of the high standards requires that the conditions of service for the locally recruited staff be determined by reference to the best prevailing conditions of service among other employers in the locality.[14]

11 UNAT No. 34, para. 32.
12 UNAT No. 34, para. 30.
13 Named after Arthur Flemming, chair of the 'Committee of Experts on Salary, Allowance, and Leave Systems', reporting to the UN General Assembly in 1949. (See UN Secretary-General's Note 1949.)
14 ILOAT No. 1000, para. 13.

However, in ILOAT Judgment No. 1519, *Prados and Others v. United Nations Educational, Scientific and Cultural Organization (UNESCO)* (1996) – repeatedly cited with approval by the Tribunal since – the claimants are unsuccessful in demonstrating that the Flemming principle has been misapplied, not least because the Tribunal emphasizes that what must be offered are 'conditions of employment on a par with the best prevailing conditions of employment in the locality' but 'without being necessarily the best local conditions'.[15]

Since compensation is legally purposive, compensation that does not achieve staff of the highest standard cannot obligate an international organization. In UNAT Judgment No. 76, *Kasyanov v. Secretary-General of the United Nations* (2010), the New York-based claimant – wrongly denied transfer to a position in Geneva – contends that they are due the better Geneva duty station post adjustment in recompense. The Tribunal finds:

> Post adjustment is not intended as a profit for a staff member but as a means of maintaining the same level of income in spite of the different costs of living at different duty stations of the [international organization]. It does not accrue unless the staff member effectively lives at the duty station.[16]

Since compensation must secure staff of the highest standard and the claimant never moved to Geneva, they are ineligible for the Geneva salary adjustment, even though wrongly denied the Geneva-based appointment.

Principle 2: Pay Must Be Equal for Equivalent Work

In ILOAT Judgment No. 2313, *ZP v. World Health Organization* (2004) – featuring one of the Tribunal's fullest discussions of unequal pay – the claimant contends that their position has been wrongly classified since its creation, therefore leading to protracted underpayment for their work. The Tribunal effectively states that the principle of equal pay for work of equivalent value – which is typically codified into the internal law of international organizations – is a manifestation of the prohibition on arbitrary administration, which 'requires that persons in like situations be treated alike and that persons in relevantly different situations be treated differently'.[17] The Tribunal emphasizes that it is the responsibility of an international organization to proactively ensure equality:

15 ILOAT No. 1519, para. 2(a).
16 UNAT No. 76, para. 27.
17 ILOAT No. 2313, para. 5.

> It is the duty of international organizations to ensure that they abide by the principle of equality and, particularly, that they comply with its requirement that there be equal pay for work of equal value. And if their rules and procedures do not ensure adherence to that principle and its requirement of equal remuneration, it is their duty to initiate procedures that do, whether by way of general rule or some specific procedure for the particular case.[18]

In WBAT Judgment No. 577, *EL v. The World Bank Group* (2018), the claimant successfully challenges the respondent international organization's failure to explain or remedy their apparent gender and nationality pay differential – between 12 and 17 per cent below their comparator cohort, according to the World Bank's own studies.[19] Albeit that salary-setting is an exercise of the discretionary authority of an international organization, the Tribunal states that breaching the principle of equal pay for work of equivalent value abuses administrative authority, holding that 'discrimination takes place where staff who are in basically similar situations are treated differently'.[20] In adhering to equal compensation for equivalent work, the determination of compensation must exhibit a reasonable basis.[21]

However, a degree of adaptability expected of international civil servants – deputizing for an absent manager, for example – is not tantamount to pay inequality. In UNAT Judgment No. 1065, *Alquza v. Secretary-General of the United Nations* (2020), the claimant unsuccessfully contends that their pay should be supplemented as a result of them assuming additional responsibilities. The Tribunal states, 'the principle of equal pay for work of equal value forbids discrimination',[22] but emphasizes that 'different treatment constitutes discrimination only when there is no lawful and convincing reason for the different treatment of staff members'.[23] Different treatment based upon impermissible distinctions – 'such as gender or race, or when there are no significant differences between the categories of staff members or staff members being treated differently' – is always abusive.[24] But, the Tribunal notes that the claimant belongs to a category of staff expected to temporarily

[18] ILOAT No. 2313, para. 7.
[19] WBAT 577, para. 58.
[20] WBAT 577, para. 44.
[21] See WBAT 577, para. 50.
[22] UNAT No. 1065, para. 36.
[23] UNAT No. 1065, para. 34.
[24] UNAT No. 1065, para. 34.

perform higher-level duties without increased compensation – their recompense is the opportunity to show aptitude for promotion.[25]

Therefore, whilst international civil servants are not all paid the same, the basis for differing pay must be related only to the difference in their work. Misclassification of position may drive unequal compensation – so that the erroneous classification leads automatically to wrongful pay. But the ordinary demands of the international civil service – adaptability and initiative, for example – are not equivalent to this. Whereas, identity-based discrimination – such as sexism or racism – is always arbitrary and compromises the legal basis of administrative action. (See Chapter 5, 'Employment-Related Dispute Resolution'.)

7.3 Legal Duties of Remuneration

Legal duties of remuneration govern the administrative authority of an international organization. These duties may be expressed as: (1) Benefits must obtain geographic diversity; and (2) Compensation revision methodology must be objective.

Duty 1: Benefits Must Ensure Geographic Diversity

Benefits – payments related to the personal circumstances of the international official – are integral to achieving a staff on as wide a geographical basis as possible. (See Chapter 3, 'International Civil Service'.) However, the starting point is the basis of recruitment: local or international. As the UN Staff Rules underscore, this distinction is drawn on the basis of the post, not the post-holder: 'All staff in the General Service … shall be recruited in the country or within commuting distance of each office, irrespective of their nationality and of the length of time they may have been in the country'.[26] All staff not subject to local recruitment, 'shall be considered as having been internationally recruited'.[27] The Staff Rules of the World Bank distinguish between positions subject to local recruitment and international recruitment in terms of whether or not 'global mobility and international experience' are or are not essential and to a subordinate extent, whether or not 'required skills' are or are not obtainable locally.[28]

[25] UNAT No. 1065, para. 36.
[26] UN Staff Rule 4.4(a).
[27] UN Staff Rule 4.5(a), first sentence.
[28] World Bank Staff Rule 4.01 'Appointment', Section 3, 'Recruitment'.

This categorization then determines benefits within the internal law of international organizations. For example, the benefits available to internationally recruited staff of the UN may include, 'payment of travel expenses upon initial appointment and on separation for themselves and their spouses and dependent children; relocation shipment; home leave; education grant; and repatriation grant'.[29] Necessarily, the internal law of the UN and other international organizations also establishes the extent and eligibility for benefits. Consequently, the legal basis of these benefits – obtaining geographic diversity – determines the interpretation of their extent, eligibility, reform or suppression.

In ILOAT Judgment No. 271, *Lopez-Vallarino v. Food and Agriculture Organization* (1976) – featuring an examination of the law underlying the extent of benefits – the claimant contends that they are entitled to full (not partial) reimbursement of home leave travel expenses, having regard to the following provision of their international organization's internal law: 'Eligible staff members shall be granted home leave once in every two years'.[30] However, as the Tribunal notes:

> [T]he grant of this benefit is by this rule made subject to certain conditions, one of which is that the grant should extend only to a point within the general area of the duty station. The result of this condition is that for staff who live outside the general area the grant covers a part only of the cost of the journey.[31]

The Tribunal finds that this is 'not to be read literally',[32] and is instead to be accorded a purposive interpretation in accordance with the legal duty that benefits must ensure geographic diversity:

> [T]he object of the [home leave benefit] is not primarily to make a monetary concession to a staff member. It is to the advantage of the [international organization] as an international body that staff members should maintain their links with their home countries and the principle of home leave has from the earliest times been justified on this ground. If the [international organization] pays for only a part of the journey, the principle of home leave will depend on the willingness and ability of the staff member to pay for the rest [themselves]. A rule which applies only to the longer journeys may result in links with the more distant countries being lost.[33]

[29] UN Staff Rule 4.5(a), second sentence.
[30] ILOAT No. 271, para. 2.
[31] ILOAT No. 271, para. 2.
[32] ILOAT No. 271, para. 3.
[33] ILOAT No. 271, para. 4.

In ILOAT Judgment No. 2638, *JDR v. World Trade Organization* (2007) – featuring an examination of the law underlying the eligibility for benefits – a Swiss claimant contests as discriminatory their ineligibility for the education benefit, as their home country (Switzerland) and country of duty station (Geneva) coincide. The Tribunal has regard to the legal basis of the education benefit:

> The main justification for granting benefits such as home leave or an education grant to some staff members is not that the beneficiaries have a particular nationality, but that their duty station is not in their recognised home country. Far from being discriminatory, such practices, which moreover exist in most international organizations, are designed to restore a degree of equality between officials serving in a foreign country and those who are working in a country where they normally have their home. The two categories cannot be regarded in identical situations. Consequently … the principle of equality must not lead to their being treated in an identical manner when a difference in treatment is appropriate and adapted.[34]

A benefit that becomes disconnected from ensuring geographic diversity may be reformed or suppressed by an international organization. In ILOAT Judgment No. 1241, *Barton and Others v. World Health Organization* (1994) – featuring an examination of the law underlying the reform or suppression of benefits – the claimants contend that means-testing their retiree health insurance premiums, no longer based on the value of their actual pension from the respondent, but instead on the value of their notional whole-career pension, is unlawful. The Tribunal determines that the former method led to an (unjustifiable) windful for the claimants: 'The whole purpose of the reform was to get them to contribute as much as other members and that is fully in line with the notion of mutual aid that underlies social security schemes'.[35] Importantly, this amended basis of pension valuation does not discriminate against the claimants: 'Its purpose was to remove an unfair advantage the [internal law] used to confer on them'.[36]

Duty 2: Compensation Revision Methodology Must Be Objective

Whilst the compensation of staff members invariably changes due to developments in their careers (transferring duties stations or being promoted,

34 ILOAT No. 2638. para. 9.
35 ILOAT No. 1241, para. 22.
36 ILOAT No. 1241, para. 24.

for example), it is also subject to revision – exercising the discretionary authority of an international organization – due to shifts in the external economic comparators used to calculate pay which is competitive and post adjustments which achieve purchasing parity.[37] Due to the complexity of these computations, many international organizations outsource the data collation and processing involved. Prominently, the International Civil Service Commission is the custodian of 'scales of salaries and post adjustments' and 'the classification of duty stations for the purposes of applying post adjustments', within the UN 'common system'.[38]

In ILOAT Judgment No. 4138, *G and Others v. World Intellectual Property Organization* (2019) – in which the Tribunal consolidates its jurisprudence on the methodology to determine post adjustments – the claimants successfully contend that their Geneva duty station post adjustment is unlawfully reduced as a result of a faulty survey methodology utilized by the International Civil Service Commission. The Tribunal states:

- First, an international organization is free to choose a methodology, system or standard of reference for determining salary adjustments for its staff provided that it meets all the principles of international [administrative] law.
- Further, the Tribunal has noted that cases such as the present can raise issues of a highly specialised nature being based on the technical judgment to be made by those whose training and experience equip them for that task and that it will not substitute its own assessment for that of the organization.
- While an international organization is free to choose a methodology, system or standard of reference for determining salary adjustments it must be a methodology which ensures that the results are stable, foreseeable and clearly understood or transparent.
- The requirement that the results must be stable, foreseeable and clearly understood or transparent does not mean a salary regime is fixed once and for all and is incapable of change, or that this requirement excludes reasonable variations in the results yielded. Moreover

[37] Since salaries cannot be set without extraneous inputs – because of the obligation to compete in the 'marketplace' for the highest standard staff – inevitably a change in the extraneous factors triggers revision. Whilst it is possible to render this as a structural term of employment that cannot be suppressed (see Chapter 11, 'Administration'), the approach of this book is that it is subsumed into the duty of an objective methodology.

[38] See, Statute of the International Civil Service Commission, Articles 10(b) and 11(c); also Article 1(2): 'The Commission shall perform its functions in respect of the United Nations and of those specialised agencies and other international organizations which participate in the United Nations common system and which accept the present statute'.

> a methodology cannot be applied without a degree of flexibility and without leaving some room for interpretation by the competent authority, which is entitled to take into account the imbalances generated by past applications of the adopted methodology in order to try to attenuate the effects thereof and properly to implement the Noblemaire principle.[39]

Similarly, in WBAT Judgment No. 149, *Kepper v. International Finance Corporation* (1996) – in which the claimant contests the timing and basis of a change to the post adjustment for Tokyo – the Tribunal holds:

> Among the factors pertinent to a change in policy and the timing thereof are considerations of cost-effectiveness, budget, administration and transition. The [international organization] did not abuse its discretion in weighing the budgetary implications, concerning both extent and timing, of the proposed change in the post allowance index against the benefits to be derived therefrom. There is no evidence that the [international organization] purposely delayed the change to the [applicable] Index in order to deprive staff members of fair compensation or to discriminate against certain groups. It was not unreasonable for the [international organization] to coordinate the implementation of the change with the budget-making process and the beginning of the fiscal year.[40]

This legal duty to ensure an objective compensation revision methodology, likewise applies to pay. In ILOAT Judgment No. 1821, *Allaert and Warmels (No. 3) v. European Southern Observatory* (1999), the claimants challenge the imposition of a salary increase of 0.7 per cent – less than the 1.3 per cent recommended as a result of the applicable salary-setting methodology at the international organization. The Tribunal is scathing of the approach by their employer and consequent arbitrariness:

> Even if it were possible to dignify the process adopted by the [international organization] by calling it a methodology for salary [revision], it obviously fails to produce results that are stable, foreseeable and clearly understood. The rule laid down by the Tribunal is simply an extension of the general principle that an organization may not act arbitrarily and must adopt an objective methodology for salary [revision]. In the case [before the Tribunal] the [international organization] has failed to demonstrate that the decision was not simply arbitrary.[41]

39 ILOAT No. 4138, para. 26, bullet points added.
40 WBAT No. 149, para. 26.
41 ILOAT No. 1821, para. 8.

Despite the invariable reliance by international organizations on data collected and expertly analyzed by external entities – such as the International Civil Service Commission – the legal duty to ensure an objective compensation revision methodology is unalterably fixed to the international organization itself. In *ILOAT No. 4138*, the Tribunal states that international organizations cannot hide behind external bodies:

> The Tribunal has recognised that the whole subject of post adjustment is of great complexity and the constant changes in the factors that are considered relevant, mean that the methodology will probably never attain perfection. However, if the [international] organization is relying on an external body for advice and assistance, it nonetheless needs to ensure these principles have been applied ... The [international] organization has the duty of checking the lawfulness of any decision by another body on which it bases its own decision. So too must it check the adequacy of action by that other body to correct any mistake it may have made, and make sure that such corrective action respects the rights of staff ... If the [International Civil Service Commission's] original reckoning was unlawful, so is a second one that fails to redress fully the wrong.[42]

The Tribunal goes on to give examples of unlawfulness in compensation revision methodology. The Tribunal has the reckoning of post adjustments in mind, but arbitrariness would result with regards to any element of compensation, if an international organization, 'overlooks or misconstrues some particular factor, or if some method is applied for the wilful contrivance of lower figures of [compensation], or if corners are cut for the sake of saving time, but to the detriment of staff interests'.[43]

In all circumstance, to exercise the discretionary administrative authority to revise compensation, an international organization must adhere to an objective methodology – even if the calculations are performed by external experts.

7.4 Tax Reimbursement

The constituent instruments of international organizations or supplementary privileges and immunities agreements commonly exempt compensation and benefits received by international civil servants from national taxation. For example, the Convention on the Privileges and Immunities of the UN states, 'Officials of the United Nations shall ... [b]e

[42] ILOAT No. 4138, paras. 26–27.
[43] ILOAT 4138, para. 28.

exempt from taxation on the salaries and emoluments paid to them by the United Nations'.[44] Nevertheless, Member States may exercise a 'reservation' to exclude this immunity, thereby subjecting their same-state nationals (but not other nationals) to taxation of their international civil service renumeration.[45] The United States of America does this uniformly.[46] The practice of other states is variable.

This presents two challenges to the premise of tax exemption of international organizations, intended to maintain their impartiality. (See Chapter 2, 'International Organizations'). First, national taxes may divert the communal financial resources of international organizations to the treasuries of taxing Member States. Second, tax exemption marries with the principle of equal pay for work of equivalent value, which is undermined if international civil service pay is subject to varying national taxation, since international organizations establish pay assuming nil national taxation.

The resolution of this impasse – providing affected staff with a tax reimbursement – compromises the first concern, whilst attempting to address the second. In WBAT Judgment No. 1, *De Merode and Others v. The World Bank* (1981) – the landmark case in which the claimants challenge the World Bank's altered approach to tax reimbursement and revision of salary – the Tribunal finds that an established practice of tax reimbursement assumes the status of a structural term of employment which cannot be suppressed (see Chapter 11, 'Administration'), but the methodology of the reimbursement is not inviolable and may be objectively reformed.[47]

7.5 The Employment Law of Remuneration

The purpose of remuneration at international organizations is not to bestow a life of privilege on international officials, but to attract people of the highest standard from every Member State, into the international civil service. Derived from the treaty-based legal obligation

[44] General Convention, Section 18(b).

[45] See Vienna Convention on the Law of Treaties, Article 2(d): '*Reservation* means a unilateral statement, however phrased or named, made by a State, when signing, ratifying, accepting, approving or acceding to a treaty, whereby it purports to exclude or to modify the legal effect of certain provisions of the treaty in their application to that State'.

[46] See, www.irs.gov, accessed 3 September 2025, 'Employees of a foreign government or international organization – Federal income tax withholding'.

[47] See WBAT No. 1, para. 82.

of an international organization to secure staff of the highest standards of efficiency and competence – utilizing pay, post adjustment and retirement payments – with due regard to recruitment on as wide a geographical basis as possible – through benefits – the applicable law may be restated as:

Legal Principles of Remuneration

- Compensation must secure staff of the highest standard.
- Pay must be equal for equivalent work.

Legal Duties of Remuneration

- Benefits must obtain geographic diversity.
- Compensation revision methodology must be objective.

Tax Reimbursement

- An established practice of tax reimbursement is a structural term of employment which cannot be suppressed, but the methodology of the reimbursement is not inviolable and may be objectively revised.

8

Performance Management

This chapter begins by describing performance management – the administrative action of appraising performance and its consequences – inherent to the continuing treaty-based obligation of international organizations to secure the highest standards of efficiency and competence of their staff. Second, the legal principles of performance management are identified, namely: (1) Absent abuse of discretion, deference is owed performance-managers; (2) Performance management defects must be manifest, to be contestable; and (3) Probationary decisions exercise the widest discretion. Third, two attendant legal duties of performance appraisal are considered, as follows: (1) Performance appraisal must be useable; and (2) Performance appraisal must afford an opportunity to respond. Fourth, the temporary intensification of performance management as the basis for termination of appointment – in the context of probation and substandard performance – is considered. Fifth, and in conclusion, this employment law of performance management at international organizations is restated.

8.1 What Is Performance Management?

The considerable effort of securing the highest standards of efficiency and competence through appointing the most able international officials – see Chapter 6, 'Selection' – and offering compelling compensation and benefits – see Chapter 7, 'Remuneration' – would be meaningless if the superior performance of international civil servants was not recognized, and unsatisfactory performance went unaddressed. Therefore, the attainment of these highest standards by employees of international organizations throughout their employment arises from the treaty-basis of multilateral institutions. This international law obligation is fulfilled by performance management.

The centrepiece of performance management at international organizations is typically an institution-wide performance management exercise – *performance evaluation* or *performance assessment* or *staff report* or similar. For most staff members, this occurs annually and tends to be a laborious affair. It may start with the self-assessment of performance, supplemented by input perhaps from co-workers, 'internal clients', 'stakeholders' or similar. Clearly, the opinion of the staff member's line-manager should be paramount. Yet, this managerial judgment must be exposed to the response and possible rebuttal of the staff member. Even this may not be the last word, since some further review by the line-manager's line-manager (known as a second-level supervisor) or Human Resources function is often required. Notwithstanding the heterogeneous functions of international organizations, all performance management is necessarily in pursuit of fact-based and constructive appraisal. The Staff Rules of the World Bank, for example, call for a meeting between a staff member and their line-manager in which the past year's 'performance, achievements, strengths, areas for improvement, and future development needs' are all addressed.[1]

In an effort to ensure both standardization and foreseeability, the principle performance metric of international civil servants is a series of objectives. In other words, previously established performance milestones and targets, tailored to the staff member's duties and responsibilities. Ideally, objective-setting cascades from an organizational strategy adopted by a governance organ, tasking the principal executive official, who then assigns their direct-reports compatible objectives and so on. This all aligns with the annual performance management cycle, enabling successes and shortcomings to be identified each year. Many international organizations then translate this individualized interaction into a *performance rating* – either a numerical score or a descriptor, like 'Fully Successful'.[2] Plainly, performance management is intended to be demonstrably objective.

But, even if the duties and responsibilities of a staff member lend themselves to quantifiable, data-driven objective-setting – and an institution-wide performance management framework is robust and commands confidence – the appraisal of performance requires considerable professional judgment by line-managers. This is now more pronounced than ever, with the addition of 'behavioural competences' – collegial and collaborative styles of working and workplace interactions – to the traditional 'technical skills', that international officials are called

[1] World Bank Staff Directive 5.03 'Performance Management Process', para. 3.01(a).

[2] See, for example, Germond and Martin 2020, 282–286.

upon to demonstrate. A notorious scenario divides opinion: the technically gifted international official, with an obnoxious interpersonal style. So, even with diligent, skilled and self-aware performance-managers, the risk of subjective preferences subverting professional judgment is only too obvious. The legal principles of performance management and the related legal duties of performance appraisal respond to this dynamic.

8.2 Legal Principles of Performance Management

As with the exercise of all discretionary administrative authority at international organizations, the foremost legal principle of performance management is absent an abuse of discretion, deference is owed performance-managers. It may then be said that, in the context of performance management, this accountability interlocks with the second principle – namely, defects in performance management must be manifest in order to be contestable. Lastly, by convention, the management of probationary performance is owed the greatest deference, so ensuring that selection errors can be remedied promptly and with minimal organizational disruption. These principles are now considered in turn.

Principle 1: Absent Abuse of Discretion, Deference Is Owed Performance Managers

Performance management exercises the discretionary authority of an international organization. In other words, the treaty-based administrative authority of the principal executive official (and their delegates) cannot be displaced. Professional judgment is called for and there are a reasonable range of outcomes in the same circumstances. Such discretionary authority is regulated in alignment with general legal principles. (See Chapter 5, 'Employment-Related Dispute Resolution'.) In ILOAT Judgment No. 3692, *B (No. 2) v. European Patent Organization* (2016) the claimant challenges – amongst other things – their annual performance appraisal wherein their 'Good' rating for one year is disparaged by an accompanying remark. The Tribunal restates its consistent approach:

> [A]ssessment of an employee's merit during a specified period involves a value judgement; for this reason, the Tribunal must recognise the discretionary authority of the bodies responsible for conducting such an assessment. Of course, it must ascertain whether the ratings given to the employee have been determined in full conformity with the rules, but it

> cannot substitute its own opinion for assessment made by these bodies of the qualities, performance and conduct of the person concerned. The Tribunal will therefore intervene in this area only if the decision was taken without authority, if it was based on an error of law or fact, a material fact was overlooked, or a plainly wrong conclusion was drawn from the facts, or if it was taken in breach of a rule of form or procedure, or if there was abuse of authority.[3]

The Tribunal adds that this limited review, 'naturally applies to both the rating given in a staff report and the comments accompanying that rating'.[4] So, in other words, the Tribunal may not overturn performance management simply because it does not share the judgment of the performance manager. Performance managers are entitled to their views.

The approach of the WBAT is the same. In WBAT Judgment No. 614, *Andriamilamina (No. 2) v. International Finance Corporation* (2019) the claimant unsuccessfully challenges their 'underrating' and allegedly unclear performance appraisal. The Tribunal sets out the basis of its limited review:

> The evaluation of staff performance is an essentially discretionary act entailing the exercise of judgment by management, which is presumed to possess the requisite familiarity with the work of all departmental staff members and to have made many comparative quality judgments. The task of the Tribunal is not to substitute its own judgment for that of the management. The proper task of the Tribunal is, rather, to determine whether or not management's acts and decisions in connection therewith constituted, or were attended by, an abuse of discretion.[5]

When dealing with performance management cases, the UNAT refers to its standard approach to the limited review of discretionary authority. For example, in UNAT Judgment No. 1047, *Al Ashhab v. Commissioner-General of the United Nations Relief and Works Agency for Palestine Refugees in the Near East* (2010), concerning a challenge to substandard performance-related termination, the Tribunal recalls:

> The Appeals Tribunal has consistently held [that] when judging the validity of the Secretary-General's exercise of discretion in administrative matters, the [first-instance] Tribunal determines if the decision is legal, rational, procedurally correct, and proportionate. The Tribunal

3 ILOAT No. 3692, para. 8.
4 ILOAT No. 3692, para. 8.
5 WBAT No. 614, para. 71.

> can consider whether relevant matters have been ignored and irrelevant matters considered, and also examine whether the decision is absurd or perverse. But it is not the role of the Tribunal to consider the correctness of the choice made by the Secretary-General amongst the various courses of action open to [them]. Nor is it the role of the Tribunal to substitute its own decision for that of the Secretary-General.[6]

In other words, to survive legal challenge before an administrative tribunal, any administrative decision on performance management must be taken: (1) by a competent authority; (2) in accordance with the applicable procedure established by the respondent international organization; and (3) not be arbitrary or otherwise abusive.

Principle 2: Performance Management Defects Must Be Manifest, to Be Contestable

Since the professional judgment – the managerial opinion – of a performance manager is not amenable to substitution by a Tribunal, in order for performance management to be contestable, defects must be manifest. In other words, faults must be noticeable without the Tribunal possessing itself of the same expertise and knowledge as management. In *WBAT No. 614*, this is vividly termed the exclusion of the 'microscopic review':

> It is not the Tribunal's role to undertake a microscopic review of the [claimant's] performance, and to substitute its own judgment about the [claimant's] performance for the Bank's. Rendering judgment on the appropriateness of a Fully Successful versus a Superior rating comes close to a microscopic review. Ordinarily, to allow petitions to the Tribunal regarding disagreements as to the correctness of 'Fully Successful' versus 'Superior' ratings would involve unwarranted intrusion on managerial discretion.[7]

Similarly, international administrative tribunals are deferential to the complexity of the comparative assessment of performance. In WBAT Judgment No. 593, *EU v. International Bank for Reconstruction and Development* (2018), the claimant challenges their annual performance management as arbitrary, in the context of a broader challenge to a series of administrative actions which appear to constitute disguised misconduct-related demotion. The Tribunal finds:

6 UNAT No. 1047, para. 42.
7 WBAT No. 614, para. 74, restating the application of this paragraph by the Tribunal on multiple occasions.

> The process of establishing performance ratings is based on a comparative assessment of staff members within the same unit. The Tribunal has recognized that given the various decisional elements that are properly taken into account in making such a comparative assessment, it is difficult to support a claim of abuse of discretion.[8]

For similar reasons, a Tribunal will not entertain a challenge based upon the subtlety that an apparently positive performance appraisal conceals some unspoken criticism. In *WBAT No. 614* the Tribunal states:

> There is no basis for considering a 'Fully Successful' rating as adverse or negative. The Bank's guidelines state that it is expected 'that most staff members on many items would be rated fully successful or fully accomplished' and 'that a few staff members on a few items would be rated superior'.[9]

Of course, there is an objective tension in supposing that 'superior' performance is elusive, since it is only the highest standards that are legally attributed to the international civil service – see Chapter 2, 'International Civil Service'.

Principle 3: Probationary Decisions Exercise the Widest Discretion

In ILOAT Judgment No. 1817, *FJ v. European Organisation for the Safety of Air Navigation* (1999), in which the claimant challenges the termination of their probationary appointment, the Tribunal restates that the administrative decision not to confirm a probationary appointment is a discretionary decision – and hence amenable to challenge. But the ILOAT emphasizes that the function of probation would be thwarted without the greatest possible deference to such decisions:

> The Tribunal will be particularly cautious in reviewing a decision not to confirm the appointment of a probationer; otherwise probation would fail to serve as a period of trial. The purpose of probation is to ensure that new staff members are the best qualified. So an organization must be allowed the widest discretion in the matter and its decision will stand unless the flaw is especially serious or glaring.[10]

This 'widest discretion' is usually rendered as an assessment of the staff member's overall suitability. This assessment of 'fit' to the international organization, includes but is not limited to performance – at the

[8] WBAT No. 593, para. 199.
[9] WBAT No. 614, para. 73.
[10] ILOAT No. 1817, para. 5.

World Bank it encompasses, 'performance, technical qualifications and professional behaviours'.[11] In WBAT Judgment No. 7, *Buranavanichkit v. International Bank for Reconstruction and Development* (1982) – repeatedly cited with approval since – in which the claimant successfully challenges the non-confirmation of their probationary appointment, the Tribunal states:

> Probation has as its purpose the determination whether the employee concerned satisfies the conditions required for confirmation. These conditions may refer not only to the technical competence of the probationer but also to [their] character, personality and conduct generally in so far as they bear on ability to work harmoniously and to good effect with supervisors and other staff members.[12]

In WBAT Judgment No. 293, *Khan v. International Bank for Reconstruction and Development* (2003), in which the claimant successfully challenges the non-confirmation of their probationary appointment, the Tribunal finds:

> [A] probationer has no right to confirmation, and the [international organization] has a considerable discretion in deciding whether or not to confirm a probationary appointment. The Tribunal has said that the position of a probationer is essentially provisional and the assessment of [their] suitability is a matter of managerial discretion. The issue is whether the probationer has proven [their] suitability to the specific requirements of the [international organization].[13]

The probationer's compatibility to the international organization is understood, not only in terms of technical competence, but also sympathetic professional traits. Since modern-day performance typically includes both technical and behavioural abilities – and given the importance of inclusivity in the workplace – it seems that a reasoned decision not to confirm a probationary appointment should today be based on factors that are amenable to performance management.

8.3 Legal Duties of Performance Appraisal

Legal duties of performance appraisal govern the administrative authority of an international organization. They impose obligations upon employing international organizations towards the international officials

[11] World Bank Staff Directive 4.02 'Probation', para. 4.01.
[12] WBAT No. 7, para. 26.
[13] WBAT No. 293, para. 58.

they employ. Although the internal law of international organizations closely regulates performance appraisal, this regulatory environment could be amended and updated at the discretion of the employer – so long as these legal duties are secured. These duties may be expressed as: (1) Performance appraisal must be useable; and (2) Performance appraisal must afford an opportunity to respond.

Duty 1: Performance Appraisal Must Be Useable

It may be recalled that performance management at international organizations is not an end to itself, but implements a treaty-based obligation. For this reason, performance appraisal must be 'useable'. If no use can be made of it – in other words, it does not obtain the highest standards of efficiency and competence of staff – then it is robbed of its legal basis. What are the attributes of useable performance appraisal? To be useable, performance appraisal must be: (1) credible and (2) timely. These are now considered in turn.

1 Performance Appraisal Must Be Credible

To be credible, performance appraisal has to possess an empirical basis which should typically be documented. In *WBAT No. 614*, the Tribunal states:

> [T]he [international organization] must be able to adduce a reasonable and objective basis for adverse judgment on a staff member's performance. The Tribunal considers that failure on the part of the [international organization] to submit a reasonable basis for adverse evaluation and performance ratings is evidence of arbitrariness in the making of such an evaluation and rating. Lack of a demonstrable basis commonly means that the discretionary act was done capriciously and arbitrarily.[14]

Performance appraisal must also be coherent and free from internal contradictions. In *ILOAT No. 3692*, the performance rating ('good') appeared to be modified by an accompanying comment – 'performance was at the lower end of the good rating'.[15] The Tribunal considers such inconsistency to compromise the lawfulness of performance appraisal: '[T]he Tribunal can only find that, although ultimately the [claimant] obtained the rating "good" for [their] productivity, the comment accompanying that rating detracted from it. In this respect the disputed staff

[14] WBAT No. 614, para. 72.
[15] ILOAT No. 3692, para. 7.

report is … unlawful'.[16] Likewise, in *WBAT No. 593*, the Tribunal states, 'performance ratings must have a reasonable and observable basis, and there is obviously a link between the performance evaluation and the performance rating'.[17]

A concomitant of this required robustness is that the performance appraisal must necessarily be balanced. In WBAT Judgment No. 211, *Lysy v. International Bank for Reconstruction and Development* (1999), in which the claimant challenges a sequence of decisions by the World Bank – including an allegedly unfair and unreasonable performance appraisal – the Tribunal states a test that it has repeatedly used since:

> A performance evaluation should deal with all relevant and significant facts, and should balance positive and negative factors in a manner which is fair to the person concerned. Positive aspects need to be given weight, and the weight given to factors must not be arbitrary or manifestly unreasonable.[18]

Since a useable performance appraisal is the object of all performance management procedures at international organizations, disregard of these procedures not only breaches the legal principle obligating adherence to the internal law – see Chapter 11, 'Administration' – but also gives rise to a consequent presumption of arbitrariness. In UNAT Judgment No. 400, *Tadonki v. Secretary-General of the United Nations* (2014) the claimant challenges the nonrenewal of their appointment. In the context of an admission by the Secretary-General that the appraisal of the staff member's performance 'did not follow the steps established in the applicable norms for the formal performance evaluation procedure',[19] the Tribunal states:

> If the [international organization] does not follow the clear norms which apply to evaluate staff members' performances, it risks arbitrariness and bears the burden of proof that an evaluation reached after an irregular procedure is nonetheless objective, fair and well based.[20]

In other words, performance management demands deductions based upon even-handed observations which are documented and free from contradiction, derived from adherence to a uniform procedure with this end in mind.

16 ILOAT No. 3692, para. 9.
17 WBAT No. 593, para. 120.
18 WBAT No. 211, para. 68.
19 UNAT No. 400, para. 51.
20 UNAT No. 400, para. 56.

2 Performance Appraisal Must Be Timely

In the same way that non-credible performance management is unusable, so too is untimely performance appraisal – no matter how persuasive it may be. To begin with, performance appraisal cannot simply be abandoned altogether by an international organization. In ILOAT Judgment No. 3846, *C v. International Telecommunication Union* (2017), in which the claimant alleges that they are overworked and their performance appraisal is overdue, the Tribunal finds:

> As to the lateness of the performance appraisal, the Tribunal draws attention to the fact that every international civil servant has the right to be informed of [their] supervisors' appraisal of [their] service. The [international] organization therefore has a duty to evaluate an official's work in a timely manner and any failure to do so is a breach of its obligations to its staff.[21]

In other words, employees are entitled to performance appraisal. The WBAT emphasizes that annual performance management does not mean that performance may be unmanaged during the rest of the year. In WBAT Judgment No. 434, *BG v. International Finance Corporation* (2010), in which the claimant challenges their annual performance appraisal – on the grounds that it is factually imbalanced and erroneous, procedurally flawed and improperly motivated – the Tribunal finds:

> Lapses in performance should be identified when they occur and should be addressed expressly and promptly. They should not be held in reserve only to be disclosed at the end of a review period. Discussion of performance does not replace the need for ongoing feedback throughout the year in question, which should be provided so that the staff member should be able to anticipate the nature of this year-end discussion and resultant ratings.[22]

Likewise, in *WBAT No. 593*, the Tribunal states:

> The Tribunal has held that ongoing feedback is necessary so as to avoid any surprises at the end of the review period. Ongoing feedback should be clear and specific so that the staff member can anticipate the nature of this year-end discussion and resultant ratings.[23]

Indeed, 'no surprises' could be considered – albeit colloquially – the meaning of timely performance appraisal: performance has to be continually appraised and faulty performance, promptly and explicitly addressed.

21 ILOAT No. 3846, para. 14.
22 WBAT No. 434, para. 40; this judgment consolidates several earlier cases.
23 WBAT No. 593, para. 129.

Duty 2: Performance Appraisal Must Afford an Opportunity to Respond

This second duty embodies a safeguard against arbitrary performance management – namely, that a staff member is afforded the opportunity to react to and – if they see fit – offer rebuttal of an adverse appraisal. This duty is typically overlaid in the internal law of an international organization as:

- An *obligation* upon performance-managers to draw faults to the notice of staff whilst allowing a reasonable period of time in which to demonstrate improved performance;[24] and
- The *opportunity* of staff members to discuss and respond to performance appraisal before it is finalized.[25]

For example, in ILOAT Judgment No. 3224, *D'A v. International Organization for Migration* (2013) the claimant challenges their sub-standard performance-related termination – principally on the grounds that this 'was not preceded by a proper warning and that it does not rest on lawful reasons, because [their] work was never assessed'.[26] The Tribunal states:

> The Tribunal recalls that a staff member whose service is not considered satisfactory is entitled to be informed in a timely manner as to the unsatisfactory aspects of [their] service, so as to be in a position to remedy the situation, and to have objectives set in advance.[27]

Similarly, in WBAT Judgment No. 624, *FH v. International Bank for Reconstruction and Development* (2020), the claimant challenges their annual performance appraisal – in which they are rated as not meeting 'expectations', but not afforded the opportunity to discuss the appraisal with their performance manager before it is finalized. The Tribunal states:

[24] For example, World Bank Staff Directive 5.03 'Performance Management Process', para. 5.01:

> If a Manager ... determines that a Staff Member's performance (which includes professional and workplace behaviour) is not satisfactory, the Manager [is to] ... Discuss and share with the Staff Member in writing: (i) the aspects of performance that are not satisfactory, (ii) guidance on what improvement is expected and by when, and (iii) the possible consequences of failure to improve.

[25] For example, World Bank Staff Directive 5.03 'Performance Management Process', para. 3.01(e): 'The Staff may submit written comments on the performance evaluation and any supplemental evaluation'.

[26] ILOAT No. 3224, para. 5.

[27] ILOAT No. 3224, para. 7.

> The staff member must be given adequate warning about criticism of [their] performance or any deficiencies in [their] work that might result in an adverse decision being ultimately reached. Second the staff member must be given adequate opportunities to defend [themselves]. The Tribunal has held that any decision to deviate from established best practices must not be arbitrary or lack a reasonable and observable basis.[28]

The Tribunal further holds 'that a staff member's performance rating must not be set before the staff member has participated in a performance discussion'.[29] In other words, performance appraisal cannot be secretive and performance-managers cannot be ignorant or indifferent to a response or rebuttal from the subject staff member.

8.4 Performance Management-Related Termination

Since the highest standards of efficiency and competence of their staff must be constantly secured by international organizations, performance that is irredeemably unsatisfactory or substandard should lead to termination of appointment. This is considered under the following headings: (1) Probation; and (2) Substandard performance.

1 Probation

Appointment to the staff of an international organization is probationary. In other words, employment begins with a trial period. This trial must be successfully completed before appointment is confirmed. However, although on the one hand, discretion is widest concerning probationary non-confirmation, on the other hand, probation does not invalidate the duty of useable appraisal. Consequently, the terms of suitability to an international organization may not be unknown or unknowable to the probationer.

In ILOAT Judgment No. 4215, *D (No. 3) v. Intergovernmental Organisation for International Carriage by Rail* (2020), in which the claimant successfully challenges the non-confirmation of their probationary appointment, the Tribunal states:

> It is well established that an [international] organization which requires a staff member to undergo a probation period on [their] appointment must, in particular, set objectives for [them] so that [they know] what criteria will

[28] WBAT No. 624, paras. 61–62.
[29] WBAT No. 624, para. 67.

> be used to assess [their] performance, assess [their] merits following the proper procedure and, if it finds [their] performance unsatisfactory, inform [them] in sufficient time for [them] to attempt to remedy the situation.[30]

Given the latitude of 'unsatisfactory' service during probation, it must be assumed that this duty to credibly appraise the probationer must include guidance on any interpersonal incompatibility to the institution. In UNAT Judgment No. 21, *Asaad v. Commissioner-General of the United Nations Relief and Works Agency for Palestine Refugees in the Near East* (2010), the Tribunal invalidates non-confirmation of probation since the claimant was not made aware of the reasons for their non-confirmation.[31]

The entire premise of probation is that during this period unsatisfactory performance by an international official risks non-confirmation of their appointment. In ILOAT Judgment No. 3440, *E v. Pan American Health Organization* (2015), the claimant unsuccessfully challenges the non-confirmation of their probationary appointment alleging they were un-warned that their probationary appointment may not be confirmed.[32] The Tribunal notes:

> [B]y its nature, a probationary period is one of trial in which it is determined whether a person is capable of carrying out the duties of a post. A probationer is quite aware that unsatisfactory performance would occasion the termination of [their] appointment. The [claimant's] letter of appointment made it clear that a decision whether to confirm [their] appointment would have been taken at the end of the probationary period, or of any extension thereto.[33]

However, an international organization must ensure that a connection is drawn between noted unsatisfactory performance and jeopardized employment. A clear warning achieves this. In *ILOAT No. 4215*, the Tribunal requires employees to be warned 'in specific terms if there is a risk that [their] appointment will not be confirmed at the end of [their] probation'.[34]

2 *Substandard Performance*

The term 'substandard performance' is used here to mean an international official – once confirmed in their appointment – deemed to

30 ILOAT No. 4215, para. 12.
31 See UNAT No. 21, para. 12.
32 See ILOAT No. 3440, para. 15.
33 ILOAT No. 3440, para. 16.
34 ILOAT No. 4215, para. 12.

be underperforming so seriously that this cannot be addressed through the mechanism of routine feedback or annual performance appraisal. Instead, the presumption of continuing employment that exists following confirmation of probation is reversed and the employee risks termination of appointment if their performance does not improve.

Whilst most international organizations recognize the gravity of these circumstances by closely regulating the management of substandard performance in their internal law, substandard performance is held accountable through the legal principles and governed by the legal duties of performance management as a whole. In *ILOAT No. 3224*, the Tribunal synopsizes this as follows:

> The Tribunal recalls that a staff member whose service is not considered satisfactory is entitled to be informed in a timely manner as to the unsatisfactory aspects of [their] service, so as to be in a position to remedy the situation, and to have objectives set in advance. It also recalls that an organization cannot base an adverse decision on a staff member's unsatisfactory performance if it has not complied with the rules governing the evaluation of that performance. Except in a case of manifest error, the Tribunal will not substitute its own assessment of a staff member's services for that of the competent bodies of an international organization. Nevertheless, such an assessment must be made in full knowledge of the facts, and the considerations on which it is based must be accurate and properly established.[35]

This is to say that lawful substandard performance-related termination must result from a process that has afforded the seriously underperforming international official:

(1) A reasonable opportunity to demonstrate improved performance. The components of which are necessarily that:
   (a) The elements of substandard performance are communicated with sufficient clarity and concreteness so as to allow them to be addressed; and
   (b) A reasonable time period is established in which to remedy the substandard performance.
(2) A demonstrable warning that unaddressed substandard performance may result in termination of appointment.

Nevertheless, the nature of the discretionary authority to terminate the appointment of an underperforming international official is no different

[35] ILOAT No. 3224, para. 7.

from the authority to adjudge their suitability for confirmation of probationary appointment, or annually appraise their performance. Unless arbitrary or otherwise abusive, substandard performance managers are entitled to their views.

8.5 The Employment Law of Performance Management

Derived from the continuing treaty-based obligations of an international organization, the employment law of performance management is composed of legal principles and attendant legal duties, which fix international organizations with accountability and govern decision-makers, securing the highest standard of efficiency and competence of staff. The applicable law may be restated as:

Legal Principles of Performance Management

- Absent abuse of discretion, deference is owed performance-managers.
- Performance management defects must be manifest, to be contestable.
- Discretion is widest concerning probationary non-confirmation.

Legal Duties of Performance Appraisal

- Performance appraisal must be useable, so must be credible and timely.
- Performance appraisal must afford an opportunity to respond.

Performance-related Termination

- Probationary status does not invalidate the duty of useable appraisal.
- Substandard performance is managed in accordance with the legal principles and duties of performance management.

PART III

Integrity and Independence

9

Standards of Conduct

This chapter begins by introducing standards of conduct – implementing the integrity and independence attributed to the international civil service by the treaty-basis of international organizations. Second, the legal principles of conduct are identified, namely: (1) The interests of the international organization are paramount; (2) Abuse of authority must be manifest, to be contestable; (3) International officials must be uncorrupted; and (4) External authority must not compromise international officials. Third, three attendant legal duties of conduct are considered, as follows: (1) Integrity requires honesty and reputability; (2) Integrity requires reserve and respect; and (3) Integrity requires discipline and hierarchical authority. Fourth, the duty to report alleged beaches of the standards of conduct (sometimes styled, 'whistleblowing') is considered. Fifth, the chapter examines the interaction between the immunity typically possessed by international officials in the course of their duties and the exercise of national legal jurisdiction, notably when crimes may have been committed in connection to the workplace. Sixth, and in conclusion, this employment law of standards of conduct at international organizations is restated. The employment law of the enforcement of integrity and the independence of the international civil service – procedures to ascertain and sanction breaches of standards of conduct – is the subject of Chapter 10, 'Misconduct'.

9.1 What Are Standards of Conduct?

Saying that someone in the workplace 'lacks integrity', is never meant as praise. But what does it mean? The dictionary definition of integrity references morality: 'Freedom from moral corruption; innocence, sinlessness. Soundness of moral principle; the character of uncorrupted virtue; uprightness, honesty, sincerity'.[1] However, in colloquial usage,

[1] *Shorter Oxford English Dictionary*: one limb of the three-part definition of 'integrity'.

the intended implication could vary, depending on the context. It could – in its mildest form – convey that someone is inconsistent. That they express different views to different audiences, or act differently in similar situations – based perhaps upon their perception of what opinions and actions are most welcome or opportune. Of course, even here, the circumstances may suggest whether this is the cause of exasperation or – if the inconsistency is reputationally or operationally damaging – the basis for rebuke.

However, it could mean that someone is self-interested. That their actions further their personal, which is to say, their private interests – not their functions entrusted by an employer – or give rise to this appearance. It could mean that someone is motivated by prejudice or cronyism. At its most extreme, to say someone 'lacks integrity', could be meant to convey dishonesty and corruption – that they abuse their position or the resources of their employer to enrich themselves (or others) or are bribed to act or influence actions in certain ways.

Exploitative and corrupt employees may afflict any employer, with potentially ruinous consequences. But if this misbehaviour goes unchecked in international officials, international organizations would become ineffective and irrelevant – their critical mandates unfulfilled. Yet, as custodians of multilateral authority, international officials are also vulnerable to pressures to distort the discharge of their duties – not for personal gain – but for their same-nationality state's perceived advantage. An international organization compromised by state patronage and partisanship erodes its multilateralism – and so too its purpose. So, international officials must be independent and resistant to efforts by external authorities to subvert their undivided loyalty to their multilateral institution and exclusive subordination to its principal executive official.

This internal order is obligated by the treaty-basis of multilateral institutions. In other words, the integrity of international officials includes adherence to a chain of command, whereby instructions (and authority) are passed hierarchically from the principal executive official, downwards. However, this structure is accompanied by the obligation of international officials to report alleged breaches of integrity internally and – in limited circumstances – externally. This is popularly termed *whistleblowing*. In the case of integrity breaches coinciding with criminality, there may be recourse to national law enforcement authorities – and hence a waiver of the functional immunity typically possessed by an international official. (See Chapter 2, 'International Organizations'.)

It is these aims – of an incorruptible, independent and disciplined international civil service – that is the object of the employment law at international organizations establishing standards of conduct.

9.2 Legal Principles of Conduct

An inextinguishable legal attribute of international civil servants is integrity, obligated by the treaty-basis of international organizations. (See Chapter 3, 'International Civil Service'.) However, the same constituent instruments do not articulate standards of conduct. The UN Charter, for example, refers simply to 'international officials [being] responsible only to the [UN]' and 'the necessity of securing the highest standards of … integrity'.[2] Rather, the administrative authority of international organizations is used to address this through internal law, comparable to the Standards of Conduct for the International Civil Service, produced by the International Civil Service Commission.[3] These standards of conduct instrumentalize treaty-based integrity. (Such enactment may also be reflected in other components of the internal law, such as *Staff Regulations* and *Financial Regulations*.)

These standards coalesce around four principles of conduct considered inherent to the treaty-based status of international civil servants. First, any private interests of international officials must give way to the interests of their employing international organization. This principle necessitates that personal and official interests cannot conflict, risk conflict, or if they come into conflict are resolved or mitigated in the interests of the multilateral institution. Second, abuse of authority – whether motivated by personal prejudice, retribution, or any type of harassment – is impermissible, but must be manifest to be contestable. Third, international officials must be uncorruptible. Transparency International defines corruption 'as the abuse of entrusted power for private gain'.[4] In other words, international officials must neither misappropriate the resources of, nor exploit their authority at, an international organization to enrich themselves or others. Fourth, international officials must be uncompromised by external authorities. Most relevant to multilateralism, the staff members of international organizations are not functionaries of their same-nationality state. Instead, they owe an undivided

[2] UN Charter, Articles 100(1) and 101(3).

[3] See Chapter 7, 'Compensation'.

[4] See www.transparency.org, accessed 3 September 2025.

duty of loyalty – in their official functions – to their employing multilateral institution. These principles are now considered in turn.

Principle 1: The Interests of the International Organization Are Paramount

How are interests conflicting with those of an international organization in the achievement of its purposes to be excluded from the conduct of international officials? This requires that conflicts of interest yield to the priorities of the international organization. The Standards of Conduct for the International Civil Service exemplify the regulation of conflicts of interest at international organizations:

> Conflicts of interest may occur when an international civil servant's personal interests interfere with the performance of [their] official duties or call into question the qualities of integrity, independence and impartiality required by the status of an international civil servant.[5]

International officials must act to avoid conflicts of interest and if one arises, promptly declare it. The Standards of Conduct state: 'If a conflict of interest or possible conflict of interest does arise, the conflict shall be disclosed and resolved in the best interest of the organization'.[6] One example of this, is the prohibition on international officials of all international organizations from appointing their friends and relatives to the international civil service. Such cronyism and nepotism would render international officials beholden to such relationships. Instead of international organizations based upon impartiality, competence and discipline, they would become 'patrimonial', founded upon personal affiliations and loyalties.[7]

In UNAT Judgment No. 935, *Jenbere v. Secretary-General of the United Nations* (2019), the claimant challenges the disciplinary sanction (of demotion and ineligibility for promotion) imposed upon them for failing to declare that they were married to a candidate they interviewed. The Tribunal finds the appeal unmeritorious: 'There is overwhelming evidence that the facts supporting the disciplinary measure had been

[5] Standards of Conduct, para. 23.

[6] Standards of Conduct, para. 23.

[7] For example, see UN Staff Rule 4.7 'Family relationships': '(a) An appointment within the same organization shall not be granted to a person who is the parent, child or sibling of a staff member'.

established and that those facts amounted to misconduct',[8] and cites the first-instance UN Dispute Tribunal's reasoning with approval:

> Circumstances advanced by [the claimant] in arguing legality of [their] conduct, that [their spouse] was qualified for the job and that the other candidate secured another position, do not remove the conflict of interest. The Tribunal reiterates that the issue lies not just in competing interests of the candidates but also in the integrity of the process as such, whose impartiality and fairness is compromised by nepotism or cronyism. Even if [their] spouse was the sole candidate for position, [they were] precluded from participating in [their] interview.[9]

In this way, conflicts of interest yield to the paramountcy of the interests of the international organization, which is sustained by the internal law and standards of conduct.

Principle 2: Abuse of Authority Must Be Manifest, to Be Contestable

The abuse of authority, however motivated, is always incompatible with administrative authority at international organizations. The international civil service must be interpersonally impartial and unprejudiced: 'It requires a willingness to work without bias with persons of all nationalities, religions and cultures'.[10] Likewise, favouritism is impermissible,[11] and retributive administrative decisions – motivated by reprisal or retaliation – also abuse authority.[12] As does any type of harassment: 'International civil servants must not abuse their authority or use their power or position in a manner that is offensive, humiliating, embarrassing or intimidating to another person'.[13]

However, such abuse of authority must be manifest, to be contestable. In ILOAT Judgment No. 4382, *B v. International Federation of the Red Cross and Red Crescent Societies* (2021), the claimant alleges that their contested performance appraisal is both 'tainted by prejudice and bias', as well as

[8] UNAT No. 935, para. 25.
[9] UNAT No. 935, para. 31.
[10] Standards of Conduct, para. 14.
[11] Standards of Conduct, para. 17.
[12] This book uses the term 'retribution' to bridge both 'reprisal' and 'retaliation', since typically these are conflated by the judgments of international administrative tribunals; but in some internal law, 'retaliation' has a special definition, meaning retribution against staff members using protected procedures, such as reporting allegations of misconduct or bringing claims before administrative tribunals. For example, see World Bank Staff Rules 3.00 and 8.02.
[13] See Standards of Conduct, para. 22.

being accompanied by a series of other defects.[14] The Tribunal recognizes that an international official acting upon prejudice would abuse the authority entrusted to them, but it acknowledges that this is seldom clearcut:

> With regard to prejudice, the Tribunal has stated that although evidence of personal prejudice is often concealed and such prejudice must be inferred from surrounding circumstances, that does not relieve the [claimant], who has the burden of proving [their] allegations, from introducing evidence of sufficient quality and weight to persuade the Tribunal. Mere suspicion and unsupported allegations are clearly not enough, the less so where the actions of the [international] organization which are alleged to have been tainted by personal prejudice are shown to have a verifiable objective justification.[15]

The allegation that personal bias influences an international official must rely on more than mere 'suspicion or unsupported allegations'.[16] Likewise, to contest an administrative decision on the grounds that it is retributive, this abuse must be evidenced.[17] In WBAT Judgment No. 677, *GL v. International Bank for Reconstruction and Development* (2022), the claimant contends that the administrative decision not to progress them to the next higher grade is – amongst other things – retributory. But the Tribunal finds that adverse administrative decisions do not amount to evident retribution:

> The Tribunal has made clear, however, that it is not enough for a staff member to speculate or infer retaliation from unproven incidents of disagreement or bad feelings with another person. The Tribunal has also recognised that, although staff members are entitled to protection against reprisal and retaliation, managers must nevertheless have the authority to manage their staff and to take decisions that the affected staff member may find unpalatable or adverse to [their] best wishes.[18]

Principle 3: International Civil Servants Must Be Uncorrupted

The incorruptibility of the international civil service mirrors a defining characteristic of the modern national civil service – that international officials cannot enrich themselves nor obtain other forms of personal

[14] ILOAT No. 4382, para. 3.
[15] ILOAT No. 4283, para. 11.
[16] ILOAT No. 4283, para. 11.
[17] See, for example, UN Staff Rule 1.2 'Basic rights and obligations of staff', (g), second sentence: 'Staff members shall not threaten, retaliate or attempt to retaliate against such individuals or against staff members exercising their rights and duties under the present Rules'.
[18] WBAT No. 677, para. 103.

benefit from possession of the public trust. In UNAT Judgment No. 98, *Masri v. Secretary-General of the United Nations* (2010), the international organization seeks to reverse upon appeal the claimant's successful challenge to their summary dismissal for corruption before the first-instance UN Dispute Tribunal. The claimant, a procurement official, is found to have received 'interest-free loans from two vendors' and to have assisted one bidder prepare a technical proposal.[19]

Whilst it finds this to be a breach of the internal law of the international organization, the Tribunal also considers this sustained by the integrity attributed to international civil servants:

> It is the view of this Tribunal that staff members exercising procurement functions are required to conduct themselves, from an objective standpoint, in an impartial and honest way and act in the interests of the [international organization] only. To comply with this duty, staff members must be seen to act with integrity, obtain no personal benefit from third parties and not engage in any conduct which could create the impression of favouring third parties.[20]

This actual and apparent incorruptibility extends to a ban – absent authorization – on gifts, honours and secondary income sources for international officials. The Standards of Conduct for the International Civil Service state:

> To protect the international civil service from any appearance of impropriety, international civil servants must not accept, without authorisation from the [principal executive official], any honour, decoration, gift, remuneration, favour or economic benefit of more than nominal value from any source external to their [international] organizations; it is understood that this includes [states] as well as commercial firms and other entities.[21]

Or in other words, as the UNAT succinctly puts it, international officials 'must be and appear to be above reproach'.[22]

Principle 4: International Civil Servants Must Be Uncompromised by External Authority

International officials uncompromised by external authority are inherent to achieving the purposes of international organizations. As

[19] See UNAT No. 98, para. 2.
[20] UNAT No. 98, para. 37.
[21] Standards of Conduct, para. 50.
[22] UNAT No. 98, para. 37.

the constituent instrument of the World Bank typifies: all 'officers and staff of the Bank, in the discharge of their offices, owe their duty entirely to the Bank and to no other authority'; this duty is of an 'international character'.[23] The Standards of Conduct for the International Civil Service emphasize:

> If the impartiality of the international civil service is to be maintained, international civil servants must remain independent of any authority outside their organization; their conduct must reflect that independence. In keeping with their oath of office, they should not seek nor should they accept instructions from any Government, person or entity external to the [international] organization.[24]

Thus, the Standards of Conduct amplify the interlocking prohibition on implementing or imposing external authority found in the constituent instruments of all international organizations. (See Chapter 3, 'International Civil Service'.) However, importantly, it also addresses – explicitly – a widespread practice in the staffing of multilateral institutions: 'It cannot be too strongly stressed that international civil servants are not, in any sense, representatives of Governments or other entities, nor are they proponents of their policies', before going on to underscore that, 'This applies equally to those on secondment from Governments and to those whose services have been made available from elsewhere'.[25]

In ILOAT Judgment No. 2232, *JMB v. Organisation for the Prohibition of Chemical Weapons* (2003), the claimant – in fact the former principal executive official – successfully contests the governance action that purportedly summarily dismissed them from office, following sustained political pressure from a Member State. The Tribunal finds:

> In accordance with the established case law of all international administrative tribunals, the Tribunal reaffirms that the independence of international civil servants is an essential guarantee, not only for the civil servants themselves, but also for the proper functioning of international organizations. In the case of [the principal executive official], that independence is protected, [amongst other things], by the fact that they are appointed for a limited term of office.[26]

The Tribunal also refutes the argument that the authority of appointment is inherently the power to summarily revoke an appointment,

[23] World Bank Articles of Agreement, Article 36(3).
[24] Standards of Conduct, para. 8.
[25] Standards of Conduct, para. 8.
[26] ILOAT No. 2232, para. 16.

since this would mean 'rendering officials vulnerable to pressures and to political change'.[27] Whilst the Tribunal contemplates that 'grave misconduct' may be the basis for termination, this 'could only be taken in full compliance with the principle of due process, following a procedure enabling the individual concerned to defend [their] case effectively before an independent and impartial body'.[28] (See Chapter 10, 'Misconduct'.)

9.3 Legal Duties of Conduct

Legal duties of conduct govern the international civil service, namely: (1) Integrity requires honesty and reputability; (2) Integrity requires reserve and respect; and (3) Integrity requires discipline and hierarchical authority.

Duty 1: Integrity Requires Honesty and Reputability

The honesty and reputability of an international civil servant is the basis for the trustworthiness with which they carry out all of their official duties. International officials must, in other words, be unimpeachable. In UNAT Judgment No. 1156, *Payenda v. Secretary-General of the United Nations* (2021), the claimant's disciplinary termination for misstating the truth on the job application for their post was upheld by the Tribunal. In addition to adhering to the internal law of the international organization – which transposes the terms of the UN Charter and states, 'Staff members shall uphold the highest standards of efficiency, competence and integrity'[29] – the Tribunal expresses an attendant legal duty, in the following terms:

> As a general rule, any form of dishonest conduct compromises the necessary relationship of trust between employer and employee and will generally warrant dismissal. [The Tribunal] reiterates that dishonest conduct by definition implies an element of intent or some element of deception. Deliberate false statements, misrepresentations and a failure to disclose required information are invariably dishonest.[30]

[27] ILAOT No. 2232, para. 16.

[28] ILOAT No. 2232, para. 16.

[29] UN Staff Regulation 1.2(b), which continues, 'The concept of integrity includes, but is not limited to, probity, impartiality, fairness, honesty and truthfulness in all matters affecting their work and status'.

[30] UNAT No. 1156, paras. 38–39.

The duty is not restricted to international officials in the course of their work, but also extends to outside the workplace. Committing a criminal offence otherwise unrelated to an international organization may nevertheless breach this duty. The Standards of Conduct for the International Civil Service state:

> Violations of the law can range from serious criminal activities to trivial offences, and [international] organizations may be called upon to exercise judgement depending on the nature and circumstances of individual cases. A conviction by a national court will usually, although not always, be persuasive evidence of the act for which an international civil servant was prosecuted; acts that are generally recognised as offences by national criminal laws will normally also be considered violations of the standards of conduct for the international civil service.[31]

In ILOAT Judgment No. 4400, *E (Nos. 1 and 2) v. International Labour Organization* (2021), the claimant unsuccessfully contests the decision to disciplinarily terminate their appointment following their criminal conviction by a French court for making death threats to and assaulting their spouse. The Tribunal emphasizes that the administrative authority implementing integrity at an international organization may rely upon the overall probity of a national court system and it need not necessarily re-try cases internally:

> It is well known that this restriction, placed on the principle in question when the [Standards of Conduct for the International Civil Service] were adopted, was solely intended by the drafters to reserve the case of convictions in States where the courts do not offer the requisite safeguards of independence and procedural fairness.[32]

In other words, the outcomes of impartial court systems may be depended upon by international organizations as a basis for internal, integrity-related administrative decisions. Since serious criminal convictions compromise both the standing of an international official involved and also the standing of their employing international organizations, the Tribunal holds:

> [W]hile international organizations cannot intrude on the private lives of their staff members, those staff members must nonetheless comply with the requirements inherent in their status as international civil servants, including in their personal conduct. … The Tribunal finds that the [claimant's] conduct was in fact such as to reflect adversely on [their] position and compromise the [international organization's] image and interests.[33]

[31] Standards of Conduct, para. 44.
[32] ILOAT No. 4400, para. 19.
[33] ILOAT No. 4400, paras. 24–25.

In this way, an international organization may have regard to the entire reputation of international officials, derived from all their activities, including personal conduct. Acting in their personal lives does not release international official from the 'moral probity and decency that all international civil servants must respect'.[34] In other words, international officials are obligated to refrain from all disreputable conduct, likely to compromise the reputations – and so effectiveness – of their employing international organization.

Duty 2: Integrity Requires Reserve and Respect

Across multiple dimensions, integrity – ensuring the independent and international character of the international civil service – necessities reserve and respect. Encoded into the internal law of international organizations, this pervasively governs how international officials behave both within and beyond the workplace. In other words, it is a standard of conduct that applies, even when some more particular rule of conduct either does not exist or is not breached.

The Standards of Conduct for the International Civil Service underpin the necessary 'tact and discretion' of international civil servants with the maintenance of confidence in international organizations: 'While their personal views remain inviolate, international civil servants do not have the freedom of private persons to take sides or to express their convictions publicly on controversial matters'.[35] In ILOAT Judgment No. 1061, *Dodi v. Food and Agriculture Organization* (1991) – in which the claimant unsuccessfully challenges their disciplinary termination for an outspoken (and unauthorized) radio broadcast, among several other grounds – the Tribunal is unpersuaded that the claimant's role as staff representative protects them:

> Freedom of speech must be protected particularly for officers of a staff association, so that they are not hampered in their task of representing the membership when in dispute with the [international organization]. But there are limits on such freedom. A staff representative's public statements must not impair the dignity of the international civil service.[36]

The Tribunal clarifies that no international official is allowed to resort to 'behaviour incompatible with the decorum appropriate to [their] status'

[34] ILOAT No. 4400, para. 25.
[35] Standards of Conduct, para. 9.
[36] ILOAT No. 1061, para. 3.

as the employees of international organizations and for this reason internal laws 'require staff to conduct themselves with decorum, reserve and tact as befitting their status and to exercise the utmost discretion in all matters of official business'.[37]

Likewise, it is always incumbent upon international officials to be respectful. In particular, all forms of harassment and any abuse of authority are incompatible with the integrity of international civil servants. The Standards of Conduct for the International Civil Service state:

> International civil servants have the right to a workplace environment free of harassment or abuse. All organizations must prohibit any kind of harassment. [International organizations] have a duty to establish rules and provide guidance on what constitutes harassment and abuse of authority and how unacceptable behaviour will be addressed.

Importantly, the absence of specific harassment does not erase an underlying obligation of respectful conduct. For example, in WBAT Judgment No. 197, *Rendall-Speranza v. International Finance Corporation* (1998) – repeatedly cited by the Tribunal with approval since – the claimant contends they are 'subjected to sexual harassment' by their supervisor and the international organization 'failed to discharge its obligation to protect [them] from such harassment'. However, the Tribunal finds:

> The independent investigator concluded that whatever the nature of the advances on the part of [the claimant's supervisor], the [claimant] did not make it clear that they were unwelcome and that [their supervisor] did not commit sexual harassment. The [international organization] endorsed these conclusions. The Tribunal concludes that the evidence justifies the [international organization's] decision.[38]

Nevertheless:

> The Tribunal also concludes, however, that this determination by the [international organization], that no sexual harassment had been committed, should not have been regarded by the [international organization] as putting an end to the matter. There are forms of improper behaviour, even though falling short of sexual harassment, that should engage the attention of the [international organization] and require action on the part of its management.[39]

Whilst not sexual harassment, the behaviour 'crossed the line separating friendly congenial relationships from improper behaviour thereby

[37] ILOAT No. 1061, para. 3.
[38] WBAT No. 197, para. 77.
[39] WBAT No. 197, para. 78.

subjecting the [claimant] to stress, confusion and other intangible [and compensable] injury'.[40] In other words, the integrity of international officials requires their reserve and respect.

Duty 3: Integrity Requires Discipline and Hierarchical Authority

As the Standards of Conduct for the International Civil Service make clear, international officials are obligated by duties of discipline and adherence to hierarchical authority: 'International civil servants must follow the instructions they receive in connection with their official functions'.[41] Only in limited circumstances – 'instructions that are manifestly inconsistent with their official functions or that threaten their safety or that of others' – should instructions be disregarded.[42] International officials may challenge instructions that they regard as contradictory to the employment law at international organizations. But this must be through the 'proper institutional mechanisms' and such protest does not entitle them to 'delay carrying out the instruction'.[43] In other words, a failure to adhere to the instructions of superiors by international officials is a breach of a legal duty obligating discipline and hierarchical authority.

For example, in ILOAT Judgment No. 4453, *G-B (No.3) v. World Tourism Organization* (2022), the claimant succeeds in having their summary dismissal – for alleged financial irregularities in their role of Director of Administration and Finance – set aside. However, the Tribunal finds:

> [A] member of staff whose duties included dealing with and managing the funds or other property of an [international] organization should adhere to normative legal or other instructional documents concerning how those funds and property should be dispersed and managed. Moreover, a failure to do so could well warrant summary dismissal. Additionally, that failure could be characterised as a serious breach of trust.[44]

Categoric non-adherence to instructions is insubordination. In UNAT Judgment No. 197, *Kamunyi v. Secretary-General of the United Nations* (2011), the claimant contests their reprimand for failing to hand over a

40 WBAT No. 197, para. 80.
41 Standards of Conduct, para. 19.
42 Standards of Conduct, para, 19.
43 Standards of Conduct, para. 19.
44 ILOAT No. 4453, para. 15.

personal firearm when instructed to do so upon entering UN premises in Kenya. The internal law of the international organization authorized confiscation, whereas the claimant considered Kenyan law to support their refusal to surrender the weapon. The Tribunal finds:

> National laws cannot apply when, as in the present case, they contradict specific administrative regulations of the United Nations. Even if [the claimant] thought that the request was unlawful, [they] had to comply with it. It was up to [them] to subsequently challenge the order through administrative proceedings. Security and safety were involved so [they] should have complied with the instruction. From the foregoing, [the claimant] was in fact insubordinate when [they] refused a direct order.[45]

In other words, the claimant could have protested the instruction they considered baseless through the proper institutional mechanism, but disobeying the instruction is impermissible. Such insubordination breaches the legal duty of integrity, obligating discipline and hierarchical authority incumbent upon international civil servants.

9.4 Whistleblowing

International officials are obligated 'to report any breach of the [international] organization's regulations and rules to the official or entity within their organizations whose responsibility it is to take appropriate action' and cooperate with ensuing investigations.[46] This duty is unmodified by the personal predispositions of international officials to tolerate – or not – misbehaviour. However, 'whistleblowing' contemplates the possibility of reporting integrity breaches outside the international organization.[47] Transparency International states: 'A whistleblower discloses information about corruption or other wrongdoing being committed in or by an organization to individuals or entities believed to be able to effect action – the organization itself, the relevant authorities, or the public'.[48]

However, this is not encouraged by the internal law of international organizations, wherein 'whistleblowing' is largely interchangeable with encouraging – and protecting from retribution – the internal reporting

[45] UNAT No. 197, para. 38.

[46] Standards of Conduct, para. 20.

[47] Whilst 'whistleblowing' is a ubiquitous term, it tends to confuse and sensationalize the obligation incumbant on international civil servants to report misconduct.

[48] See www.transparency.org, accessed 3 September 2025.

of allegations of misconduct.[49] At the World Bank, for example, external reporting is restricted to limited circumstances, necessitating the avoidance of a 'significant threat to public health or safety', 'substantive damage' to operations, or 'violation of national or international law', when the 'established internal mechanisms' are inadequate.[50]

In WBAT Judgment No. 543, *Houdart v. International Bank for Reconstruction and Development* (2016), the claimant contests the imposition of disciplinary sanctions upon them in connection with disclosing non-public information. The Tribunal notes that the disclosure of non-public information is not countenanced by the claimant as 'whistleblowing' and finds:

> Even assuming, for the sake of argument, that [the claimant] engaged in some kind of whistleblowing and further assuming that somehow [they] made a [on the face of it] case of retaliation, the record provides a legitimate non-retaliatory basis for the Bank's actions to conclude that the same employment action would have been taken absent the staff member's protected activity.[51]

In other words, even if made out, whistleblowing only disables retributive actions by international officials against whistleblowers. In this case, the investigation into the disclosure of non-public information is not targeting the claimant: 'The record shows that the investigation was not about the [claimant] but rather it was about the leak of a number of confidential documents that resulted in, in the Bank's view, embarrassment and reputational harm to the Bank'.[52]

In ILOAT Judgment No. 4376, *P v. World Intellectual Property Organization* (2021), the claimant contends that the international organization failed to appropriately protect them after they made a report of misconduct. The claimant considers themselves insufficiently compensated for the mishandling of their report, including the failure to

[49] For example, World Bank Staff Rule 8.08 'Protections and Procedures for Reporting Misconduct (Whistleblowing)', para. 2.02, 'Reporting Channels', allows for a range of routes to report misconduct, but none of these routings legitimize reporting outside the institution.

[50] World Bank Staff Rule 8.08, 'Protections and Procedures for Reporting Misconduct (Whistleblowing)', Section 4, 'External Reporting' and para. 4.01: 'Because a primary objective of this Rule is to enable the Bank Group to take institutional measures necessary to remedy misconduct, Staff Members are generally required to report suspected misconduct under this Rule through the internal mechanisms'.

[51] WBAT No. 543, para. 165.

[52] WBAT No. 543, para. 166.

maintain their anonymity.[53] The Tribunal disagrees and absent evidence of the retributive use of administrative authority, 'an alleged failure by [an international organization] to take interim protective measures' is not compensable.[54]

9.5 Waiver of Immunity

International officials – in accordance with the privileges and immunities extended to international organizations by Member States – typically possess functional immunity from the jurisdiction of national laws. (See Chapter 2, 'International Organizations'.) This immunity is coextensive with their duties, the maintenance of their independence and hence the impartiality of the international organizations they instrumentalize. (Sometimes, very senior officials are also accorded personal immunity, comparable to diplomats.)[55] But this does not release international officials from local laws unrelated to their duties or exempt them from personal obligations, as the Standards of Conduct for the International Civil Service state:

> The privileges and immunities that international civil servants enjoy are conferred upon them solely in the interests of [international] organizations. They do not exempt international civil servants from observing local laws, nor do they provide an excuse for ignoring private legal or financial obligations. It should be remembered that only the [principal executive official] is competent to waive the immunity accorded to international civil servants or to determine its scope.[56]

What is the situation of an international official with immunity if they commit a crime in the course of carrying out their duties? As the Standards of Conduct recall, the immunity of international officials may always be waived and this may attend reporting the matter to national law enforcement authorities.[57] Typically, this is framed by

[53] See ILOAT No. 4376, para. 1.

[54] ILOAT No. 4376, para. 15.

[55] See, for example, General Convention, Section 19: 'the Secretary-General and all Assistant Secretaries-General shall be accorded in respect of themselves, their spouses and minor children, the privileges and immunities, exemptions and facilities accorded to diplomatic envoys, in accordance with international law'.

[56] Standards of Conduct, para. 43.

[57] See, for example, General Convention, Section 21: 'The United Nations shall co-operate at all times with the appropriate authorities of Members to facilitate the proper administration of justice, secure the observance of police regulations and prevent the occurrence

international law. For example, the Convention on the Privileges and Immunities of the UN, states:

> Privileges and immunities are granted to officials in the interests of the United Nations and not for the personal benefit of the individuals themselves. The [UN] Secretary-General shall have the right and the duty to waive the immunity of any official in any case where, in [their] opinion, the immunity would impede the course of justice and can be waived without prejudice to the interests of the United Nations. In the case of the [UN] Secretary-General, the [UN] Security Council shall have the right to waive immunity.[58]

However, in ILOAT Judgment No. 2190, *FZ v. World Health Organization* (2003) – concerning a serious traffic accident involving on-duty international officials, investigated by national law enforcement authorities – the Tribunal establishes that whilst an international organization 'has a discretion to assess, in the context of its relations with a [Member State] ... whether it is appropriate to lift the immunity from legal process of its employees', this is 'beyond the jurisdiction of the Tribunal'.[59] In other words, the waiver of such immunity is not an administrative decision subject to the jurisdiction of international administrative tribunals.

9.6 The Employment Law of Standards of Conduct

Derived from the continuing treaty-based obligations of an international organization to secure the highest standard of integrity and the independence of staff, the employment law of the standards of conduct is composed of legal principles and attendant legal duties. These are complemented by the obligation to report integrity breaches and the authority of international organizations to on occasion waive immunity and report allegedly criminally liable international officials to national law enforcement authorities. The applicable law may be restated as:

Legal Principles of Conduct

- The interests of the international organization are paramount and conflicts of interest must yield to the priorities of the international organization.

of any abuse in connection with the privileges, immunities and facilities [accorded by the General Convention]'.

[58] General Convention, Section 20.

[59] ILOAT No. 2190, para. 3.

- Whilst impermissible, to be contested, abuse of authority – occasioned by personal bias, retribution or any type of harassment – must be manifest.
- International officials must be uncorrupted.
- External authority must not compromise international officials.

Legal Duties of Conduct

- Integrity requires honesty and reputability.
- Integrity requires reserve and respect.
- Integrity requires discipline and hierarchical authority.

Whistleblowing

- It is incumbent upon international officials to report allegations of misconduct, either through internal mechanisms or – exceptionally – through external recourse.

Waiver of Immunity

- The waiver of immunity of international officials is not an administrative decision, within the jurisdiction of international administrative tribunals.

10

Misconduct

This chapter begins by introducing misconduct – as the enforcement of standards of conduct at international organizations – comprising a series of actions intended to dependably investigate, attribute responsibility and consequently sanction integrity breaches by international officials. Second, the legal principles of misconduct are identified, namely: (1) The facts of misconduct must be established; (2) The established facts must legally constitute misconduct; and (3) Disciplinary sanction must possess a legal basis. Third, three attendant legal duties of misconduct are considered, as follows: (1) Proof of misconduct must be compelling; (2) Alleged misconduct must afford an opportunity to respond; and (3) Misconduct may only be sanctioned proportionately. Fourth, the chapter considers obligations towards staff who allege that they have been subjected to interpersonal misconduct – notably sexual harassment and bullying – and their capability to challenge and obtain information concerning related administrative decisions. Fifth, and in conclusion, this employment law of misconduct at international organizations is restated. The standards of conduct implementing the treaty-attributed integrity and independence of the international civil service are the subject of Chapter 9, 'Standards of Conduct'.

10.1 What Is Misconduct?

The standards of conduct implementing the integrity of the international civil service – see Chapter 9, 'Standards of Conduct' – would be aspirational at best, and immaterial at worst, if there was no mechanism to enforce them. Conversely, if such enforcement was either undependable or oppressive, this would be ruinous to the independence of the international civil service and compromise the impartiality and effectiveness of international organizations. Therefore, to charge an international official with a breach of standards of conduct and consequently sanction their misbehaviour – potentially terminating their employment – clearly requires the formation of both a robust factual and reasoned legal basis.[1]

In practice, this enforcement mechanism comprises successive stages, closely regulated by the internal law of international organizations. Broadly, these five stages are: (1) an intake stage, to preliminarily examine the allegation of misconduct – which may result in unsupported allegations being dismissed; (2) an investigatory stage, during which evidence is gathered and witnesses are interviewed, intended to substantiate – or indeed, disprove – the alleged misconduct; (3) an accusatory stage, in which the accusation and evidence of misconduct is formally put to the staff member and they may respond to and rebut these charges; (4) a decision-making stage, when the ultimate determination of whether misconduct took place is decided; and (5) in the event that the decision-maker finds misconduct proven, a sanction stage, in which an appropriate punishment is decided and imposed.[2]

Most international organizations have established a dedicated investigatory function, attributed exclusive authority to intake allegations of misconduct and conduct resultant investigations (stages one and two). The results of such investigations are usually reported to the chief human resources officer who is invested with the authority – delegated from the principal executive official – to decide, first, whether the report is sufficiently compelling to form the basis of an accusation of misconduct; second, whether misconduct is established, following an opportunity for the accused staff member to respond; and third, if they find misconduct to be established, what commensurate punishment should be imposed (stages three to five). This separation between investigation and decision-making is an important safeguard, first to ensure that relevant facts are established diligently; and second, to ensure the decision-maker is uninvolved in assembling the underlying evidence they are required to evaluate, retaining their neutrality and detachment.

Whilst standards of conduct must be enforced at international organizations, it is often the case that misconduct will have adversely impacted others – and this is most often, a fellow staff member – allegedly harmed by the misbehaviour. This is especially apparent in interpersonal circumstances where colleagues are subject to abuse of

[1] For example, see UN Staff Rule 10.2 'Disciplinary Measures'; sanctions include: written censure; suspension without pay for a specified period; fine; and dismissal.

[2] See, for example, ILO Staff Regulations, Article 12.3, 'Procedure for the application of disciplinary measures'.

authority – for example, personal prejudice, retribution and harassment. (See Chapter 9, 'Standards of Conduct'.) In particular, as intolerance of the scourge of sexual harassment intensifies, international organizations confront demands from complainants, contending not only that they are entitled to be informed about the enforcement of the alleged misconduct they report, but also that they are entitled to challenge any such enforcement they regard as lenient and owed some remedy, if misconduct is established.

Together, the components of this enforcement mechanism – their operation and interaction – and the interrelationship between international officials accused of misconduct, the complainants of integrity breaches and multilateral institutions, must be thorough, dependable and command confidence. This then is the preoccupation of the attendant employment law of misconduct.

10.2 Legal Principles of Misconduct

Enforcing standards of conduct at international organizations engages strict adjudicative and legal frameworks. Whereas an international administrative tribunal defers to discretionary administrative authority to manage international officials – limiting itself to overruling manifest abuses – the procedures authorizing sanction for misconduct of international officials are subject to denser legal review.

In WBAT Judgment No. 665, *GK v. World Bank Group* (2021) – in which the claimant unsuccessfully contests the finding that they committed misconduct and their consequent sanction – the Tribunal restates its 'well-established' approach, namely the 'scope of review in disciplinary cases is not limited to determining whether there has been an abuse of discretion'.[3] Instead, the Tribunal will examine the entire factual and legal sufficiency of the case. Nevertheless, the Tribunal will not reinvestigate the misconduct allegations:

> The Tribunal has also stated that its role is to ensure that a disciplinary measure falls within the legal powers of the Bank. This, however, does not mean that the Tribunal is an investigative agency. The Tribunal simply takes the record as it finds it and evaluates the fact-finding methodology, the probative weight of legitimately obtained evidence, and the inherent rationale of the findings in the light of that evidence.[4]

[3] WBAT No. 665, para. 74.
[4] WBAT No. 665, para. 76.

In UNAT Judgment No. 956, *Ladu v. Secretary-General of the United Nations* (2019), the claimant unsuccessfully challenges their misconduct sanction – termination of appointment – for attempted theft of UN property. As with the WBAT, the UNAT follows a 'settled and unambiguous' approach, namely: 'Judicial review of a disciplinary case requires the [first-instance UN Dispute Tribunal] to consider the evidence adduced and the procedures utilized during the course of the investigation by the [UN]'.[5]

Therefore, three legal principles underpin the full review of misconduct by an administrative tribunal. First, facts substantiating misconduct must be established by the available evidence; second, these established fact must legally constitute misconduct; and third, the misconduct sanction imposed must have a lawful basis. These principles are now considered in turn.

Principle 1: The Facts of Misconduct Must Be Established

The starting point for international administrative tribunals is to examine 'the existence of the facts' sustaining the misconduct sanction.[6] Or, in other words, to examine 'whether the facts on which the sanction is based have been established'.[7] The burden of proving the existence of these facts falls to the employing international organization. It is not an international official that must disprove allegations of misconduct against them – although the internal law of international organizations uniformly obligates 'cooperation' by all staff members with misconduct investigations.[8]

In *WBAT No. 665*, the Tribunal states: 'The Tribunal has held that the burden of proof in misconduct cases lies with the respondent organization. It has also stipulated on several occasions that there must be substantial evidence to support the finding of facts which amount to misconduct'.[9] Similarly, in *UNAT No. 956*, the Tribunal states that the international organization 'bears the burden of establishing that the alleged misconduct for which a disciplinary measure has been taken against a staff member occurred'.[10]

5 UNAT No. 956, para. 15.
6 WBAT No. 665, para. 74.
7 UNAT No. 956, para. 15.
8 For example, World Bank Directive 'Conduct of Disciplinary Proceedings for [Ethics and Business Conduct] Investigations', para. B(1): 'Staff members must cooperate fully with requests for assistance made by investigators throughout the disciplinary proceedings'.
9 WBAT No. 665, para. 75.
10 UNAT No. 956, para. 15.

Likewise, in ILOAT Judgment No. 4461, *Z v. International Organization for Migration* (2022) – wherein the claimant challenges termination of their appointment, the sanction imposed for them insubordinately refusing to report from Moscow to Geneva when ordered to do so – the Tribunal states, 'the burden of proof rests on an [international] organization to prove the allegations of misconduct'.[11] However, the Tribunal looks at this from the standpoint of the decision-maker, consistent with it not undertaking its own reinvestigation. In ILOAT Judgment No. 4362, *S (No. 2) v. International Criminal Court* (2020) – where the claimant successfully challenges their misconduct-related termination of appointment – the Tribunal emphasizes: 'The role of the Tribunal in a case such as the present is not to assess the evidence itself and determine whether the charge of misconduct has been established … but rather to assess whether there was evidence available to the relevant decision-maker to reach that conclusion'.[12]

Principle 2: The Established Facts Must Legally Constitute Misconduct

Once the first legal principle of misconduct is satisfied, the second is applicable: do the facts depended upon amount to misconduct within the internal law of the international organization? In other words, an international administrative tribunal examines 'whether they legally amount to misconduct',[13] or 'whether the established facts qualify as misconduct' under the internal law.[14]

This question is addressed by the reviewing administrative tribunal through considering the evidentiary record, not reconstructing the mindset of the decision-maker. In WBAT Decision No. 671, *GR v. International Bank for Reconstruction and Development* (2022), the claimant unsuccessfully challenges the finding of misconduct – for an overbearing management style – and consequent sanction, demoting them. The Tribunal first marshals the available evidence, then determines whether this amounts to misconduct:

> In the present case, the record and established facts … demonstrate that the [claimant's] actions as Country Manager, which included asking staff to perform tasks of a personal nature, raising [their] voice and speaking

[11] ILOAT No. 4461, para. 6.
[12] ILOAT No. 4362, para. 7.
[13] WBAT No. 665, para. 74.
[14] UNAT No. 956, para. 15.

> angrily to staff, and confronting staff about [their] 360 assessment, made staff feel afraid, uncomfortable, and intimidated ... This behaviour is incompatible with the professional and ethical conduct expected of staff in general, and especially that of a Country Manager who is in a position of power and authority over local country staff.[15]

Consequently, the Tribunal 'finds that there is substantial evidence in the record to support a finding that the [claimant's] conduct constituted a failure to identify and observe generally applicable norms of prudent professional conduct' – in other words, the duty that integrity obligates reserve and respect – in breach of proscribed standards of conduct.[16] (See Chapter 9, 'Standards of Conduct'.)

Principle 3: Disciplinary Sanction Must Possess a Legal Basis

The third principle, 'whether the sanction imposed is provided for in the [internal] law' of the international organization,[17] excludes both improvised punishments on the one hand – sanctions not transparently available to the institution for misconduct – and on the other hand, imposing a disciplinary sanction without first adhering to the internal law basis for establishing misconduct. In WBAT Judgment No. 593, *EU v. International Bank for Reconstruction and Development* (2018), the claimant – an asset management team leader – challenges a series of adverse administrative actions which include taking away their managerial and trading responsibilities. Whilst the Tribunal finds this to effectively be reassignment,[18] it has before it evidence that the international organization regarded 'reassignment [to be] preferable to a period of warning or other sanction and that the [claimant's] actions constituted misbehaviour which is not acceptable'.[19] Consequently, '[t]he Tribunal finds that the [claimant's] reassignment was a disguised disciplinary sanction, imposed without any of the safeguards provided for in the disciplinary process',[20] and was therefore 'neither reasonable nor fair' and hence, abusive.[21]

[15] WBAT No. 671, para. 184.
[16] WBAT No. 671, para. 185.
[17] WBAT No. 665, para. 74.
[18] See WBAT No. 593, para. 141.
[19] WBAT No. 593, para. 163.
[20] WBAT No. 593, para. 163.
[21] WBAT No. 593, para. 165.

10.3 Legal Duties of Misconduct

Whereas the legal principles of misconduct sustain a dense legal review by administrative tribunals, the attendant legal duties govern misconduct-related administrative decisions. Although the internal law of international organizations closely aligns to the legal principles of misconduct, the related legal duties are broadly substantiated by the judgments of international administrative tribunals. Three settled legal duties of misconduct are: (1) Proof of misconduct must be compelling; (2) Alleged misconduct must afford an opportunity to respond; and (3) Misconduct may only be sanctioned proportionately.

Duty 1: Proof of Misconduct Must Be Compelling

If the 'proof' of misconduct at multilateral institutions was weak or one-sided, then confidence in the enforcement of conduct standards at international organizations would be undermined and the independence of international officials would be jeopardized. As already noted, the burden of proving misconduct falls to the employing international organization. But to what probabilistic *standard* must misconduct be proven?

Two dominant concepts are available to draw upon from national legal traditions. On the one hand, is a lower standard – on the balance of probabilities – often applied to fix civil liability. It means that, on balance, a liable act (which is amenable only to financial compensation) is more likely than not to have occurred. On the other hand, a higher standard – beyond all reasonable doubt – is applied to fix criminal liability. The rationale for the higher criminal standard is the possible deprivation of liberty (or indeed life) that may ensue, together with the resources of the state being deployed by criminal prosecution. With regards to misconduct by international civil servants, national civil or criminal liability is seldom involved, but where the standard of proof is set is integral to the influence of an integrity enforcement mechanism at an international organization. In this regard, the administrative tribunals of the World Bank, UN and ILO each formulate their own probabilistic standards of proof. The articulation of each is now considered in turn.

First, the WBAT states, 'there must be substantial evidence to support the finding of facts which amount to misconduct. In other words, the standard of evidence in disciplinary decisions leading to misconduct and disciplinary sanctions must be higher than a mere balance of probabilities'.[22] This then renders 'substantial evidence' as higher than the balance of probabilities, but suggests that the certainty of beyond all reasonable doubt need not be attained.

Second, the UNAT weights the standard to the gravest sanction: 'When termination is a possible outcome, misconduct must be established by clear and convincing evidence, which means that the truth of the facts asserted is highly probable'.[23] This, too, renders 'clear and convincing evidence' as higher than mere likelihood, but suggests that certainty need not be attained – highly probable being stricter than on the balance of probabilities.

However, differently to the WBAT, the UNAT implies that the standard may shift, depending on the severity of the alleged misconduct and hence whether the staff member risks disciplinary termination of appointment. Third, the ILOAT states: 'The relevant legal standard is beyond reasonable doubt'.[24]

On their face, these three administrative tribunals seem to adhere to dissimilar approaches to the standard to which misconduct must be proven. However, in their practical application, these three approaches may be seen as more convergent than at first appears. The WBAT refers to 'substantial evidence' to mean 'higher than a mere balance of probabilities'. In effect, this pushes the standard closer to 'beyond reasonable doubt', since after more likely than not, there is no way to articulate some middle ground. The UNAT's use of 'highly probable' seems intended to enhance the standard of mere likelihood in the same way – finding events 'highly probable', must surely exclude any 'reasonable doubt'. Likewise, although the ILOAT's standard seems borrowed from the national criminal context, the Tribunal disavows this:

> Rather the standard involves the recognition that often disciplinary proceedings can have severe consequences for the affected staff member, including dismissal and potentially serious adverse consequences on the reputation of the staff member and [their] career as an international civil servant, and in these circumstances it is appropriate to require a high level of satisfaction on the part of the [international organization] that the disciplinary measure is justified because the misconduct has been proved.

Importantly, 'beyond reasonable doubt' is not the exclusion of any and all doubt, but the exclusion of *reasonable* doubt. The safeguards afforded

22 WBAT No. 665, para. 152.
23 UNAT No. 956, para. 15.
24 ILOAT No. 4362, para. 7.

staff members would render a finding of misconduct oppressive, if the decision-maker weighing the facts, concluded a breach of standards of conduct, whilst nevertheless possessing 'reasonable doubts' about the probity of the evidence. In this sense, despite varying articulations, the applicable standard of proof – ultimately derived from a uniform treaty-basis – may be said to converge: it is an obligation upon international officials exercising administrative authority reasonably to determine misconduct to a standard of compelling proof. As the ILOAT notes: 'The [mere] likelihood of misconduct having occurred is insufficient and does not afford appropriate protection to international civil servants'.[25]

Duty 2: Alleged Misconduct Must Afford an Opportunity to Respond

Whilst administrative tribunals examine 'whether the requirements of due process were observed' during misconduct proceedings,[26] they underscore how this is adapted to the administrative, not adjudicatory, character of these processes.[27] Thus, in this context, it means, an opportunity to respond to allegations of misconduct. For example, in WBAT Judgment No. 197, *Rendall-Speranza v. International Finance Corporation* (1998) – regularly cited with approval by the Tribunal since – the claimant challenges the investigative finding that they were not sexually harassed, contrary to their allegation. The Tribunal clarifies:

> In order to assess whether the investigation was carried out fairly, it is necessary to appreciate the nature of the investigation and its role within the context of disciplinary proceedings. After a complaint of misconduct is filed, an investigation is to be undertaken in order to develop a factual record on which the [international organization] might choose to implement disciplinary measures. The investigation is of an administrative, and not an adjudicatory, nature … The purpose is to gather information, and to establish and find facts, so that the [international organization] can decide whether to impose disciplinary measures or to take any other action pursuant to the [internal law]. The concerns for due process in such a context relate to the development of a fair and full record of facts, and to the conduct of the investigation in a fair and impartial manner. They

[25] ILOAT No. 4362, para. 8.

[26] WBAT No. 665, para. 74.

[27] This book prefers the term 'opportunity to respond' over 'due process', which whilst frequently used in case law, risks overstatement – and misaligned expectations – given that administrative tribunals consistently emphasize that the full safeguards of judicial proceedings are inappropriate to the administration and resolution of employment-related disputes at international organizations.

> do not necessarily require conformity to all the technicalities of judicial proceedings.[28]

In other words, misconduct allegations must afford an opportunity to respond, including testing the evidence of alleged misconduct. This satisfies the WBAT: 'The record shows that the investigator gave both sides, the [claimant] and [the staff member investigated for alleged misconduct], ample opportunity to be heard, and an equally ample opportunity to try to corroborate their respective versions of the events'.[29]

Likewise, in UNAT Judgment No. 761, *Michaud v. Secretary-General of the United Nations* (2017), the claimant appeals their disciplinary sanction of a written reprimand, alleging that they were 'not afforded due process before the decision to issue a reprimand was taken'.[30] The Tribunal finds: 'Procedural fairness is a highly variable concept and is context specific. The essential question is whether the staff member is adequately apprised of any allegations and had a reasonable opportunity to make representations before action was taken against [them]'.[31]

In ILOAT Judgment No. 3863, *MS v. International Criminal Court* (2017), the claimant challenges the disciplinary termination of their employment – a sanction for a breach of confidentiality related to a case before the International Criminal Court – contending that 'due process' was violated. The Tribunal summarizes:

> [A]s a general rule, a staff member must have access to all evidence on which the authority bases (or intends to base) its decision against [them]. Under normal circumstances, such evidence cannot be withheld on grounds of confidentiality. The [staff member] is also entitled to have an opportunity to test the evidence and produce evidence to the contrary.[32]

In other words, the enforcement of standards of conduct cannot result in secretive or unsubstantiated allegations of misconduct – the accused international official is entitled to the opportunity to respond in an informed and explicit way to the allegations against them.

However, the UNAT considers: 'A lack or a deficiency in due process will be no bar to a fair or reasonable administrative decision or disciplinary action should it appear at a later stage that fuller or better due process

[28] WBAT No. 197, para. 57.
[29] WBAT No. 197, para. 59.
[30] UNAT No. 761, para. 55.
[31] UNAT No. 761, para. 56.
[32] ILOAT No. 3863, para. 18.

would have made no difference'.[33] This only 'applies exceptionally where the ultimate outcome is an irrefutable foregone conclusion' such as 'where a gross assault is widely witnessed' or misconduct is admitted.[34] So a prudent decision-maker would nevertheless afford a staff member an opportunity to respond to allegations of misconduct – although serious misconduct allegations may always be accompanied by immediate suspension from duty.[35]

Duty 3: Misconduct May Only Be Sanctioned Proportionately

The treaty-based 'necessity of securing the highest standards of … integrity' at international organizations,[36] both enables and constrains the mechanisms enforcing standards of conduct to achieve only this. Disproportionately severe misconduct sanctions would be intimidatory and disproportionately lax misconduct sanctions would not dissuade breaches of standards of conduct. Hence, misconduct may only be sanctioned proportionately. Consequently, decision-makers may not impose a sanction 'significantly disproportionate to the offence'.[37] In other words, sanctioning misconduct is the exercise of discretionary administrative authority which may be set aside by an international administrative tribunal if found to be arbitrary. In *WBAT No. 665*, the Tribunal states the corresponding approach to proportionality:

> [I]n order for a sanction to be proportionate, there must be some reasonable relationship between the staff member's delinquency and the severity of the discipline imposed by the Bank. The Tribunal has the authority to determine whether a sanction imposed by the Bank upon a staff member is significantly disproportionate to the staff member's offense, for if the Bank were so to act, its action would properly be deemed arbitrary or discriminatory.[38]

Or, in other words, the Tribunal's 'job is not to decide what sanction the Tribunal would impose or whether the [international organization] chose the best penalty, but, rather, whether the [international

[33] UNAT No. 761, para. 60.

[34] UNAT No. 761, para. 60.

[35] See, for example, UN Staff Rule 10.4(a): 'A staff member may be placed on administrative leave, under conditions established by the Secretary-General, at any time after an allegation of misconduct and pending the completion of a disciplinary process. Administrative leave may continue until the completion of the disciplinary process'.

[36] UN Charter, Article 101(3).

[37] WBAT No. 665, para. 74.

[38] WBAT No. 665, para. 132.

organization] reasonably exercised [its] discretion in this matter'.[39] In *UNAT No. 956*, the Tribunal examines 'whether the sanction is proportionate to the offence' and states,[40] 'the determination of the degree of the sanction is usually reserved for the [international organization], which has discretion to impose a measure that it considers adequate to the circumstances of the case in light of the actions and behaviour of the staff member involved'.[41] This discretionary administrative authority includes, 'the discretion to weigh aggravating and mitigating circumstances when deciding upon the appropriate sanction to impose'.[42]

When is the harshest punishment – termination of employment – proportionate? In ILOAT Judgment No. 203, *Ferrecchia v. International Labour Organization* (1973) – featuring a full discussion of proportionality – the claimant successfully contests as disproportionate their termination for repeatedly falling asleep at their work as a night-time security guard. The Tribunal finds:

> [T]he Staff Regulations of the [international organization] provides for the imposition of the disciplinary sanctions of warning, reprimand, censure, reduction of salary and demotion, discharge, and summary dismissal. By depriving [the staff member] of [their] employment the two latter measures may cause serious harm to the staff member concerned and to [their] family. In accordance with the principle that the penalty should be proportionate to the fault, they should, therefore, as a general rule be imposed only on a staff member whose conduct appears to be incompatible with the performance of [their] duties.[43]

In other words, as a disciplinary sanction, termination of appointment is proportionate to misconduct so serious that the international official's continued employment by an international organization could not be contemplated.

10.4 Obligations to Complainants Alleging Misconduct

The legal principles and duties extended to international officials investigated for and accused of misconduct are extensive. But what obligations are owed to international officials to vindicate their complaints of alleged misconduct?

[39] WBAT No. 665, para. 133.
[40] UNAT No. 956, para. 15.
[41] UNAT No. 956, para. 39.
[42] UNAT No. 956, para. 40.
[43] ILOAT No. 203, para. 2.

In ILOAT Judgment No. 1899, *Boivin v. European Organisation for the Safety of Air Navigation* (2000) – repeatedly cited with approval since – the claimant alleges a fellow employee falsified an in-time challenge to their appointment to a vacant position. The Tribunal finds:

> Disciplinary relations between an [international] organization and a staff member do not directly concern other members of staff or affect their position in law. Consequently, a decision regarding a disciplinary inquiry or a disciplinary measure relating to one staff member will not adversely affect other staff, so the latter will have no cause of action for challenging a disciplinary sanction or a refusal to impose one.

However, complainant staff members who allege harassment in the workplace are not considered simply bystanders to whom no obligations are owed. For example, in WBAT Judgment No. 649, *FW and FX v. International Bank from Reconstruction and Development* (2021), the claimants contend that they are the victims of workplace sexual harassment, unprotected by the international organization and failed by a flawed misconduct investigation. Whilst 'complainants in sexual harassment cases or other similar cases cannot dictate the outcome of the investigation or what disciplinary measures ought to be imposed',[44] the Tribunal finds:

> Generally, in the context of misconduct 'against the individual,' the complainant is not merely a reporter of misconduct but one who has alleged a personal harm from the conduct reported. As such, any alleged unfair or biased investigation, or unreasonable and unobservable decisions made thereon, if substantiated, might reasonably affect the rights of the complainant.[45]

In UNAT Judgment No. 787, *Auda v. Secretary-General of the United Nations* (2017), the claimant – who contends that they are the victim of bullying – contests the decision of the international organization to close the investigation into their complaint, without further action. The Tribunal summarizes:

> As a general principle, the instigation of disciplinary charges against a staff member is the privilege of the [international organization] itself, and it is not legally possible to compel the [organization] to take disciplinary action. The [organization] has a degree of discretion as to how to conduct a review and assessment of a complaint and whether to undertake an investigation regarding all or some of the allegations.[46]

44 WBAT No. 649, para. 149.
45 WBAT No. 649, para. 145.
46 UNAT No. 787, para. 30.

However, the Tribunal goes on to identify that this is the exercise of discretionary administrative authority, hence it is nevertheless amenable to limited review by an administrative tribunal and would be invalidated by arbitrariness. (See Chapter 5, 'Employment-Related Dispute Resolution'.) Reasonable allegations of grave misconduct must be investigated:

> Only in particular situations ([that is], in a case of a serious and reasonable accusation) does a staff member have a right to an investigation against another staff member which may be subject to judicial review [by the Tribunal]. However, the [international organization's] discretion can also be confined in the opposite direction. There are situations where the only possible and lawful decision of the [international organization] is to deny a staff member's request to undertake a fact-finding investigation against another staff member.

Similarly, ILOAT Judgment No. 4207, *GM v. International Atomic Energy Agency* (2020), the claimant alleges sexual harassment by a supervisor and successfully challenges the international organization's determination that the allegations could not be established. The Tribunal finds:

> Given the serious nature of a claim of harassment, an international organization has an obligation to initiate the investigation itself. Moreover, the investigation must be initiated promptly, conducted thoroughly and the facts must be determined objectively and in their overall context. Upon the conclusion of the investigation, the complainant is entitled to a response from the [international organization] regarding the claim of harassment … an international organization must take proper actions to protect a victim of harassment.[47]

Importantly, in the context of such misconduct allegations: 'It is noted that the Tribunal has specifically rejected this assumption that intent on the part of the alleged perpetrator is required in order to establish harassment'.[48]

In ILOAT Judgment No. 4378, *YT v. World Health Organization* (2021), the claimant – who contends that they are harassed by the investigative function of their international organization – alleges (amongst several allegations) that their right to respond to misconduct allegations is violated by a refusal to allow them to comment on an external report, commissioned to investigate the investigators over these allegations. The Tribunal finds this contention unfounded and clarifies that the legal duty that misconduct allegations must afford an opportunity to respond,

[47] ILOAT No. 4207, para. 15.
[48] ILOAT No. 4207, para. 20

protects international officials investigated for and accused of misconduct, not international officials *complaining* of misconduct by others: 'Given that the [claimant], in this case, was not the subject of the investigation process and, therefore, was not in an adversarial situation … the principle of due process and the right to be heard are not applicable in these circumstances'.[49] (See also, Chapter 9, 'Standards of Conduct'.)

10.5 The Employment Law of Misconduct

Derived from the necessity to enforce the treaty-based highest standards of integrity and the independence of officials at international organizations, the employment law of misconduct is composed of legal principles on the one hand – that hold an international organization accountable for fixing employees with liability for misconduct – and legal duties on the other hand – that safeguard employees from unsubstantiated allegations and disproportionate punishment. This is complemented by the obligation owed international officials who complain of misconduct, to address their allegations and afford them a response and appropriate protections.

The applicable law may be restated as:

Legal Principles of Misconduct

- The facts of misconduct must be established.
- The established facts must legally constitute misconduct.
- Disciplinary sanction must possess a legal basis.

Legal Duties of Misconduct

- Misconduct must be compellingly proven.
- Staff members must be allowed an opportunity to respond to misconduct allegations.
- Misconduct may only be sanctioned proportionately.

Obligations to Complainants Alleging Misconduct

- It is incumbent upon international organizations to address complaints of misconduct from staff members, affording them a response and appropriate protections.

[49] ILOAT No. 4378, para. 25.

PART IV

Administrative Authority

11

Administration

This chapter begins by introducing administration – in terms of issuing and adhering to binding and impersonal instructions – as the exercise of authority attributed by the treaty-basis of international organizations to the principal executive official and regulating governance organ. Second, the legal principles of administration are identified, namely: (1) Administrative authority is unilateral, but may not be arbitrary; (2) Internal law must be adhered to, but may be amended; and (3) Structural terms of employment cannot be suppressed. Third, two attendant legal duties of administration are considered, as follows: (1) Administration must be diligent; and (2) Administration must ensure safety. Fourth the relevance of practice to administration is examined. Fifth, and in conclusion, this employment law of administration at international organizations is restated.

11.1 What Is Administration?

Notwithstanding their multitudinous mandates, many may think of administration – bureaucracy – as the common, unifying feature of all international organizations. Even though the feat of a multinational staff cooperating together to achieve some multilateral aim may be remarkable, the result has a reputation for being organizationally unresponsive and procedurally fixated.[1] This may be attributed to the way in which multilateral institutions tend to be administered – often a fluctuating mixture of national civil service cultures, contemporary private sector influences and plenty of organizational heritage. Yet, although the treaty-basis of international organizations possesses the governance organ that supervises the principal executive official with the

[1] See Sinclair 2017, 268.

authority – and obligation – to issue written employment-related regulations, the manner in which the authority of the principal executive official to instruct their staff is exercised, is unspecified. (See Chapter 3, 'International Civil Service'.)

Obviously, no matter how energetic and charismatic the leader of an international organization may be – or think themselves – it would be fanciful to instruct the work of every staff member in person, even in the smallest multilateral institution. So, instead, written instructions, or in other words internal law – *Staff Rules, Administrative Circulars, Directives* and so forth – are also issued by the principal executive official (and their authorized delegates) to govern the employment of international officials. The action of issuing the internal law and how it is adhered to – in application to the staff of an international organization as a collective body, rather than the individualized administrative actions described in preceding chapters – is what is here meant as 'administration'.

Such powers of administration appear, on their face, unconstrained by the constituent instruments of international organizations but are in fact regulated by international law. Broadly, these constraints can be understood as falling into two categories. On the one hand, there are limitations that accompany the attribution itself of unilateral powers to the principal executive official. Since legal authority is constrained by its lawful purposes – in other words, arbitrariness invalidates authority (see Chapter 5, 'Employment-Related Dispute Resolution') – from this derives the prohibition on arbitrary administration, including administration that disregards an international organization's own internal law.

On the other hand, there are limitations inherent to the purposes of appointment to the international civil service, as empowered by the treaty-basis of international organizations. From this may be said to be derived the duties of diligent administration and administration that ensures the safety of international officials, together with the impermissibility of suppressing structural terms of employment which are of fundamental significance in the employment of international officials.

Similarly, the administrative practices of a multilateral institution are not unbounded. The way in which the internal law is administered and supplemented by unwritten practices must ensure a uniformity of treatment between similarly situated international officials, and cannot override contradictory provisions of the written internal law itself. Taken together, this comprises the employment law of administration.

11.2 Legal Principles of Administration

The competence of administration, to instruct staff through issuance of an internal law – distinct from governance and regulatory arrangements – is attributed to the principal executive official by the treaty-basis of international organizations. The only limit placed upon this administrative authority by the express treaty text is the subjugation of the principal executive official to the governance organ competent to supervise their work. (See Chapter 3, 'International Civil Service'). Inherent to this administrative authority is its legal regulation. Hence, the first legal principle of administration is that whilst administrative authority is unilateral – in other words, internal lawmaking does not require the consent of staff – it cannot be used arbitrarily. An internal law either unrelated to, or incapable of achieving, the purposes of an international organization would be arbitrary – it would exceed the limited functional powers of international organizations (see Chapter 2, 'International Organizations') – and hence a legal nullity. Second, although possessed of the authority to make and remake the internal law, this does not release an international organization from the obligation to adhere to it. Third, there are certain terms and conditions of the employment of the international civil service, which even supposing their revocation and replacement were to be non-arbitrary, are so fundamental – *structural* – to the employment relationship that they cannot be suppressed. These principles are now considered in turn.

Principle 1: Administration Is Unilateral, but May Not Be Arbitrary

Upon successfully applying for a post at an international organization, most soon-to-be international officials are sent a written offer of employment, setting out terms and conditions of appointment – including at least their job title, starting pay and benefits, along with details of the institutional rules and regulations, 'incorporated by reference' – that they are invited to accept. Once they do, this then instigates a legal relationship between them and their employer and appoints them to the international civil service. These referenced rules and regulations – the internal law of an international organization (see Chapter 2, 'International Civil Service') – are neither fixed to the date their employment begins, nor does their amendment by an international organization need the employee's consent.[2]

[2] However, typically a provision of the internal law obligates the *consultation* of staff – especially through formal staff representatives – before administrative authority is used to revise

In WBAT Judgment No. 1, *de Merode and Others v. The World Bank* (1981) – a canonical examination of the administrative authority of an international organization, in the context of the claimants' challenge to any alteration to the way the taxes on their salaries are reimbursed – the Tribunal finds:

> [T]he fact that the Bank's employees enter its service on the basis of an exchange of letters does not mean that these contractual instruments contain an exhaustive statement of all relevant rights and duties … The contract may be the [indispensable basis][3] of the [employment relationship], but it remains no more than one of a number of elements which collectively establish the ensemble of conditions of employment operative between the Bank and its staff members. In the case of other [international] organizations one looks for these other elements principally in the constituent instrument of the organization and in its Staff Rules and Regulations.[4]

However, the treaty-basis and internal lawmaking authority of an international organization are not part of any individualized bargain. Instead, as the WBAT puts it, 'The applicability of these to the employee is … the consequence of their objective existence as part of the legal system to which the staff member becomes subject by entering into a contract with the organization'.[5] Consequently, the Tribunal finds:

> [T]he Bank possesses, in common with other international organizations, an inherent power to change … the general and impersonal rules establishing the rights and duties of the staff. It is a well-established legal principle that the power to make rules implies in principle the right to amend them.[6]

Hence, 'the administrative authority of an international organization is unilateral' – it could be understood as analagous to a statutory (public law), not a contractual (private law), status.[7] But this unilateral administrative authority is not the same as unconstrained authority: 'Discretionary power is not absolute power', the Tribunal observes.[8] In other words,

and reissue the internal law itself. See, for example, World Bank Staff Rules, Principle 10, second sentence: 'In recognition of the right of the staff to associate, the President shall establish appropriate mechanisms to consult with representative members of the staff selected by the staff about the establishment of and changes in personnel policies, conditions of employment, general questions of staff welfare, and the establishment, amendment or revocation of Principles and of Staff Rules.'

3 The Tribunal uses the legal Latin, *sine qua non*.

4 WBAT No. 1, para. 18.

5 WBAT No. 1, para. 29.

6 WBAT No. 1, para. 31.

7 WBAT No. 1, para. 35.

8 WBAT No. 1, para. 45.

the treaty-based lawful purposes of an international organization, which possess it of this authority over staff, also govern its administration. The Tribunal identifies a number of limitations upon administrative authority of international organizations to issue and reissue the internal law:

> Changes must be based on a proper consideration of relevant facts. They must be reasonably related to the objective which they are intended to achieve. They must be made in good faith and must not be prompted by improper motives. They must not discriminate in an unjustifiable manner between individuals or groups within the staff. Amendments must be made in a reasonable manner seeking to avoid excessive and unnecessary harm to the staff. In this respect, the care with which a reform has been studied and the conditions attached to a change are to be taken into account by the Tribunal.[9]

The Tribunal also considers a prohibition on retroactivity to be an incontrovertible attribute of the employment law of international organizations. It finds, 'no retroactive effect may be given to any amendments adopted by the Bank. The Bank cannot deprive staff members of accrued rights for services already rendered'.[10]

However, the fundamental constraint – which may be said to subsume all other limitations – is inherent to the possession of all legal powers: 'The Bank would abuse its discretion if it were to adopt such changes [to its internal law] for reasons alien to the proper functioning of the organization'.[11] A proper functioning international organization must adhere to its treaty-basis in pursuit of its purposes – administration is necessarily an exercise of the functional powers of a multilateral institution, governed by the achievement of their mandates (see Chapter 2, 'International Organizations') and the special status of the international civil service (see Chapter 3, 'International Civil Service').

Principle 2: Internal Law Must Be Adhered to, but May Be Amended

Inherent to the power of international organizations to introduce internal law – and hence the attendant power to amend the same internal law – is the concurrent obligation to adhere to this internal law. In ILOAT Judgment No. 1896, *Cervantes and Others (No. 3) v. European Patent Office* (2000) – repeatedly cited with approval by the Tribunal since – the claimants successfully challenge the decision of the international organization's 'Administrative

[9] WBAT No. 1, para. 47.
[10] WBAT No. 1, para. 46.
[11] WBAT No. 1, para. 47.

Council' not to include staff representation, despite a provision of the internal law – a 'Service Regulation' – obligating such inclusion. The Tribunal considers the plain interpretation of the Service Regulation admitting staff representation to be clear, finding: 'The written law must … be applied, in particular by the authority having enacted it, as long as it has not been repealed or modified for the sake of the principle that similar acts require similar rules'.[12] Notably, if the internal law is ambiguous, then the interpretation most favourable to the staff member – not the employing international organization – applies.[13]

In ILOAT Judgment No. 2170, *A E L v. International Telecommunication Union* (2003) – repeatedly cited with approval by the Tribunal, in combination with *ILOAT No. 1896* – the claimant successfully challenges the failure of the international organization to appraise their performance, but then awarding them a (minimal) performance appraisal-related annual pay increment. The Tribunal finds: 'An international organization has a duty to comply with its own internal rules and to conduct its affairs in a way that allows its employees to rely on the fact that these will be followed'.[14]

In *WBAT No. 1*, the Tribunal states, 'because every authority is bound by its own rules for so long as such rules have not been amended or abrogated[,] individual decisions must conform to the general rules'.[15] In other words, the administrative authority of an international organization is obligated by the internal law, until such time as this law is revoked or reissued.

Principle 3: Structural Terms of Employment Cannot Be Suppressed

Whilst the administrative authority of international organizations is unilateral not contractual, there are certain structural terms of employment.[16] These relate to the fundamental relationship accepted by all international

[12] ILOAT No. 1896, para. 5(d).

[13] See ILOAT Judgment No. 3355, *BC v. European Organisation for the Safety of Air Navigation* (2014), para. 16, '[I]t is well established in the Tribunal's case law that when the regulations or rules of an international organization are ambiguous they must in principle be construed in favour of the interests of its staff and not those of the organization itself.'

[14] ILOAT No. 2170, para. 14.

[15] WBAT No. 1, para. 30.

[16] Although this concept is ubiquitous, terminology differs between administrative tribunals. This book uses the expression, 'structural terms', drawing upon the phrase 'structure of the contract' used by the ILOAT; for example, in ILOAT No. 832, paras. 12–13.

officials as employees – essential inducements to enter into and remain in the employ – of international organizations. This may be understood as purposeful interpretation of the power of appointment attributed by the treaty-basis of international organizations, in accordance with international law. Although difficult to define, these structural terms cannot be suppressed.

In ILOAT Judgment No. 832, *Ayoub and Others v. International Labour Organization* (1987) – in which the Tribunal considers structural terms of employment – the claimants unsuccessfully contend that their employer has unlawfully reduced the proportion of their compensation which qualifies as pensionable renumeration, alleging that this is a non-suppressible term of their employment. The Tribunal refers to structural terms of employment as 'acquired rights', stating:

> [A]n acquired right is one the staff member may expect to survive any amendment of the rules … the amendment of a rule to an official's detriment and without [their] consent amounts to breach of an acquired right when the structure of the contract of appointment is disturbed or there is impairment of any fundamental term of appointment in consideration of which the official accepted appointment.[17]

Most structural terms of employment exist at the time they persuade an international official to take on their appointment. But they may also be established subsequently, convincing a staff member to continue in employment with an international organization. The Tribunal develops this further:

> Although there will be breach of an acquired right only if one of two conditions is fulfilled, the two are in fact but one. Disturbance of the structure of the contract posits impairment of a fundamental term, and the latter the former. A somewhat broader framing of the doctrine is wanted so that it will cover not just terms of appointment that were in effect at recruitment but also terms that were brought in later and were calculated to induce the staff member to stay on.[18]

The Tribunal emphasizes that this does not give rise to a subjective, individualized test – the question is not, 'did this term or that actually make the staff member sign on or decide to stay?'[19] But rather, the Tribunal scrutinizes terms which might objectively be said to 'sway' such a decision.[20] Importantly, it is the case that both 'the existence of

17 ILOAT No. 832, paras. 12–13.
18 ILOAT No. 832, para. 13.
19 ILOAT No. 832, para. 13.
20 ILOAT No. 832, para. 13.

a particular term of appointment' may be non-suppressible, as well as 'arrangements for giving effect to the term'.[21] The Tribunal also distinguishes this principle from the prohibition of retroactivity. Namely, 'the doctrine [of acquired rights] is broader than the rule against retroactivity. Whereas the doctrine looks to the future as well as to the past, the rule merely forbids altering what already belongs to the past'.[22]

In UNAT Judgment No. 840, *Alcañiz and Others v. Secretary-General of the United Nations* (2018), the claimants unsuccessfully contend that the abolition of separate pay scales for international officials with and without dependants (splitting this element off from compensation, into a dependents-related benefit) and consequent reduction of their salary, suppresses a structural term of employment. The Tribunal, having regard to the case law and nomenclature of the ILOAT, states:

> An 'acquired' right should be purposively interpreted to mean a vested right; and employees only acquire a vested right to their salary for services already rendered. Promises to pay prospective benefits, including future salaries, may constitute contractual promises, but they are not acquired rights until such time as the quid pro quo for the promise has been performed or earned. Moreover, the fact that increases have been granted in the past does not create an acquired right to future increases or pose a legal bar to a reduction in salary.[23]

However, the UNAT is an outlier, in not regarding the principle of structural terms as categorically distinct from the prohibition of retroactivity: 'In the final analysis, the doctrinal protection of acquired rights is essentially an aspect of the principle of non-retroactivity. The aim is to protect individuals from harm to their vested entitlements caused by retrospective statutory instruments'.[24] Nevertheless, if retroactive adverse administration is understood as one of the many dimensions of arbitrariness – and so necessarily prohibited – then non-suppressible structural terms go to a functionally different restraint upon administrative authority.[25]

[21] ILOAT No. 832, para. 13.
[22] ILOAT NO. 832, para. 13.
[23] UNAT No. 840, para. 90.
[24] UNAT No. 840, para. 91.
[25] Whilst administrative tribunals theorize about structural terms, they do not often identify them. But essentially the principle of non-suppressible structural terms involves imagining a change to the employment relationship so profound that the unilateral administrative authority of an international organization however non-arbitrarily exercised, is insufficient to secure lawfulness, and the agreement of staff must be obtained to proceed.

In *WBAT No. 1*, the Tribunal regards terms and conditions of appointment to be divisible into those that may and may not, be unilaterally changed. It finds:

> The Tribunal considers that in examining the numerous and varied elements of the conditions of employment, a major distinction must be drawn. Certain elements are fundamental and essential in the balance of rights and duties of the staff member; they are not open to any change without the consent of the staff member affected. Others are less fundamental and less essential in this balance; they may be unilaterally changed by the Bank in the exercise of its power, subject to the limits and conditions [of the employment law of international organizations]. In various forms and with differing terminology this distinction is found in the [j]urisprudence of other international administrative tribunals.[26]

However, whilst the Tribunal regards it as impossible 'to describe in abstract terms the line between essential and non-essential elements', it shares the ILOAT's preparedness to protect both substantive terms of employment as well as the way in which those terms are implemented.[27] *WBAT No. 1* states:

> Sometimes it will be the principle itself of a condition of employment which possesses an essential and fundamental character, while its implementation will possess a less fundamental and less essential character. In other cases, one or another element in the legal status of a staff member will belong entirely – both principle and implementation – to one or another of these categories. In some cases the distinction will rest upon a quantitative criterion; in others, it will rest on qualitative considerations. Sometimes it is the inclusion of a specific and well-defined undertaking in the letters of appointment and acceptance that may endow such an undertaking with the quality of being essential.[28]

The Tribunal finds that protected – structural – terms 'may not be amended unilaterally' by an international organization.[29] However, *WBAT No. 1* highlights the important distinction between a particular term of employment and arrangements for giving effect to this term. The Tribunal finds the term of employment constituted by tax reimbursement is structural, but the methodology to give effect to this term is not – in other words, the way in which the reimbursement is calculated may be amended unilaterally, albeit not arbitrarily.[30]

[26] WBAT No. 1, para. 42.
[27] WBAT No. 1, para. 43.
[28] WBAT No. 1, para. 43.
[29] WBAT No. 1, para. 45.
[30] WBAT No. 1, para. 82.

11.3 Legal Duties of Administration

The legal principles of administration hold to account the internal law-making competence at international organizations, where treaty-based administrative authority is exercised through written instructions of impersonal application. Although this authority may only be exercised in accordance with the employment law at international organizations, there is plainly an imbalance of resources and compulsion between an employing international organization and the international officials it employs. Legal duties of administration govern decision-makers, obligating international organizations to a 'duty of care', 'good faith', 'fairness' and 'good administration' – or in terms less embedded in national laws, a 'duty of carefulness'. This may be expressed as: (1) Administration must be diligent; and (2) Administration must ensure safety.

Duty 1: Administration Must Be Diligent

What is diligent administration? *Diligence* means 'careful attention', 'heedfulness', 'caution'.[31] This quality must be characteristic of the administration of international organizations. Complementing adherence to the internal law and evidence-based (non-arbitrary, purposive) administrative decisions, the duty to administer an international organization with diligence obligates a multilateral institution not to be careless, reckless or haphazard.

In ILOAT Judgment No. 4411, *D v. Food and Agriculture Organization* (2021), the claimant successfully contests the abolition of their position as unlawful, in circumstances where the international organization can adduce no documentary evidence as to the supposed necessity of this action. Relatedly but separately, the claimant contends that a feature of this abolition – its suddenness – was undignified and careless. The ILOAT finds, 'it is well established in the Tribunal's case law that international organizations are bound to refrain from any type of conduct that may harm the dignity or reputation of their staff members'.[32] The Tribunal finds the unexpected and sudden abolition of the claimant's position – or in other words, the absence of any diligent administration – an unlawful affront to their dignity.[33]

[31] *Shorter Oxford English Dictionary*; and *heed* means 'careful attention, observation, regard' and 'have a care, pay attention, take notice'.

[32] ILOAT No. 4411, para. 22.

[33] See ILOAT No 4411, para. 22.

In ILOAT Judgment No. 4494, *M (No. 2) v. European Patent Office* (2021), the claimant unsuccessfully challenges the delay to implementing a recommendation to retire them on grounds of invalidity, alleging bad faith. The Tribunal states the obligation of the conduct of administration owed to staff of an international organization:

> The Tribunal recalls that the principle of good faith and the concomitant duty of care demand that international organizations treat their staff with due consideration in order to avoid causing them undue injury; an employer must consequently inform employees in advance of any action that may imperil their rights or harm their rightful interests ... the duty of care is greater in a rather opaque or particularly complex legal situation, as is often the case when it is necessary to determine staff rights in technical fields, such as the determination of pension rights.[34]

In other words, murky and neglectful administration is antithetical to the special status of the international civil service and breaches a duty of diligence that obligates all administration by international organizations.

Duty 2: Administration Must Ensure Safety

The legal duty of an international organization to ensure the safety of its employees arises – given the global service of international civil servants – both in the context of the duties they perform in the course of their employment (when they are 'on-duty') and by their presence generally at a (possibly dangerous) duty station to which they are deployed. (When outside work, they are said to be carrying on their private lives, 'off-duty'). Consequently, administration by a multilateral institution must ensure the safety of international officials by protecting them against both: (1) foreseeable on-duty risks; and (2) abnormal off-duty risks. These are now considered in turn.

1 Foreseeable On-Duty Risks Must Be Prevented

As between all employers and employees, it is uncontentious – and prescribed by their internal law – that international organizations must provide international civil servants with a safe and healthy workplace. For example, UN Staff Regulations state:

> Staff members are subject to the authority of the Secretary-General and to assignment by [them] to any of the activities or offices of the United

[34] ILOAT 4494, para. 9.

> Nations. In exercising this authority, the Secretary-General shall seek to ensure, having regard to the circumstances, that all necessary safety and security arrangements are made for staff carrying out the responsibilities entrusted to them.[35]

Breach of this obligation has been termed 'negligence'. In ILOAT Judgment No. 4239, *L v. World Health Organization* (2019), the claimant – who suffered a brain injury in a car accident whilst on-duty in India – contests their health-related termination of appointment and injury-related compensation as inadequate. The Tribunal enumerates the legal and factual elements of a failure to protect against foreseeable on-duty risks – in other words, alleged negligence – as follows:

> - The first is that the [international] organization has failed to take reasonable steps to prevent a foreseeable risk of injury.
> - The second is that liability in negligence is occasioned when the failure to take such steps causes an injury that was foreseeable … the word 'injury' in this context is not used in any technical, legal or medical sense. Equally apt and often used is the word 'damage', which may be physical (including psychological), financial or, as is often the case, both. In the context of employment with an international organization, physical damage or injury is more likely to be foundational to the claim though the damage could well be … consequential financial damage occasioned by loss of earning capacity flowing from the physical injury.
> - However, another essential element of the cause of action is that the negligent act or omission caused the damage. That is to say, there must be a causal link between the conduct complained of and the damage suffered.[36]

The burden of demonstrating these three elements – (1) failure to prevent foreseeable on-duty risk, (2) causing damage or injury, and (3) a causal link between the two – falls upon 'the person seeking damages for negligence'.[37]

2 Abnormal Off-Duty Risks Must Be Prevented

In ILOAT Judgment No. 402, *Grasshoff (Nos. 1 and 2) v. World Health Organization* (1980) – featuring a full examination of the safety of international officials off-duty – the claimant (a doctor) successfully

[35] UN Staff Regulation 1.2(c).
[36] ILOAT No. 4239, paras. 14–15, bullet points added.
[37] ILOAT No. 4239, para. 15.

contends that they be compensated for loss of earnings occasioned by their injury in a bomb explosion whilst deployed to a south-east Asian state experiencing civil war. The Tribunal states:

> It is a fundamental principle of every contract of employment that the employer will not require the employee to work in a place which [they know] or ought to know to be unsafe. [The internal law] is to be read subject to this principle. If there is doubt about the safety of a place of work, it is the duty of the employer to make the necessary inquiries and to arrive at a reasonable and careful judgment, and the employee is entitled to rely upon [the employer's] judgment.[38]

Consequently, if the employing international organization's judgment is defective in this regard, the international official is 'entitled to be indemnified in full against the consequences of the misjudgement'.[39] However, this exercise of judgment is contextualized by the nature of the occupation of the employee:

> This principle is to be applied with due regard to the nature of the employment. In some employments there are unavoidable risks. A doctor may have to risk infection and a soldier or a policeman to risk bombs. The question in each case is whether the risk is abnormal having regard to the nature of the employment.[40]

The Tribunal notes that the claimant, 'was employed in the branch concerned with malaria eradication and did not therefore by the nature of [their] employment accept the risk of hostilities in an area of civil war'.[41]

In WBAT Judgment No. 643, *FM v. International Bank for Reconstruction and Development* (2020) – in which the Tribunal cross-refers to *ILOAT No. 402* – one of the claimant's contentions is that they be compensated for contracting an endemic mosquito-borne illness whilst on deployment to Sierra Leonne. The Tribunal finds the claimant (a health specialist) is 'required to demonstrate that contraction of malaria and dengue fever arose out of and in the course of [their] employment and not as a result of general exposure to hazards prevalent [at their] duty station'.[42] The Tribunal concludes:

[38] ILOAT No. 402, para. 1.
[39] ILOAT No. 402, para. 1.
[40] ILOAT No. 402, para. 2.
[41] ILOAT No. 402, para. 3.
[42] WBAT No. 643, para. 136.

> The Tribunal is not convinced that the Bank acted negligently toward the [claimant] or otherwise breached its duty of care in this regard. Mosquito-related illnesses are a known risk of living in Sierra Leone. While such a risk cannot be entirely avoided, the question is whether the Bank was required to take specific measures, in conjunction with a reasonable exercise of its general duty of care to staff, to mitigate those risks.[43]

The Tribunal notes that it is not contended that the claimant was infected whilst on the premises of the World Bank nor that their employer failed to take reasonable steps to ensure such premises were free from mosquito infestation.[44] In other words, mosquitos are regarded as a normal hazard in West Africa (including for health specialists), whereas bomb explosions are an abnormal risk (for malaria-eradication doctors) to run in south-east Asia.

11.4 Administrative Practice

Even in the most densely regulated international organization, there is a considerable amount of repetitive administrative activity which comprises an unwritten institutional practice. This chiefly arises in two contexts – both intended to achieve uniformity of administration. First, when an internal law admits such a range of outcomes that the results may be erratic – unless supplemented by some settled practical approach. Second, where administration encounters a domain that is either sufficiently novel or insufficiently regulated to achieve predictability – unless, here again, supplemented by some consistent practice. Where this is the case, international officials may, on the one hand, (1) depend upon this practice and hence an equality of treatment – it would be arbitrary if similarly situated staff members were not administered similarly. But, on the other hand, (2) practice is undependable if it is unlawful. In other words, if a practice contravenes the written internal law of an international organization, then the written internal law prevails and no reliance can be placed on the practice – since it has no legal significance. These dynamics are now considered in turn.

1 *Administrative Practice Must Treat Similarly Situated Staff Similarly*

Inequality of treatment and discrimination – both evidence of arbitrary administration – are closely regulated and proscribed by the internal law

[43] WBAT No. 642, para. 143.
[44] See WBAT No. 642, para. 143.

of international organizations. For example, the UN Staff Regulations state, ‘staff members shall exhibit respect for all cultures; they shall not discriminate against any individual or group of individuals or otherwise abuse the power and authority vested in them’.[45] However, a difference in treatment is not necessarily discriminatory treatment.

In ILOAT Judgment No. 2704, *AGS v. United Nations International Development Organization* (2008) – in which the Tribunal elaborates on the concept of discrimination – the claimant successfully contends that they are unlawfully denied a merit-based promotion in circumstances of inequality of treatment. The Tribunal finds:

> The Tribunal has consistently held that discrimination occurs when persons who are in the same situation in fact and law are treated differently. The principle of equality not only requires that situations which are the same or similar be governed by the same rules, but that dissimilar situations be governed by rules that take account of the dissimilarity. However, the principle of equality may be infringed if the rules that govern dissimilarity are not appropriate and adapted to the dissimilarity. That is because, if they are not appropriate and adapted, they may have a discriminatory effect or a disproportionate impact on different members of the same class.[46]

Since the performance of the claimant – as head of the international organization’s staff representative body – was unsupervised and unassessed (a prerequisite for such merit-based promotion, in practice), the Tribunal finds this discriminatory.[47]

In ILOAT Judgment No. 4029, *A v. World Health Organization* (2018), the claimant challenges the decision not to grant them an in-grade promotion for meritorious long service. The Tribunal finds, ‘the principle of equality requires that persons in the same position in fact and in law must be treated equally’.[48] Since the international organization awarded an in-grade promotion to all other long-serving similarly situated staff, there is no basis to withhold it from the claimant:

> [T]he principle of equality requires that persons in the same position in fact and in law must be treated equally. The failure to grant the complainant the two-step within-grade increase that at the material time was given to other long-term short-term staff members, who were in the same position as the [claimant], constitutes unequal treatment.[49]

[45] UN Staff Regulation 1.2(a), second sentence.
[46] ILOAT No. 2704, para. 7.
[47] ILOAT No. 2704, para. 6.
[48] ILOAT No. 4209, para. 20.
[49] ILOAT No. 4209, para. 20.

Hence, even when a multilateral institution repeatedly acts upon initiative – rather than upon the obligation of the internal written law – it cannot exercise this administrative authority inconsistently.

2 *Unlawful Administrative Practice Is Undependable*

In *ILOAT No. 4029* the international organization attempts to escape the obligation to treat similarly situated staff similarly, by arguing that the practice contravenes the written internal law and hence, is undependable. The Tribunal finds:

> It is well settled in the case law that a practice cannot become legally binding if it contravenes a written rule that is already in force. The Tribunal [has] explained that a practice which is in violation of a rule cannot have the effect of modifying the rule itself. In this case, [the international organization] initiated a practice for the benefit of long-term short-term staff members to address the concern that these staff members were not given any within-grade increases.[50]

Although this practice was not contemplated by the internal law of the international organization, the Tribunal finds that it supplements – but does not contravene – the internal law. Consequently, it is a lawful – and hence a dependable – administrative practice: 'The benefit provided in the application of that practice went beyond and was in addition to the provisions in [the internal law]. The practice did not modify [the internal law] or affect the rights of other … staff members. Accordingly, the Tribunal concludes that the practice was legally binding'.[51]

11.5 The Employment Law of Administration

Consistent with the treaty-based authority of the principal executive official of an international organization to direct the work of the staff, their written instructions to all international officials assume the status of internal law. The unilateral authority to administer the staff of an international organization is subject to limitations both inherent to possession of that authority – the prohibition of both arbitrary administration and administration that disregards the internal law – and to the purpose of the employment relationship with international officials – the non-suppressibility of structural terms of employment and the duties

[50] ILOAT No. 4209, para. 19.
[51] ILOAT No. 4209, para. 19.

of diligence and ensuring the safety of international civil servants. This is complemented by the obligation to ensure that administrative practice does not occasion inequality and whilst it may supplement, it cannot contradict, the internal law of a multilateral institution.

The applicable law may be restated as:

Legal Principles of Administration

- Administrative authority is unilateral, but may not be arbitrary.
- Internal law must be adhered to, but may be amended.
- Structural terms of employment cannot be suppressed.

Legal Duties of Administration

- Administration must be diligent.
- Administration must ensure safety, so foreseeable on-duty and abnormal off-duty risks must be prevented.

Administrative Practice

- The administrative practice of an international organization must treat similarly situated staff similarly, but no dependence may be placed on administrative practice that contravenes the internal law.

12

Ending Service

This chapter begins by describing ending service – the automated discontinuance of the employment of international officials, administrated to achieve an adaptable, effective and highly efficient international organization. (Differently, administrative action may terminate employment as a consequence of performance management – see Chapter 8, 'Performance Management' – and as a consequence of the enforcement of standards of conduct – see Chapter 10, 'Misconduct' – at international organizations.) Second, the legal principles of ending service are identified, namely: (1) Absent abuse of discretion, deference is owed organizational restructuring; (2) Absent abuse of discretion, deference is owed appointment nonrenewal; and (3) Mutually agreed termination may obtain legal release. Third, the related governance of ending service is considered, namely the legal duties that: (1) Abolition of post must be credible; and (2) Recourse to redundancy must exhaust practicable alternatives. Fourth, the chapter addresses service ending in circumstances of an international official no longer being able to perform – as a result of illness or injury – or being unwilling to perform their duties. Fifth, service ending upon attainment by a staff member of a mandatory retirement age is examined. Sixth, and in conclusion, this employment law of ending service at international organizations is restated.

12.1 What Is Ending Service?

The longevity of international organizations is alone sufficient to suggest that they are institutionally adaptable. The longest-established international organizations now number their existence over centuries, not decades.[1] Even the UN and the institutions established in the immediate

[1] For example, the International Bureau of Weights and Measures remains governed by its constituent instrument – the Metre Convention and Annexed Regulations – signed in 1875, with limited amendment in 1921.

aftermath of World War II are older than many of their Member States. Hence, the adaptiveness of international organizations is apparent, even before the many examples of multilateral institutions that periodically equip themselves with new capabilities are considered – for example, the now commonplace 'Blue Helmet' UN peacekeeping operations are an innovation, unmentioned in the Charter of the UN.[2]

Such periodic institutional redeployment – maintaining the utility and relevance of international organizations – would be stymied if the international civil service could not be organizationally restructured. Inevitably, not all international officials possess the skills needed indefinitely by an adaptable international organization. Entire functions could be suppressed – the UN has no need today for specialists to staff the colonial-era Trusteeship Council, for example. Or, new functions may be created – such as when the UN Security Council instituted the UN International Criminal Tribunals for the Former Yugoslavia and Rwanda (and indeed, later disbanded these courts). Or, a so-called operational 'business model' could be reconfigured – the World Bank's shift to 'global practices' from a 'geographical matrix', for example.[3] Although much about this adaptation may mean many international officials are newly appointed and current international officials are promoted or reassigned, an invariable consequence is that following the abolition of their positions, international officials are also made redundant.[4] An employing international organization possesses the authority to do this, inherent to the principal executive official's competence to appoint, organize and dismiss the staff. However, this authority must be exercised in accordance with the institution's internal law and cannot be abused or used carelessly – so, the abolition of posts must be credible and redundancies must be practicably unavoidable.

The inevitability of adaptation by international organizations – and the expense associated with redundancy payments – leads multilateral institutions to appoint many – and sometimes, most – of their staff on

[2] However, for an explanation of the functional powers of international organizations, see Chapter 2, 'International Organizations'.

[3] See *Financial Times* 2014: 'Mr Kim [the World Bank's then President] rightly argues that the bank's value should be through the quality of advice it provides, rather than its cost of capital. But it is unclear whether his reorganisation is any better than the bank's previous geography-based structure. Mr Kim is replacing the six regional departments with 14 "global practices."'

[4] Terminologically, posts or positions may be *abolished*, but people are made *redundant*.

fixed-term contracts.[5] In other words, rather than being appointed open-endedly (potentially until retirement), the staff member's appointment term – their length of service – is for a fixed time period. In practice, this usually varies from one year to as many as four or five. These term appointments are emblazoned with warnings to international officials that they may have no 'legitimate expectation' of reappointment when the appointment expires – despite the fact that the majority of such staff members experience (repeated) contract term extensions. This then leads staff whose fixed-term appointments are not renewed (*nonrenewal* or *non-extension*, as distinct from premature *termination* of appointment) – especially after several extensions – to allege that fixed-term contracting is a legal fiction. In other words, the law and reality part ways – entitling them to continuing employment.

Given the contentiousness involved in reforming and restructuring international organizations and the high degree of disruptiveness that this could entail, many institutions will be prepared to arrive at individual agreements with staff members to govern the terms of their amicable exit. These 'mutually agreed separations' (MAS) trade advantageous terms for the international civil servant in exchange for releasing their employer from any legal liability. In other words, these terms bar subsequent claims before an international administrative tribunal – and any national judicial forum. Such agreements also represent a bargain that staff members may come to regret and then seek to overturn, alleging that some unlawful factor compromises their agreement. Of course, in all this and at any stage, nothing prevents an international official from simply resigning their appointment, in accordance with any applicable notice requirement.

Although the continued relevance of an international organization is an institutional necessity, so too is ongoing efficiency and effectiveness. Consequently, the basis for ending service includes ending service when a staff member is either unable to go on working – *invalidity*, due to a lasting serious illness or career-ending injury – or unwilling to go on working (but absent their resignation), so-called *abandonment of position*. Both depend upon factually clear circumstances that the staff member is no longer available to an international organization to perform their

[5] Good governance also plays a role in certain circumstances – for example, ensuring that in senior leadership positions turnover, integrity functions are refreshed and international organizations maintain political neutrality. As does avoiding acrimonious, damaging and high-profile disputes before international administrative tribunals.

assigned duties and responsibilities. More happily, service ends irrevocably for international civil servants upon their retirement. This usually occurs because they attain a mandatory retirement age, set out in the internal law of the international organization. The compulsory retirement of international civil servants is often represented as an indispensable way to renew an institution and hence sustain the achievement of its object and purposes. However, shifting societal norms result in challenges to compulsory retirement as ageist. Together, these differing but related circumstances underly the employment law of ending service.

12.2 Legal Principles of Ending Service

The administrative action of ending service to achieve organizational flexibility – redundancy, related to organizational restructuring, appointment expiration, or MAS – exercises the discretionary authority of an international organization, attributed to the principal executive official. Since this competence to deploy international civil servants is discretionary, the law is not capable of determining how international officials should be organized, contracted, or amicably exited. Deference is due to the judgment of administrative decision-makers. Hence, international administrative tribunals exercise a restrained review, consistent with the irreplaceable authority of the principal executive official: absent arbitrariness or other abuses, the related administrative decision to end the service of staff members is lawful. The accountability of an international organization when ending service in these circumstances arises through three legal principles.

Principle 1: Absent Abuse of Discretion, Deference Is Owed Organizational Restructuring

In ILOAT Judgment No. 2830, *SGG v. World Intellectual Property Organization* (2009) – repeatedly cited with approval by the Tribunal since – the claimant successfully contests the termination of their appointment as a consequence of organizational restructuring. The Tribunal sets out the scope of an international organization's discretionary authority in this regard:

> An international organization may find that it has to reorganise some or all of its departments or units. Reorganisation measures may naturally entail the abolition of posts, the creation of new posts or the

> redeployment of staff. The steps to be taken in this respect are a matter for the [international organization's] discretion and are subject to only limited review by the Tribunal.[6]

In ILOAT Judgment No. 2510, *WG v. World Telecommunication Union* (2006) – featuring an emphatic statement on the Tribunal's non-intrusion into organizational restructuring – the claimant unsuccessfully contests the loss of their managerial responsibilities, resulting from a reorganization. The Tribunal is not competent to overrule the structural design adopted by an international organization:

> [A]n international organization necessarily has power to restructure some or all of its departments or units, including by the abolition of posts, the creation of new posts and the redeployment of staff ... the Tribunal may not supplant an organization's view with respect to these matters, and decisions on them are discretionary and subject to limited review.[7]

In WBAT Judgment No. 657, *Andriamilamina (No. 4) v. International Finance Corporation* (2021), the claimant challenges their redundancy, resulting from an extensive exercise described by the organization as, 'workforce planning ... to recalibrate our staffing pyramid so that we are more efficient and that we appropriately leverage senior resources with more junior staff'.[8] The Tribunal restates its approach: '[T]he decision to declare a staff member's employment redundant is an exercise of managerial discretion'.[9] Or, in other words, 'the Tribunal reviews such decisions for abuse of discretion, that is, the Tribunal examines whether a decision is arbitrary, discriminatory, improperly motivated or carried out in violation of a fair and reasonable procedure'.[10]

In UNAT Judgment No. 764, *Zachariah v. Secretary-General of the United Nations* (2017) – in which the claimant challenges the abolition of their post by the UN General Assembly – the Tribunal similarly finds:

> The [international organization] has broad discretion to reorganise its operations and departments to meet changing needs and economic realities. As the [UN] Appeals Tribunal has recognised, an international organization necessarily has power to restructure some or all of its departments or units, including the abolition of posts, the creation of new posts and the redeployment of staff.[11]

6 ILOAT No. 2830, para. 6.
7 ILOAT No. 2510, para. 10.
8 WBAT No. 657, para. 5.
9 WBAT No. 657, para. 131.
10 WBAT No. 657, para. 131.
11 UNAT No. 764, para. 26.

Principle 2: Absent Abuse of Discretion, Deference Is Owed Appointment Nonrenewal

In WBAT Decision No. 602, *GF v. International Bank for Reconstruction and Development* (2019), the claimant challenges the nonrenewal of their fixed-term appointment. The claimant's letter of appointment states:

> Your appointment will terminate at the end of this two-year period unless it is extended or a new appointment is made. The World Bank has no obligation to extend the appointment or to offer a new appointment, even if your performance is outstanding, but it may do so if agreed in writing at the time of the expiration of the appointment.[12]

In view of these contractual terms, the Tribunal finds:

> With respect to the renewal or extension of term appointments … [a] staff member appointed to serve for a fixed period is not entitled, absent unusual circumstances, to the extension or renewal of that appointment … A fixed-term contract is just what the expression says: it is a contract for a fixed period of time. Even so, the decision not to extend a [fixed-term] contract, like all decisions by the Bank, must be reached fairly and not in an arbitrary manner.[13]

Importantly, non-extension of an expiring appointment represents an administrative decision (see Chapter 5, 'Employment-Related Dispute Resolution') that is amenable to judicial review by an international administrative tribunal. Or, in other words, the nonrenewal of a fixed-term appointment is not beyond the jurisdiction of an administrative tribunal – an international organization cannot portray it as inadmissible automatic appointment expiration.

However, '[t]he Tribunal will not interfere in management's decisions about the staffing needs of a unit, unless abuse of discretion is apparent'.[14] Reasonable justifications for nonrenewal emphasize achieving the adaptation of an international organization – for example, 'a skills mismatch'[15] and 'changing business needs'[16] are credible grounds for non-extension. However, to the extent that a skills mismatch is performance-based, the staff member must have this drawn to their attention with sufficient candour that 'notice of imminent nonrenewal' is not mistaken for ongoing 'areas for improvement', within the context

12 WBAT No. 602, para. 71.
13 WBAT No. 602, para. 72.
14 WBAT No. 602, para. 97.
15 WBAT No. 602, para. 75.
16 WBAT No. 602, para. 76.

of a renewed appointment and continuing performance management.[17] To depend upon performance-related nonrenewal, the 'staff member's need to obtain or demonstrate certain skills and the consequences of the failure to do so' must be put to them unambiguously.[18]

In WBAT Judgment No. 556, *DW v. International Bank for Reconstruction and Development* (2017) – in which the claimant unsuccessfully challenges the nonrenewal of their appointment – the Tribunal also underscores that (inevitably) this discretionary authority cannot be used arbitrarily:

> That discretionary authority to renew or not to renew a contract at the expiration of its predetermined date is not, however, absolute and unlimited; it may not be exercised in an arbitrary manner … the decision not to renew or extend a contract may not be based on considerations unrelated to the functioning of the institution, such as racial discrimination. Another kind of restriction upon the Bank's discretionary authority … arises when circumstances are shown which reasonably warrant the inference by a staff member that the Bank in fact made a promise to extend or renew [their] appointment either expressly or by unmistakable implication.[19]

However, in UNAT Judgment No. 522, *Munir v. Secretary-General of the United Nations* (2015) – in which the claimant challenges the nonrenewal of their appointment on the basis that 'they had a legitimate expectation of a one-year extension'[20] – the Tribunal emphasis that: 'In order for a staff member's claim of legitimate expectation of a renewal of appointment to be sustained, it must not be based on mere verbal assertion, but on a firm commitment to renewal revealed by the circumstances of the case.'[21]

In ILOAT Judgment No. 4363, *CM v. International Labour Organization* (2020) – in which the claimant contests the defunding of their position and expiration of their fixed-term appointment – the Tribunal emphasizes the limitations of its review:

> [The] scope of review is limited as an [international] organization enjoys wide discretion in deciding whether or not to extend a fixed-term appointment and … the exercise of such discretion is subject to limited review because the Tribunal respects an [international] organization's freedom to determine its own requirements and the career prospects of staff.

17 WBAT No. 602, para. 123.
18 WBAT No. 602, para. 126.
19 WBAT No. 556, para. 65.
20 UNAT No. 522, para. 10.
21 UNAT No. 522, para. 24.

> Accordingly, the Tribunal will not substitute its own assessment for that of the [international] organization and a decision in the exercise of this discretion may only be quashed or set aside for unlawfulness or illegality.[22]

In ILOAT Judgment No. 3353, *HPW and HM v. International Telecommunication Organization* (2014), the claimants contest the allegedly baseless rationale for not renewing their fixed-term contracts, namely 'a complete reorientation of Telecom activities and consequently a restructuring of the Telecom Secretariat'.[23] The Tribunal finds that a legal feature of restructuring, correspondent to the limited review of discretionary authority, is that 'a decision not to renew a fixed-term contract must be based on objective and valid grounds'.[24] The Tribunal is persuaded that such basis underlies the decision not to renew the claimants' appointments:

> The obvious aim was to achieve greater efficiency in [the international organization's] … operations in keeping with immediate and projected market and competitive needs. Notwithstanding that there was no apparent reduction in staff, the new staffing structure … as well as other documents, support this. The evidence shows that the functions for which new staff members were recruited required qualifications, expertise and experience that the [claimants] did not have. Accordingly, the restructuring involving a decision to abolish the [claimants'] posts, was within the discretion of the [international organization].[25]

In other words, the decision to allow a fixed-term appointment to expire possesses three legal features: (1) it exercises discretionary administrative authority, amenable to limited judicial review; (2) it must be related to the functioning of an international organization; and (3) it must be credibly explained.

Principle 3: Mutually Agreed Termination May Obtain Legal Release

All international civil servants are entitled to resign their post and exit their employing international organization, typically subject to giving written notice, as set forth in the institution's internal law.[26] However,

[22] ILOAT No. 4363, para. 10.
[23] ILOAT No. 3353, para. A.
[24] ILOAT No. 3353, para. 15.
[25] ILOAT No. 3353, paras. 21–22.
[26] For example, UN Staff Rule 9.2:

> (a) A resignation, within the meaning of the Staff Regulations and Rules, is a separation initiated by a staff member. (b) Unless otherwise specified in their letters of appointment, staff members shall give written notice of resignation according

amicable termination of their appointment in other – incentivized – circumstances, necessitates a bargain being reached between employee and employer. These terms are usually set out in a written contractual document and referred to as an MAS. This contract typically settles arrangements for the exit of the staff member from the international organization and incorporates a provision barring the international official from either challenging the terms of the exit or bringing any other employment-related claims before an international administrative tribunal.

In WBAT Judgment No. 508, *Tweedle v. International Bank for Reconstruction and Development* (2015), the claimant unsuccessfully contends that they lacked the capacity to enter into an MAS and only did so under duress. The Tribunal upholds the legitimacy of this organizational tool:

> An MAS is a matter of contract between the Bank and a staff member. The Tribunal in the past has accepted the validity of, and given effect to, MAS agreements between the Bank and staff members including the provision on the release of claims against the Bank … It would unduly interfere with the constructive and efficient resolution of [employment-related] claims if the Bank could not negotiate – in exchange for concessions on its part – for a return promise from the staff member not to press [their] claim further.[27]

However, 'no release or settlement of claims should be given effect if concluded under duress'.[28] A staff member may seek to set aside the MAS on these grounds before the Tribunal, but claimants 'must comply with the [admissibility] requirements of the Tribunal's Statute'.[29] In other words, 'duress' cannot be pleaded long after it allegedly becomes apparent, as it is time-barred. (See Chapter 4, 'International Administrative Tribunals'.)

In ILOAT Judgment No. 4223, *L v. United Nations Educational, Scientific and Cultural Organization (UNESCO)* (2020), the claimant contends that they are entitled to an unpaid allowance, unmentioned in the MAS which served as the basis for their departure from employment. The ILOAT confirms the enforceability of a 'clause preventing any challenge or appeal by the [claimant] concerning the terms of [their] departure from [the international organization]' and hence the

to their type of appointment … The Secretary-General may accept resignations on shorter notice. (c) The Secretary-General may require the resignation to be submitted in person in order to be acceptable.

[27] WBAT No. 508, para. 21.

[28] WBAT No. 508, para. 22.

[29] WBAT No. 508. para. 23.

challenge is irreceivable.[30] Thus, only when such agreement is the result of 'misrepresentation or duress' practiced upon the staff member will the Tribunal set aside the exclusion of jurisdiction integral to an MAS.[31]

An example of such misrepresentation is afforded by ILOAT Judgment No. 4072, *P (No. 2) v. Global Fund to Fight AIDS, Tuberculosis and Malaria* (2019), in which the claimant successfully contends that they were induced to enter into an MAS when they were 'called to a meeting either to sign a mutual separation agreement or to accept the transfer to [a] new post, with the strong likelihood of having to participate in a performance improvement plan'.[32] The Tribunal finds the evidence proves that the claimant's 'performance evaluation could not, at least not at the time of the meeting with [them], have had the effect of initiating a performance improvement plan on account of past services rendered',[33] nor could such a plan be used to assess future performance.[34] Consequently, the Tribunal finds the claimant is 'placed ... under undue pressure which persuaded [them] to accept the separation agreement'[35] and consequently, the MAS is set aside.[36]

12.3 Legal Duties of Ending Service

The legal duties of ending service govern both the administrative authority to abolish posts at international organizations on the one hand, and the resulting redundancy of international officials on the other hand. These duties may be expressed as: (1) Abolition of post must be credible; and (2) Recourse to redundancy must exhaust practicable alternatives.

Duty 1: Abolition of Post Must Be Credible

To be credible, the abolition of a post – the position an employee encumbers – cannot be arbitrary. It must have an objective, reasoned, evidenced basis. It must also be procedurally transparent and not conceal illegitimate motives.

In ILOAT Judgment No. 1231, *Richard v. International Criminal Police Organization* (1993) – featuring a full discussion of pretextual

30 ILOAT No. 4223, para. 5.
31 ILOAT No. 4223, para. 6.
32 ILOAT No. 4072, para. 5.
33 ILOAT No. 4072, para. 11.
34 See ILOAT No. 4072, para. 14.
35 ILOAT No. 4072, para. 17.
36 See ILOAT No. 4072, para. 18.

redundancy – the claimant successfully contends that the abolition of their position is a ruse to terminate the appointment of an unwanted employee. The Tribunal finds:

> [T]here must be objective grounds for abolition, which must not be used as a pretext for dislodging undesirable staff ... a distinction must be drawn between the post, the content of which depends on the [international] organization's structure and requirements, and the staff member's position as holder of the post. Although the staff member's lot depends on the post [they hold], conversely the [international] organization may not set up or do away with a post on personal grounds. The distinction is between the post, which must be created, defined and abolished according to objective criteria that are subject to judicial review, and the personal position of the incumbent. It is a guarantee that the international civil service affords against the risk of dismissal without due cause or reason on grounds of abolition or reform of posts.[37]

The Tribunal also makes clear that non-arbitrariness is not satisfied by mere 'broad allusion to the [international organization's] service requirements or interests'.[38] Rather, it finds:

> Such terms are meaningless unless there is a fuller explanation enabling the staff member and, if need be, the Tribunal to grasp the actual reasons, especially where the outcome is as drastic as abolition of post and dismissal. A reference to an [international] organization's general interests is not to serve as an all-purpose catch-phrase to make any sort of administrative action pass muster.[39]

As well as clear and non-pretextual reasons, any post abolition procedure must also be transparent. In *WBAT No. 657* the Tribunal states:

> [I]t is incumbent on the Tribunal to require the strictest observance of fair and transparent procedures in implementing the [internal law] dealing with redundancy ... to be upheld, the redundancy decision in question must be based on a legitimate rationale and must have been made in the interests of efficient administration.[40]

In *UNAT No. 764*, the Tribunal states: '[E]ven in a restructuring exercise, the [international organization] has the duty to act fairly, justly and transparently in dealing with its staff members.'[41]

[37] ILOAT No. 1231, paras. 26–27.
[38] ILOAT No. 1231, para. 23.
[39] ILOAT No. 1231, para. 23.
[40] WBAT No. 657, paras. 132–133.
[41] UNAT No. 764, para. 26.

Duty 2: Recourse to Redundancy Must Exhaust Practicable Alternatives

The internal law of international organizations allow the termination of appointment of a staff member following abolition of their post. For example, the ILO Staff Regulations state that the principal executive official 'may terminate the appointment of an established official if the necessities of the service require a reduction of staff involving a reduction in the number of posts'.[42] However, first there is an obligation – typically codified in the internal law – to try to find this international official an alternative position. In other words, recourse to redundancy must be the last practicable resort, once efforts to reassign them are unsuccessful.[43]

In ILOAT Judgment No. 3901, *M v. Centre for the Development of Enterprise* (2017) – in which the claimant challenges the failure to assign them from an abolished post in a discontinued international organization to a new post in the successor institution – the Tribunal finds:

> A steady line of precedent has it that while it is true that international organizations have the right to restructure their operations, abolish posts if necessary and consequently terminate the appointment of their staff members who are affected by the planned restructuring, they cannot simply terminate their appointment – at least not if they hold an appointment of indeterminate duration – without first taking suitable steps to find them alternative employment. Only when reassignment proves impracticable may it have recourse to the … measure of terminating their appointment.[44]

In WBAT Judgment No. 226, *Marshall v. International Bank for Reconstruction and Development* (2000) – repeatedly cited by the Tribunal with approval since – the claimant challenges the 'failure to assist [them] in obtaining an alternative position', in contravention of a legal obligation upon the international organization.[45] The Tribunal finds the international organization insufficiently energetic in its discharge of this obligation, but also 'notes, however, that the job-search

[42] ILO Staff Regulations, Article 11(5)(a), second sentence.

[43] See, for example, UN Staff Rule 9(6)(c): 'staff members shall be retained in the following order of preference: (i) Staff members holding continuing appointments; (ii) Staff members recruited through competitive examinations for a career appointment serving on a two-year fixed-term appointment; (iii) Staff members holding fixed-term appointments.'

[44] ILOAT No. 3901, para. 6.

[45] WBAT No. 226, para. 2.

exercise requires efforts from both sides, and that the [claimant] was overly passive in this regard' by being unresponsive and failing to apply for suitable vacancies.[46] In other words, the international official is expected to be as engaged as their employer, in the mutual effort to identify a suitable alternative assignment.

However, in downsizing exercises – also termed a 'reduction in force' –, preferment to avoid redundancy is not without consideration of the relative performance of affected staff members. This may be reflected in the internal law of an international organization. For example, UN Staff Rules provide 'that due regard shall be given in all cases to relative competence' in the alternative assignment of staff, subsequent to the abolition of posts.[47]

Likewise, in WBAT Judgment No. 292, *del Campo v. International Bank for Reconstruction and Development* (2003) – featuring the Tribunal's first and full examination of the legitimate role of performance in redundancy – the claimant contends that consideration of their performance is wrongfully incorporated into the administrative decision to make them redundant. Yet the applicable internal law states: 'The selection of staff members whose employment is redundant shall be made on the basis of managerial judgment about the skills needed by the [Bank] to carry out its work effectively, taking into account' several factors, including, the 'performance of staff members.'[48]

The Tribunal finds that performance cannot be *unrelated* to redundancy, since if it were, superior performers would be immune to redundancy and this is plainly not the case.[49] Consequently, 'while unsatisfactory performance alone cannot furnish a basis for terminating service on the ground of redundancy (because such a termination would not be properly classifiable as a redundancy), performance or skill may be taken into account when deciding who should be retained'.[50]

In *UNAT No. 764*, the Tribunal restates the legal basis for obligating the search for an alternative posting to avoid redundancy:

> It is important to keep in mind the reasons for the creation and existence of an institute of permanent staff in the context of an international organization such as the United Nations. Staff members of the [UN] owe their allegiance to no national government. Having complied with all the necessary

[46] WBAT No. 226, para. 45.
[47] UN Staff Rule 9(6)(c).
[48] WBAT No. 292, para. 6.
[49] See WBAT No. 292, para. 51.
[50] WBAT No. 292, para. 52.

> requirements and criteria for a permanent appointment, and having received such an appointment, they become entitled to certain legal protections and advantages as articulated in the [UN's internal law].[51]

This then recognizes the ways in which international civil servants, serving a multilateral mandate and deployed globally, demonstrate a commitment and adaptation to the international organization, which the international organization is expected – so far as is consistent with its efficiency and effectiveness – to reciprocate.

12.4 Unable or Unwilling to Perform Duties

The circumstances in which an international official becomes unable – due to physical or mental impairment – or unwilling to perform their duties are almost always fraught. An inability to go on working occasioned by invalidity will usually intersect with insurances intended to address this (see Chapter 7, 'Remuneration') and is closely regulated by the internal law of international organizations.[52] The application of the employment law at international organizations to these circumstances is usually based upon incontrovertible medical findings, as determined by processes established by the employing international organization.

By contrast, so-called abandonment of position – in other words, an unwillingness to go on working, signified by extended, unexcused absence from duty – may involve an administrative tribunal establishing and interpreting the relevant facts. In WBAT Judgment No. 478, *Tanner v. International Bank for Reconstruction and Development* (2013), the claimant unsuccessfully contests the termination of their appointment on the grounds of abandonment of position. The claimant's duty station is Washington, DC, to which they are recalled following a discontinued period of remote working in New Zealand.[53] The Tribunal considers the revocation of authorization to work remotely to be clear:

> The Tribunal finds that the [claimant's] failure to report for duty in Washington, DC amounted to an abandonment of office notwithstanding [their] assertion that [they were] able to perform [their] tasks outside [their] duty station. It is insufficient for the [claimant] to state that [they] could have performed [their] duties in Auckland, New Zealand. That

[51] UNAT No. 764, para. 30.

[52] See, for example, ILO Staff Regulations, Chapter VIII, 'Social security'.

[53] See WBAT No. 478, para. 21.

> option was not available to [them] once the Telecommuting Agreement was terminated. The [claimant] was thus no longer authorised to work away from [their] duty station which was Washington, DC.[54]

In other words, although staff members may have demonstrated that other formats of working are feasible – especially during the global Covid-19 pandemic – the international organization unilaterally determines the mode and place from which the international official performs their duties.

Nor does an unsubstantiated assertion that a staff member is unfit for duty confound the legal assessment of abandonment. In UNAT Judgment No. 1081, *Da Silveira v. Secretary-General of the United Nations* (2021) – in which the claimant contests the administrative decision to terminate their appointment for abandonment of position, following the expiration of certified sick leave – the Tribunal finds: 'During that time, [the claimant] had failed to show up and perform the work that had been assigned to [them], and that altogether, [the claimant's] actions were consistent with a concluded intent to not return to [the duty station], no matter the lack of basis.'[55] Consequently, the termination of appointment for abandonment of position is lawful.

12.5 Retirement

The basis for the compulsory departure from employment of all international civil servants is attaining their employer's mandatory retirement age. Yet in an aging and ageism-conscious society, this is not uncontentious. In WBAT Judgment No. 391, *Oinas v. International Bank for Reconstruction and Development* (2009) – in which the claimant calls upon the Tribunal to order the international organization to either abolish or raise its mandatory retirement age – the Tribunal begins by delimiting its judicial functions:

> The Tribunal is mindful of the limits of its powers. It is not a policy-making or a policy-reviewing institution. These functions fall within the discretionary ambit of the powers of the Bank and its governing institutions. It is also well-established that in respect of policy-making it is not for the Tribunal to override the Bank's considered judgment and to replace it with its own, nor to consider which alternative would have been best or more effective to attain the desired objectives of reform.[56]

[54] WBAT No. 478, para. 31.
[55] UNAT No. 1081, para. 34.
[56] WBAT No. 391, para. 27.

Consequently, the Tribunal is not possessed of the authority to grant the relief sought by the claimant but is able to test for alleged abuse of administrative authority.[57] However, in assessing the mandatory retirement age for unlawfulness, the Tribunal finds that this differentiation based upon age does not constitute unlawful discrimination, since 'discrimination takes place where staff who are in basically similar situations are treated differently'.[58] In other words, the Tribunal finds that a mandatory retirement age is not arbitrary, since all staff members, similarly situated – in other words, of the same age – are treated alike, and compelled to retire.

In ILOAT Judgment No. 4531, *S (No. 2) v. World Health Organization* (2022), the claimant challenges the termination of their appointment upon achieving the mandatory retirement age and denial of their request for an exceptional extension of their appointment, beyond the retirement age. However, the ILOAT defers to 'the wide discretionary power acknowledged and accepted by the Tribunal vested in an executive head to make decisions to retain officials beyond the normal retirement age and the concomitant limits on review by the Tribunal', in upholding the termination decision by the principal executive official.[59]

12.6 The Employment Law of Ending Service

Consistent with the adaptability, efficiency and effectiveness of international organizations, principal executive officials possess a treaty-based competence to organize and dismiss – as well as to appoint – staff members. The employment law of ending service is composed of legal principles that regulate this discretionary authority to terminate appointments consequent to organizational restructuring, fixed-term appointment nonrenewal and mutual agreement incorporating legal release. This is checked by the legal duties to ensure that the abolition of posts is credible, consistent with non-arbitrary and transparent administration and any resulting redundancy first exhausts practicable alternatives. This is complemented by the administrative authority to compulsorily terminate the appointment of staff members who are either unable or unwilling to perform their duties, or have achieved the organization's policy-based mandatory retirement age.

[57] See WBAT No. 391, para. 28.
[58] WBAT No. 391, para. 32.
[59] ILOAT No. 4531, para. 12.

The applicable law may be restated as:

Legal Principles of Ending Service

- Absent abuse of discretion, deference is owed organizational restructuring.
- Absent abuse of discretion, deference is owed appointment nonrenewal.
- Mutually agreed termination may obtain legal release.

Legal Duties of Ending Service

- The abolition of a post must be credible, by being non-arbitrary and substantively and procedurally transparent.
- Recourse to redundancy must first exhaust practicable alternative assignments, whilst weighing relative performance.

Unable or Unwilling to Perform Duties

- An international organization may unilaterally determine conditions of service – including fitness, format and place – and in accordance with its internal law, terminate the appointment of staff who do not adhere to these conditions.

Retirement

- An international organization may unilaterally determine a mandatory retirement age policy.

13

Conclusion

This chapter begins by outlining the past trends and the present trajectory of employment-related dispute resolution at international organizations. Second, the historic evolution of the statutory basis of administrative tribunals at the UN is analysed – suggesting that Member State governance organs are prepared to revise procedures, but remain reluctant to address the transparency of employment law at international organizations. Third, and in conclusion – extending this book's emphasis on concisely and comprehensibly introducing the employment law at international organizations – the incorporation of general legal principles of international administrative law into the Statutes of international administrative tribunals is proposed.

13.1 What Is Trending for Employment-Related Dispute Resolution at International Organizations?

Over the past century, international administrative law has secured the treaty-based status of the international civil service, in conjunction with the administrative authority at international organizations, through adjudication by international administrative tribunals. The ad hoc committee of jurists that considered the first recorded application of international administrative law was soon superseded in 1927 by the League of Nations Administrative Tribunal, re-established twenty years later as the International Labour Organization Administrative Tribunal (ILOAT). (See Chapter 4, 'International Administrative Tribunals'.)

At the UN, administrative justice has passed through two institutional eras. The United Nations Administrative Tribunal (UNAdT) – established shortly after the UN itself – adhered to the statutory one-stage template of its predecessors.[1] Whereas in 2009, it was superseded when the UN General

[1] Albeit for a time, there was an appeals procedure using the Advisory Opinion jurisdiction of the International Court of Justice – see Section 13.2.

Assembly adopted a two-tier arrangement: the first-instance United Nations Dispute Tribunal (UNDT) – with several chambers, located in New York, Geneva and Nairobi – and the terminal United Nations Appeals Tribunal (UNAT). Most other international organizations not coupled to the jurisdiction of either the ILOAT or UNAT – with a handful of enterprising exceptions – have long since established their own proprietary administrative tribunal – such as the World Bank Administrative Tribunal, founded in 1980 – to independently and judicially resolve their employment-related disputes.[2]

Present-day international organizations complement these independent, judicial and binding administrative tribunals with extensive non-judicial dispute-resolution facilities. The traditional, quasi-judicial processes which inform a final administrative decision of the principal executive official – challengeable to an administrative tribunal – are now complemented by more informal apparatus.[3] These alternative dispute resolution procedures are intended to amicably settle workplace disagreements, without recourse to adjudication – and the application of international administrative law.

Most pervasively, international organizations retain ombudspersons and mediators. At large-scale multilateral institutions, these informal systems may be equivalent in sophistication to formal dispute resolution. For example, accompanying the introduction of the UN's two-tier formal justice system, the General Assembly affirms, 'that the informal resolution of conflict is a crucial element of the system of administration of justice, and emphasizes that all possible use should be made of the informal system in order to avoid unnecessary litigation'.[4]

Together this suggests tendencies both towards formally and independently judicializing employment-related dispute resolution on the one hand, whilst also affording non-judicial dispute resolution services for international civil servants on the other hand.[5] Ahead may be anticipated developments to this twofold, formal and informal approach.

[2] Several international organizations refer challenges to the administrative decisions of their principal executive official to arbitration, providing the functional equivalent of an international administrative tribunal judge sitting alone – see for example, Permanent Court of Arbitration, Response to the International Law Commission (2024), para. 10.

[3] See, for example, ILO Staff Regulations Article 10.5(1): 'A Joint Advisory Appeals Board shall be established to assist the [principal executive official] in making any final administrative decisions'.

[4] UN General Assembly Res. 63/253 (2008), para. 18.

[5] International organizations laggard in establishing an administrative tribunal tend to be galvanized by the risks of national courts seizing jurisdiction, following the line of reasong in, for example, ECtHR *Waite and Kennedy*.

Formal dispute resolution could – albeit contentiously –be reformed to include: the extension of the jurisdiction of administrative tribunals to contract disputes involving consultants and other 'non-staff' engaged by an international organization; the adoption of two-tier judicial systems, based upon the UN model; and access to national employment tribunals of Member States as an alternative to resorting to administrative tribunals.[6] The feasibility of coordinating or combining the ILOAT and UN administrative justice system into a single administrative tribunal has been repeatedly studied, set aside and then reconsidered.[7] Whereas, non-binding dispute resolution may yet become complemented by enabling tribunal judges to engage in informal judicial resolution.[8]

These trends demonstrate Member States preoccupied with enhancing the effectiveness of employment-related dispute resolution at international organizations. But, to date, no amendment aimed at adding to the transparency of international administrative law has been attempted. To understand the potential of past and prospective reforms to employment law at international organizations, recalling the track record of the UN General Assembly is informative.

13.2 Amending the Administration of Justice at the UN

The UN General Assembly has been engaged in assessing and amending the statutory basis of administrative justice at the UN throughout the organization's history.[9] Albeit for about the first forty-five years, the Statute of the UNAdT was revised only twice, the statutory basis of the UNAdT in its final decade and since then, the UNAT, has been altered on average every three or so years.

The Statute of the UNAdT was adopted by resolution of the General Assembly and entered into force on 1 January 1950.[10] The first amendment adjusts how the UNAdT's authority to set a financial sum in the alternative to the UN Secretariat performing a specific remedial administrative

6 For example, see generally, Gulati 2022.

7 See generally, United Nations, Report of the Secretary-General (2021).

8 See considerations at UN General Assembly Res. 79/254 (2024), para. 26.

9 Since adoption in 1946, the International Labour Conference has amended the Statute of the ILOAT eight times, in 1949, 1986, 1992, 1998, 2008, 2016, 2019 and 2021. Since adoption in 1980, the Board of Governors of the World Bank has amended the Statute of the WBAT twice, in 2001 and 2009. See ILOAT Statute and WBAT Statute, respectively.

10 UN General Assembly Res. 351 (1949).

action was exercised.[11] Henceforth, the Tribunal was obligated to fix a financial award at the time of judgment – and this was limited to two years net base pay – and the test for the Secretariat deciding to commute the administrative relief, in favour of a financial award, was changed from 'exceptional circumstances' to the less demanding, 'interests of the United Nations'.

The second amendment follows the Advisory Opinion, *Effects of Awards*, by the International Court of Justice (ICJ) confirming the General Assembly's authority to establish the UNAdT to resolve employment-related disputes.[12] The General Assembly created a mechanism allowing review of the Tribunal's judgments through a 'Committee on Applications for Review of Administrative Tribunal Judgements' requesting an Advisory Opinion from the ICJ – emulating a feature the ILOAT temporarily possessed.[13] Such appellate procedure could be utilized on grounds that the Tribunal 'exceeded its jurisdiction or competence or that the Tribunal has failed to exercise jurisdiction vested in it, or has erred on a question of law relating to the provisions of the Charter of the United Nations, or has committed a fundamental error in procedure which has occasioned a failure of justice'. (This second amending resolution also empowers the Tribunal to address the revision of mistaken judgments.) The third amendment suppresses the appellate mechanism – after forty years, the General Assembly finds it 'has not proved to be a constructive or useful element in the adjudication of staff disputes' at the UN.[14]

The fourth amendment enlarges the jurisdiction of the UNAdT by adding jurisdiction over the staff of the ICJ Registry and UN Joint Staff Pension Fund; it also enables jurisdiction to 'be extended to international organizations and entities participating in the common system of conditions of service'.[15] The fifth amendment introduces qualification criteria for UNAdT judges, namely that they 'possess the requisite qualifications and experience, including, as appropriate, legal qualifications and experience'.[16] The judicial appointment term of three years – with no reappointment limit – is increased to four years, with eligibility for reappointment restricted to once. The same reform also introduces the ability for the usual three-judge panel of the Tribunal

[11] UN General Assembly Res. 782 (1953).
[12] See Chapter 4, 'International Administrative Tribunals'.
[13] UN General Assembly Res. 957 (1955).
[14] UN General Assembly Res. 50/54 (1995).
[15] UN General Assembly Res. 52/166 (1998).
[16] UN General Assembly Res. 55/159 (2000).

to be substituted for a panel of all seven judges – with five judges of the UNAdT needing to agree to this.

The sixth amendment revisits – not for the last time – the qualification criteria for UNAdT judges. It states: 'Members shall possess judicial or other relevant legal experience in the field of administrative law or its equivalent within the [Member States'] national jurisdiction'.[17] The seventh reform once again revises the qualification criteria for Tribunal judges and henceforth: 'Members shall possess judicial experience in the field of administrative law or its equivalent within their national jurisdiction'.[18] However, this resolution also, regrets 'that the present system of administration of justice in the Secretariat continues to be slow, cumbersome and costly'. Consequently, the General Assembly instructs the UN Secretary-General 'to form a panel of external and independent experts to consider redesigning the system of administration of justice'.

The seventh amendment then incorporates the decision, 'that the United Nations Administrative Tribunal shall cease to accept new cases as of 1 July 2009' and to abolish the UNAdT as of 31 December 2009.[19] In place of the UNAdT, the General Assembly establishes the present-day administrative justice system, constituted by the Statutes of the UNDT/ATs, whilst affirming that these new Tribunals 'shall not have any powers beyond those conferred under their respective statutes'.

The eighth amendment – continuing the evolution of the UN's paramount administrative tribunal, now the UNAT – extends the appellate deadline from 45 to 60 days and establishes a 30-day deadline for appealing provisional orders.[20] The ninth amendment underscores that the UNAT is limited to ordering remedies specified by the Statute – namely, administrative relief or financial awards. The latter are now limited to redressing 'harm supported by evidence'.[21] This amendment – together with the next, ninth amendment – also revises the qualification criteria for UNAT judges, amending the original provision – 'Possess at least 15 years of judicial experience in the field of administrative law, or the equivalent within one or more national jurisdictions' – so it now reads:

> Possess at least 15 years of aggregate judicial experience in the field of administrative law, employment law or the equivalent within one or more

[17] UN General Assembly Res. 58/87 (2003).
[18] UN General Assembly Res. 59/283 (2005).
[19] UN General Assembly Res. 63/253 (2008).
[20] UN General Assembly Res. 66/237 (2012).
[21] UN General Assembly Res. 69/203 (2015).

> national or international jurisdictions. Relevant academic experience, when combined with practical experience in arbitration or the equivalent, may be taken into account towards 5 of the qualifying 15 years.[22]

The ninth amendment also aligns the privileges and immunities of UNAT judges to the Convention on the Privileges and Immunities of the UN (the 'General Convention'). The tenth – and latest – amendment adds to the Statute of the UNAT, 'The President shall have the authority, inter alia, to monitor the timely delivery of judgments'.[23]

Plainly, the UN General Assembly is capable of both continual and comprehensive amendment to the statutory basis of administrative justice at the UN. However, in revising the Statutes of first the UNAdT and then the UNAT – ten times over three-quarters of a century – the Member States of the UN have approached the apparent inadequacies of administrative tribunals primarily in terms of judicial procedure and personnel. In doing so, any inefficiency and uncertainty arising from an applicable law lacking in transparency has yet to be addressed.

13.3 Transparency and International Administrative Law

There is no Statute of any international administrative tribunal that incorporates a statement of applicable general legal principles of international administrative law. The Statute of the UNAT possesses the Tribunal with the authority to pass judgment on an appeal alleging errors 'on a question of law' – but does not include this law. The Statute of the ILOAT states: 'The Tribunal shall be competent to hear complaints alleging non-observance, in substance or in form, of the terms of appointment of officials of the International Labour Office'.[24] The Statute of the WBAT states: 'The Tribunal shall hear and pass judgment upon any application by which a member of the staff of the Bank Group alleges non-observance of the contract of employment or terms of appointment of such staff member'.[25]

The Statutes of these three international administrative tribunals do not say what law the tribunal applies. Several administrative tribunals go as far as the Statute of the IMF Administrative Tribunal, which states: 'In deciding on an application, the Tribunal shall apply the internal law

[22] UNAT Statute, Article 3(b).
[23] UN General Assembly Res. 71/266 (2016).
[24] ILOAT Statute, Article II(1).
[25] WBAT Statute, Article II(1), first sentence.

of the Fund, including generally recognised principles of international administrative law concerning judicial review of administrative acts'. Yet what these principles are is unstated by the Statute.

This lack of transparency surely cannot enhance the effectiveness of the international civil service. Likely, the inability of tribunal users to rely upon general principles clearly established in the Statutes of administrative tribunals causes a series of inefficiencies. There is a temptation to over-plead cases, since neither claimant nor respondent are able to apply concise and codified principles. In turn, judgments are extensive. Tribunals must summarize expansive pleadings and then reassemble general principles by sampling their often considerable case law. The absence of a doctrine of controlling legal precedents compounds these challenges. The timetable for submitting pleadings and time allowed for judgment-writing are necessarily prolonged. Both international civil servants and international organizations may then experience this as protracted administrative uncertainty, demoralizing employment relations and unanticipated tribunal judgments.

The incorporation of general legal principles into the Statutes of international administrative tribunals could follow the model of the treaty-basis of the International Criminal Court – the Rome Statute sets out a series of applicable 'General Principles of Criminal Law'.[26] Comparably, this book has identified general legal principles applied by administrative tribunals to the review of challenged administrative decisions and related questions of evidence (see Chapter 5, 'Employment-Related Dispute Resolution'). These are, in outline:

- Only adverse administrative decisions may be contested;
- Deference is owed discretionary authority;
- Arbitrariness invalidates authority;
- Claimants must establish arbitrariness;
- Unreasoned administrative decisions are evidently arbitrary; and
- Administrative decisions cannot be based on withheld evidence.

Enhancing the transparency of international administrative law in this way would strengthen both the legitimacy of administrative tribunals and their contribution to the effectiveness and accountability

[26] These are stated at Articles 22 to 33 of the Rome Statute and encompass, for example, Article 22 'Nullum crimen sine lege': 'A person shall not be criminally responsible under this Statute unless the conduct in question constitutes, at the time it takes place, a crime within the jurisdiction of the Court'.

of international organizations. Consequently, the encounter between treaty-based employees and employers – between the status of the international civil service and the administrative authority of international organizations – secured by international administrative tribunals, would rest on a clearly communicated legal approach. Such a proposed reform to the administration of justice at international organizations also converges with the central theme of this book: that the shared understanding of international administrative law must match the enormity of the endeavours entrusted to the international civil service.

Annex 1

Compendium of Employment-Related Clauses from Constituent Instruments

This annex is a compendium of employment-related clauses from the constituent instruments of selected international organizations, addressing the status of the international civil service and governance of administrative authority.

African Development Bank (AfDB)

Agreement Establishing the AfDB (1963)

Article 37:

(2) The President shall be chief of the staff of the Bank and shall conduct, under the direction of the Board of Directors, the current business of the Bank. He shall be responsible for the organization of the officers and staff of the Bank, including Vice-Presidents, whom he shall appoint, fix their terms of employment, and release in accordance with the rules and regulations adopted by the Bank, provided that he shall act in consultation with the Board of Directors in the exercise of his powers of appointment and release of Vice-Presidents.

(5) In appointing the officers and staff, the President shall make it his foremost consideration to secure the highest standards of efficiency, technical competence and integrity, and recruit them on as wide a geographical basis as possible, paying full regard to the regional character of the Bank, as well as the participation of non-regional states.

Article 38:

(3) The President, Vice-Presidents, officers and staff of the Bank, in discharge of their offices, owe their duty entirely to the Bank and to no other authority. Each member of the Bank shall respect the international character of this duty and shall refrain from all attempts to influence any of them in the discharge of their duties.

Asian Development Bank (ADB)

Agreement Establishing the ADB (1966)

Article 34:

(5) The President shall be chief of the staff of the Bank and shall conduct, under the direction of the Board of Directors, the current business of the Bank. He shall be responsible for the organization, appointment and dismissal of the officers and staff in accordance with regulations adopted by the Board of Directors.

(6) In appointing the officers and staff, the President shall, subject to the paramount importance of securing the highest standards of efficiency and technical competence, pay due regard to the recruitment of personnel on as wide a regional geographical basis as possible.

Article 36:

(3) The President, Vice-President(s), officers and staff of the Bank, in the discharge of their offices, owe their duty entirely to the Bank and to no other authority. Each member of the Bank shall respect the international character of this duty and shall refrain from all attempts to influence any of them in the discharge of their duties.

Food and Agriculture Organization (FAO)

Constitution of the FAO (1945)

Article VIII:

(1) The staff of the Organization shall be appointed by the Director-General in accordance with such procedure as may be determined by rules made by the Conference.

(2) The staff of the Organization shall be responsible to the Director-General. Their responsibilities shall be exclusively international in character and they shall not seek or receive instructions in regard to the discharge thereof from any authority external to the Organization. The Member nations undertake fully to respect the international character of the responsibilities of the staff and not to seek to influence any of their nationals in the discharge of such responsibilities.

(3) In appointing the staff the Director-General shall, subject to the paramount importance of securing the highest standards of efficiency and of technical competence, pay due regard to the importance of selecting personnel recruited on as wide a geographical basis as is possible.

International Labour Organization (ILO)

Constitution of the ILO (1919)

Article 9:

(1) The staff of the International Labour Office shall be appointed by the Director-General under regulations approved by the Governing Body.

(2) So far as is possible with due regard to the efficiency of the work of the Office, the Director-General shall select persons of different nationalities.

(3) A certain number of these persons shall be women.

(4) The responsibilities of the Director-General and the staff shall be exclusively international in character. In the performance of their duties, the Director-General and the staff shall not seek or receive instructions from any government or from any other authority external to the Organization. They shall refrain from any action which might reflect on their position as international officials responsible only to the Organization.

(5) Each Member of the Organization undertakes to respect the exclusively international character of the responsibilities of the Director-General and the staff and not to seek to influence them in the discharge of their responsibilities.

International Monetary Fund (IMF)

Articles of Agreement of the IMF (1944)

Article XII, Section 4:

(b) The Managing Director shall be chief of the operating staff of the Fund and shall conduct, under the direction of the Executive Board, the ordinary business of the Fund. Subject to the general control of the Executive Board, he shall be responsible for the organization, appointment, and dismissal of the staff of the Fund.

(c) The Managing Director and the staff of the Fund, in the discharge of their functions, shall owe their duty entirely to the Fund and to no other authority. Each member of the Fund shall respect the international character of this duty and shall refrain from all attempts to influence any of the staff in the discharge of these functions.

(d) In appointing the staff the Managing Director shall, subject to the paramount importance of securing the highest standards of efficiency and of technical competence, pay due regard to the importance of recruiting personnel on as wide a geographical basis as possible.

World Bank

Articles of Agreement of the International Bank for Reconstruction and Development (1944)

Article V, Section 5:

(b) The President shall be chief of the operating staff of the Bank and shall conduct, under the direction of the Executive Directors, the ordinary business of the Bank. Subject to the general control of the Executive Directors, he shall be responsible for the organization, appointment and dismissal of the officers and staff.

(c) The President, officers and staff of the Bank, in the discharge of their offices, owe their duty entirely to the Bank and to no other authority. Each member of the Bank shall respect the international character of this duty and shall refrain from all attempts to influence any of them in the discharge of their duties.

(d) In appointing the officers and staff the President shall, subject to the paramount importance of securing the highest standards of efficiency and of technical competence, pay due regard to the importance of recruiting personnel on as wide a geographical basis as possible.

UN Educational, Scientific and Cultural Organization (UNESCO)

Constitution of UNESCO (1945)

Article VI:

(4) The Director-General shall appoint the staff of the Secretariat in accordance with staff regulations to be approved by the General Conference. Subject to the paramount consideration of securing the highest standards of integrity, efficiency and technical competence, appointment to the staff shall be on as wide a geographical basis as possible.

(5) The responsibilities of the Director-General and of the staff shall be exclusively international in character. In the discharge of their duties they shall not seek or receive instructions from any government or from any authority external to the Organization. They shall refrain from any action which might prejudice their positions as international officials. Each State Member of the Organization undertakes to respect the international character of the responsibilities of the Director-General and the staff, and not to seek to influence them in the discharge of their duties.

United Nations (UN)

Charter of the UN (1945)

Article 97:

The Secretariat shall comprise a Secretary-General and such staff as the Organization may require. The Secretary-General shall be appointed by the General Assembly upon the recommendation of the Security Council. He shall be the chief administrative officer of the Organization.

Article 100:

(1) In the performance of their duties the Secretary-General and the staff shall not seek or receive instructions from any government or from any other authority external to the Organization. They shall refrain from any action which might reflect on their position as international officials responsible only to the Organization.

(2) Each Member of the United Nations undertakes to respect the exclusively international character of the responsibilities of the Secretary-General and the staff and not to seek to influence them in the discharge of their responsibilities.

Article 101:

(1) The staff shall be appointed by the Secretary-General under regulations established by the General Assembly.

(3) The paramount consideration in the employment of the staff and in the determination of the conditions of service shall be the necessity of securing the highest standards of efficiency, competence, and integrity. Due regard shall be paid to the importance of recruiting the staff on as wide a geographical basis as possible.

World Health Organization (WHO)

Constitution of the WHO (1946)

Article 35:

The Director-General shall appoint the staff of the Secretariat in accordance with staff regulations established by the Health Assembly. The paramount consideration in the employment of the staff shall be to assure that the efficiency, integrity and internationally representative character of the Secretariat shall be maintained at the highest level. Due regard shall be paid also to the importance of recruiting the staff on as wide a geographical basis as possible.

Article 37:

In the performance of their duties the Director-General and the staff shall not seek or receive instructions from any government or from any authority external to the Organization. They shall refrain from any action which might reflect on their position as international officers. Each Member of the Organization on its part undertakes to respect the exclusively international character of the Director-General and the staff and not to seek to influence them.

Annex 2

Summary of International Administrative Law

This annex summarizes the interpretative framework – comprising legal principles and duties – of international administrative law, established by Chapters 5–12. It does not reproduce the full range of legal determinations developed in those chapters.

I. Legal Basis

Employment-Related Dispute Resolution

Chapter 5

General Legal Principles of Review:

1. Only adverse administrative decisions may be contested.
2. Deference is owed discretionary authority.
3. Arbitrariness invalidates authority.

General Legal Principles of Evidence:

1. Claimants must establish arbitrariness.
2. Unreasoned administrative decisions are evidently arbitrary.
3. Administrative decisions cannot be based on withheld evidence.

II. Efficiency, Competence & Geographic Diversity

Selection

Chapter 6

Legal Principles of Selection:

1. Absent abuse of discretion, deference is owed selecting managers.
2. Vacancy announcements must be adhered to, but may be revoked.
3. Selection defects must be manifest, to be contestable.

Legal Duties of Selection:

1. Selection must be competency-based.
2. All candidates are entitled to consideration, but not selection.

Remuneration

Chapter 7

Legal Principles of Remuneration:

1. Compensation must secure staff of the highest standard.
2. Pay must be equal for equivalent work.

Legal Duties of Remuneration:

1. Benefits must obtain geographic diversity.
2. Compensation adjustment methodology must be objective.

Performance Management

Chapter 8

Legal Principles of Performance Management:

1. Absent abuse of discretion, deference is owed performance managers.
2. Performance management defects must be manifest, to be contestable.
3. Probationary decisions exercise the widest discretion.

Legal Duties of Performance Appraisal:

1. Performance appraisal must be useable.
   1.1 Performance appraisal must be credible.
   1.2 Performance appraisal must be timely.
2. Performance appraisal must afford an opportunity to respond.

III. Integrity & Independence

Standards of Conduct

Chapter 9

Legal Principles of Conduct:

1. The interests of the international organization are paramount.
2. Abuse of authority must be manifest, to be contestable.

3. International civil servants must be uncorrupted.
4. International civil servants must by uncompromised by external authority.

Legal Duties of Conduct:

1. Integrity requires honesty and reputability.
2. Integrity requires reserve and respect.
3. Integrity requires discipline and hierarchical authority.

Misconduct

Chapter 10

Legal Principles of Misconduct:

1. The facts of misconduct must be established.
2. The established facts must legally constitute misconduct.
3. Disciplinary sanction must possess a legal basis.

Legal Duties of Misconduct:

1. Proof of misconduct must be compelling.
2. Alleged misconduct must afford an opportunity to respond.
3. Misconduct may only be sanctioned proportionately.

IV. Administrative Authority

Administration

Chapter 11

Legal Principles of Administration:

1. Administration is unilateral, but may not be arbitrary.
2. Internal law must be adhered to, but may be amended.
3. Structural terms of employment cannot be suppressed.

Legal Duties of Administration:

1. Administration must be diligent.
2. Administration must ensure safety.
   2.1 Foreseeable on-duty risks must be prevented.
   2.2 Abnormal off-duty risks must be prevented.

Administrative Practice:

1. Administrative practice must treat similarly situated staff similarly.
2. Unlawful administrative practice is undependable.

Ending Service

Chapter 12

Legal Principles of Ending Service:

1. Absent abuse of discretion, deference is owed organizational re-structuring.
2. Absent abuse of discretion, deference is owed appointment nonrenewal.
3. Mutually agreed termination may obtain legal release.

Legal Duties of Ending Service:

1. Abolition of post must be credible.
2. Recourse to redundancy must exhaust practicable alternatives.

REFERENCES

African Development Bank, Agreement Establishing (signed 4 August 1963, entered into force 10 September 1964) 510 UNTS 3.

Ago S, 'What Is "International Administrative Law"? The Adequacy of This Term in Various Judgments of International Administrative Tribunals' in Quayle P (ed.), *The Role of International Administrative Law at International Organizations* (Brill Nijhoff 2020).

Agreement between the United Nations and the United States of America Regarding the Headquarters of the United Nations (signed 26 June 1947, entered into force 21 November 1947) 308 UNTS 1966.

Agreement Regarding the Headquarters for the World Food Programme (signed 15 March 1991) 1773 UNTS 30879.

Akehurst M, *The Law Governing Employment in International Organizations* (Cambridge University Press 1967).

Amerasinghe CF, *The Law of the International Civil Service: As Applied by International Administrative Tribunals* (Oxford University Press 1994).

Amerasinghe CF, *Principles of the Institutional Law of International Organizations* (Cambridge University Press 2005).

Asian Development Bank, Agreement Establishing (signed 4 December 1965, entered into force 22 August 1966) 571 UNTS 123.

Convention on the Privileges and Immunities of the Specialized Agencies (signed 21 November 1947, entered into force 2 December 1948) 33 UNTS 261.

Convention on the Privileges and Immunities of the United Nations (adopted 13 February 1946, entered into force 17 September 1946) 1 UNTS 15 (General Convention).

Conway E, *The Summit* (Little, Brown Book Group 2014).

Daugardis K and Schuricht S, 'Breaking the Silence: Why International Organizations Should Acknowledge Customary International Law Obligations to Provide Effective Remedies' in Quayle P (ed.), *The Role of International Administrative Law at International Organizations* (Brill Nijhoff 2020).

de Cooker C, 'Proliferation of International Administrative Tribunals' (2022), 12 *Asian Journal of International Law* 1.

Drummond E, 'The Secretariat of the League of Nations' (1931), 103 *Public Administration* https://doi.org/10.1111/j.1467-9299.1931.tb02023.x, accessed 3 September 2025.

Dworkin R, *Law's Empire* (Bloomsbury 1986).

Financial Times (London), 'Restructuring Hell at the World Bank' 9 April 2014.

Food and Agriculture Organizations of the United Nations, Constitution (signed and entered into force 16 October 1945) 1 UNTS 207.

Germond L and Martin E, 'Macro-Trends in the Performance Management of International Civil Servants and Their Legal Implications' in Quayle P (ed.), *The Role of International Administrative Law at International Organizations* (Brill Nijhoff 2020).

Global Fund to Fight AIDS, Tuberculosis and Malaria (Global Fund), By-Laws (2022) www.theglobalfund.org/media/6007/core_globalfund_bylaws_en.pdf, accessed 3 September 2025.

Gulati, R, *Access to Justice and International Organisations: Coordinating Jurisdiction between the National and Institutional Legal Orders* (Cambridge University Press 2022).

Hammarskjöld D, *The International Civil Servant in Law and Fact – Lecture Delivered to Congregation at Oxford University, 30 May 1961* (Oxford University Press/Dag Hammarskjöld Foundation 2021).

International Bureau of Weights and Measures, Metre Convention and Annexed Regulations (signed 20 May 1875) www.bipm.org/en/metre-convention, accessed 3 September 2025.

International Criminal Court, Rome Statute (adopted 17 July 1998, entered into force 1 July 2002) 2187 UNTS 38544.

International Labour Organization, Constitution (incorporated into the Peace Treaty of Versailles, signed 28 June 1919).

International Labour Organization, Convention (No. 100) Concerning Equal Remuneration for Men and Women Workers for Work of Equal Value (adopted 29 June 1951, entered into force 16 November 1973) 165 UNTS 303.

International Law Commission, 'Draft Articles on Responsibility of International Organizations, with Commentaries' (2011) UN Doc A/66/10.

Jenks W, *The Proper Law of International Organisations* (Stevens 1962).

Klabbers J, *An Introduction to International Organizations Law* (Cambridge University Press 2022).

League of Nations, Covenant (incorporated into the Peace Treaty of Versailles, signed 28 June 1919) https://libraryresources.unog.ch/ld.php?content_id=32971179, accessed 3 September 2025.

League of Nations, 'Report of the Committee of Enquiry Adopted by the League of Nations Council, 17 June 1921' (1921), 1921 *League of Nations Official Journal* 651.

League of Nations, 'Conclusions of the Committee for Whose Appointment Provision Was Made in the Council Resolution of 8 June 1925, Relating to a Claim Submitted by M. Monod' (1925), 1925 *League of Nations Official Journal* 1441.

Macfadyen D, Davies M, Carr M and Burley J, *Eric Drummond and His Legacies: The League of Nations and the Beginnings of Global Governance* (Palgrave Macmillan 2019).

Permanent Court of Arbitration, Response to the International Law Commission (2024) https://legal.un.org/ilc/sessions/75/pdfs/english/sdio_pca.pdf, accessed 3 September 2025.

Petrović D, 'Longest-Existing International Administrative Tribunal: History, Main Characteristics and Current Challenges' in Petrović D (ed.), 90 *Years of Contribution of the Administrative Tribunal of the International Labour Organization to the Creation of International Civil Service Law* (2017) https://tinyurl.com/49vz4kaa, accessed 3 September 2025.

Politakis G, 'Administrative Tribunal: International Labour Organization (ILO)' in Peters A (ed.) Max Planck Encyclopedia of Public International Law (Oxford University Press 2021).

Quayle P, 'Treaties of a Particular Type: The ICJ's Interpretative Approach to the Constituent Instruments of International Organizations' (2016), 29 *Leiden Journal of International Law* 853.

Sands P and Klein P, *Bowett's Law of International Institutions* (Sweet and Maxwell 2009).

Schermers H and Blokker N, *International Institutional Law* (Brill Nijhoff 2018).

Shorter Oxford English Dictionary (Oxford University Press 2007).

Sinclair GF, *To Reform the World: International Organizations and the Making of Modern States* (Oxford University Press 2017).

Sinclair GF, 'The International Civil Servant in Theory and Practice: Law, Morality, and Expertise' (2015) 26 *European Journal of International Law* 747.

Standards of Conduct for the International Civil Service, issued by the International Civil Service Commission (2013) https://icsc.un.org/Resources/General/Publications/standardsE.pdf, accessed 3 September 2025.

Statute of the Gavi Alliance (2008) https://tinyurl.com/mssxen74, accessed 3 September 2025.

Statute of the International Civil Service Commission (ICSC) https://icsc.un.org/Resources/General/Publications/statute.pdf, accessed 3 September 2025.

Statute of the International Court of Justice (ICJ) www.icj-cij.org/statute, accessed 3 September 2025.

Statute of the International Law Commission (ILC) https://legal.un.org/ilc/texts/instruments/english/statute/statute.pdf, accessed 3 September 2025.

Statute of the International Monetary Fund Administrative Tribunal (IMFAT) www.imf.org/external/imfat/statute.htm, accessed 3 September 2025.

Statute of the Organisation for Economic Co-operation and Development Administrative Tribunal (OECDAT) www.oecd.org/en/about/administrative-tribunal.html, accessed 3 September 2025.

Statute of the United Nations Appeals Tribunal (UNAT) www.un.org/en/internaljustice/unat/unat-statute.shtml, accessed 3 September 2025.

Statute of the United Nations Dispute Tribunal (UNDT) www.un.org/en/internaljustice/undt/undt-statute.shtml, accessed 3 September 2025.

Statute of the World Bank Administrative Tribunal (WBAT) https://tribunal.worldbank.org/statute, accessed 3 September 2025.

Tams C, 'League of Nations' in Peters A (ed.) *Max Planck Encyclopedia of Public International Law* (Oxford University Press 2007).

Thomas M and Elias O, 'The Role of International Administrative Law' in Elias O (ed.), *The Development and Effectiveness of International Administrative Law* (Brill Nijhoff 2012).

United Nations, Charter (signed 26 June 1945, entered into force 24 October 1945) 1 UNTS 16.

United Nations, Note by the Secretary-General, 'Report of the Committee of Experts on Salary, Allowance, and Leave Systems' (1949) UN Doc A/C.5/331.

United Nations, Report of the Joint Inspection Unit, 'Review of the state of the investigation function: progress made in the United Nations system organizations in strengthening the investigation function' (2020) UN Doc JIU/REP/2020/1.

United Nations, Report of the Secretary-General, 'Initial review of the jurisdictional set-up of the United Nations common system' (2021) UN Doc A/75/690.

United Nations Educational, Scientific and Cultural Organization, Constitution (adopted 16 November 1945, entered into force 4 November 1949) 4 UNTS 52.

United Nations Educational, Scientific and Cultural Organization, *Constitution* (adopted 16 November 1945, entered into force 4 November 1946) 4 UNTS 275.

United Nations Framework Convention on Climate Change (adopted 9 May 1992, entered into force 21 March 1994) 1771 UNTS 107.

United Nations General Assembly Res 351 (24 November 1949) UN Dox A/RES/351(IV)[A].

United Nations General Assembly Res 50/54 (29 January 1996) UN Doc A/RES/50/54.

United Nations General Assembly Res 52/166 (30 January 1998) UN Doc A/RES/52/166.

United Nations General Assembly Res 55/159 (12 December 2000) UN Doc A/RES/55/159.

United Nations General Assembly Res 58/87 (9 December 2003) UN Doc A/RES/58/87.

United Nations General Assembly Res 59/283 (2 June 2005) UN Doc A/RES/59/283.

United Nations General Assembly Res 63/253 (24 December 2008) UN Doc A/RES/63/253.

United Nations General Assembly Res 66/237 924 December 2011 UN Doc A/RES/66/237.

United Nations General Assembly Res 69/203 (18 December 2014) UN Doc A/RES/69/203.

United Nations General Assembly Res 69/321 (22 September 2015) UN Doc A/RES/69/321.

United Nations General Assembly Res 71/266 (23 December 2016) UN Doc A/RES/71/266.

United Nations General Assembly Res 75/286 (24 June 2021) UN Doc A/RES/75/286.

United Nations General Assembly Res 782 (9 December 1953) UN Doc A/RES/782(VIII).

United Nations General Assembly Res 957 (3 November 1955) UN Doc A/RES/957(X).

United Nations General Assembly Res 3357/XXIX (18 December 1974) UN Doc A/RES/3357(XXIX).

United Nations Staff Regulations and Rules (2023) UN Doc ST/SGB/2023/1/Rev.1.

Vienna Convention on the Law of Treaties (adopted 23 May 1969, entered into force 27 January 1980) 1155 UNTS 331.

World Bank, 'Guidance: Use of Short-Term Temporary/Consultant, Extended-Term Temporary/Consultant and Term Appointment Types' (2024) https://ppfdocuments.azureedge.net/c47007ee-caa6-48e6-9ba5-8bd3f9c1f797.pdf, accessed 3 September 2025.

World Bank (International Bank for Reconstruction and Development), *Articles of Agreement* (adopted 22 July 1944, signed and entered into force 27 December 1945) 2 UNTS 134.

World Bank Staff Rules and Directives, https://policies.worldbank.org/en/policies, accessed 3 September 2025.

World Food Programme, General Regulations and General Rules (2022) https://executiveboard.wfp.org/document_download/WFP-0000141150, accessed 3 September 2025.

World Health Organization, Constitution (signed 22 July 1946, entered into force 7 April 1948) 14 UNTS 185.

Zeidan F and Abboud J, 'The Global Fund to Fight AIDS, Tuberculosis and Malaria: The Journey of a Public-Private Partnership' in Quayle P (ed.), *The Role of International Administrative Law at International Organizations* (Brill Nijhoff 2020).

TABLE OF CASES

International Administrative Tribunals

International Labour Organization Administrative Tribunal (ILOAT)

United Nations Appeals Tribunal (UNAT)

World Bank Administrative Tribunal (WBAT)

Other Administrative Tribunals

Other International Courts and Tribunals

European Court of Human Rights (ECtHR)

International Court of Justice (ICJ)

INDEX

For EU product safety concerns, contact us at Calle de José Abascal, 56–1°,
28003 Madrid, Spain or eugpsr@cambridge.org.

www.ingramcontent.com/pod-product-compliance
Ingram Content Group UK Ltd.
Pitfield, Milton Keynes, MK11 3LW, UK
UKHW021546180726
473428UK00010B/478

* 9 7 8 1 1 0 8 7 2 9 2 1 5 *